LEARN
Excel 2000

John Preston
Sally Preston
Robert Ferrett

**PRENTICE
HALL**

Learn Excel 2000

©1999 by Prentice Hall
A division of Pearson Education
Upper Saddle River, NJ 07458

All rights reserved. Printed in the United States of America. No part of this book may be used or reproduced in any form or by any means, or stored in a database or retrieval system, without prior written permission of the publisher, except in the case of brief quotations embodied in critical articles and reviews. Making copies of any part of this book for any purpose other than your own personal use is a violation of United States copyright laws. For information, address Prentice Hall, 1 Lake Street, Upper Saddle River, New Jersey, 07458.

Library of Congress Catalog No: 98-88899

ISBN:1-58076-261-1

This book is sold as is, without warranty of any kind, either express or implied, respecting the contents of this book, including but not limited to implied warranties for the book's quality, performance, merchantability, or fitness for any particular purpose. Neither Prentice Hall nor its dealers or distributors shall be liable to the purchaser or any other person or entity with respect to any liability, loss, or damage caused or alleged to be caused directly or indirectly by this book.

02 01 00 99   4 3 2 1

Screens reproduced in this book were created using Collage Plus from Inner Media, Inc., Hollis, NH.

Credits

Publisher:
Robert Linsky

Executive Editor:
Alex von Rosenberg

Operations Manager:
Christine Moos

Series Editors:
John Preston, Sally Preston, Robert L. Ferrett

Senior Project Manager:
Cecil Yarbrough

Senior Development Editor:
Rebecca Johnson

Senior Editor:
Karen Walsh

Project Editor:
Laura N. Williams

Copy Editor:
Lunaea Hougland

Proofreader:
Cynthia Fields

Indexer:
Larry Sweazy

Marketing Team:
*Nancy Evans
Susan L. Kindel
Kris King*

Software Specialist:
Angela Denny

Team Coordinator:
Melody Layne

Editorial Assistant:
Jennifer Surich

Designer:
Louisa Klucznik

Production:
Jeannette McKay

About the Authors

John Preston is an Associate Professor at Eastern Michigan University in the College of Technology, where he teaches microcomputer application courses at the undergraduate and graduate levels. He has been teaching, writing, and designing computer training courses since the advent of PCs, and has authored and co-authored more than two dozen books on Microsoft Word, Excel, Access, and PowerPoint. He is a series editor for the Learn 97 and Learn 2000 books. He has received grants from the Detroit Edison Institute and the Department of Energy to develop Web sites for energy education and alternative fuels. He has also developed one of the first Internet-based microcomputer applications courses at an accredited university. He has a B.S. from the University of Michigan in Physics, Mathematics, and Education, and an M.S. from Eastern Michigan University in Physics Education. He is A.B.D. in the Ph.D. degree program in Instructional Technology at Wayne State University.

Sally Preston is president of Preston & Associates, a computer software-training firm. She utilizes her extensive business experience as a bank vice-president in charge of branch operations along with her skills in training people on new computer systems. She provides corporate training through Preston & Associates and through the Institute for Workforce Development at Washtenaw Community College, where she also teaches computer courses part-time. She has co-authored more than 20 books on Access, Excel, PowerPoint, and Word, including the Learn 97 books, Learn 2000 books, Office 2000 Essentials and Access 2000 Essentials books. She has an M.B.A. from Eastern Michigan University.

Robert L. Ferrett is the director of the Center for Instructional Computing at Eastern Michigan University. His center provides computer training and support to faculty at the university. He has authored or co-authored nearly 30 books on Access, PowerPoint, Excel, and Word, and was the editor of the *1994 ACM SIGUCCS Conference Proceedings*. He has been designing, developing, and delivering computer workshops for more than a decade. He has a B.A. in Psychology, an M.S. in Geography, and an M.S. in Interdisciplinary Technology from Eastern Michigan University. He is A.B.D. in the Ph.D. program in Instructional Technology at Wayne State University.

Trademark Acknowledgments

All terms mentioned in this book that are known to be trademarks or service marks have been appropriately capitalized. Prentice Hall cannot attest to the accuracy of this information. Use of a term in this book should not be regarded as affecting the validity of any trademark or service mark.

Philosophy of the Learn Series

The Learn Series has been designed for the student who wants to master the basics of a particular software package quickly. The books are very visual in nature because each step is accompanied by a figure that shows the results of the step. Visual cues are given to the student in the form of highlights and callouts to help direct the student to the location in the window that is being used in a particular step. Explanatory text is minimized in the actual steps, but is included where appropriate in additional pedagogical elements. Every lesson includes a variety of exercises to immediately give the student a chance to practice the skills that have just been learned.

Structure of a Learn Series Book

Each of the books in the Learn Series is structured the same way. The following elements comprise the series:

Introduction

Each book has an introduction. This consists of an introduction to the series (how to use this book), a brief introduction to the Windows operating system, and an introduction to the software.

Lesson introduction

The introduction to each lesson includes a lesson number, title, a list of tasks covered in the lesson, and a brief introduction to the main concept or purpose of the lesson.

Task introduction

The tasks included in a lesson are shown on the opening page of the lesson. As you proceed through the lesson, the purpose of each task is explained in the "Why would I do this?" section at the beginning of the task.

Visual summary

A screen capture or printout of the results of the lesson is included at the beginning of the lesson to provide an example of what is accomplished in the lesson.

"Why would I do this?"

At the beginning of each task is a "Why would I do this?" section, which is a short explanation of the relevance of the task. The purpose is to show why this particular element of the software is important and how it can be used effectively.

Figures

Each step has an accompanying figure that is placed below the step. Each figure provides a visual reinforcement of the step that has just been completed. Buttons, menu choices, and other screen elements used in the task are highlighted or identified.

Pedagogical elements

Three recurring elements are found in the Preston Ferrett Learn Series:

Glossary

New words or concepts are printed in italics the first time they are encountered. Definitions of these words or phrases are included in the glossary at the back of the book.

End-of-lesson material

The end-of-lesson material consists of four elements: Comprehension Exercises, Reinforcement, Challenge, and Discovery exercises.

Comprehension Exercises are designed to check the student's memory and understanding of the basic concepts in the lesson. Next to each exercise is a notation that references the task number in the lesson where the topic is covered. The student is encouraged to review the task referenced if he or she is uncertain of the correct answer. The Comprehension Exercises section contains the following three elements:

- True/False There are ten true/false questions that test the understanding of the new material in the lesson.

- Visual Identification A captured screen or screens gauge the familiarity with various screen elements introduced in the lesson.

- Matching Ten matching questions are included to check familiarity with concepts and procedures introduced in the lesson.

Reinforcement Exercises provide practice in the skills introduced in the tasks. These exercises generally follow the sequence of the tasks in the lesson. Since each exercise is usually built on the previous exercise, it is a good idea to do them in the order in which they are presented.

Challenge Exercises test the student's ability to apply skills to new situations with less detailed instruction. These exercises challenge students to expand their skill set by using commands similar to those they've already learned.

Discovery Exercises are designed to help students learn how to teach themselves new skills. In each exercise, the student discovers something new that is related to the topic taught in the lesson.

Welcome to the Learn On-Demand Series

Congratulations on choosing the Learn On-Demand Series from Prentice Hall. The On-Demand software in the back of your book gives you the opportunity to learn while you work. This unique software provides computer-based training using the content from this book. To learn more, read the product information booklet included with the CD.

Annotated Instructor's Manual

If you have adopted this text for use in a college classroom, you will receive, upon request, an Annotated Instructor's Manual (AIM) at no additional charge. The Annotated Instructor's Manual is a comprehensive teaching tool that contains the student text with margin notes and tips for instructors and students. The AIM also contains suggested curriculum guides for courses of varying lengths, answers to the end-of-chapter material, test questions and answers, and PowerPoint slides. Data files and solutions for each tutorial and exercise, along with a Windows NT presentation, are included on disk with the AIM. Please contact your local representative or write to us at Prentice Hall, 1 Lake Street, Upper Saddle River, NJ, 07458.

Managing Files with Windows Explorer

Throughout most of this book, you work in the Microsoft Word program. At times, however, you may need to find, retrieve, and rename files on your CD-ROM disc or a hard disk. The figures that are shown are from the Windows 95 operating system, but procedures are the same whether you are using Windows 95, Windows 98, or Windows NT.

Launch Windows Explorer

You can usually perform any operation in the Windows operating system or in Microsoft applications in two or three ways. Many people place a Windows Explorer (not to be confused with Internet Explorer!) icon on the Windows desktop. If this icon is available, double-click it. Windows Explorer is launched.

If the icon does not exist, move to the taskbar at the bottom of the screen. The taskbar contains the Start button, buttons for any open applications, and the time. The taskbar may appear at the bottom of the screen, or it may be hidden. If it is hidden, move the pointer to the bottom of the screen and it should pop up.

Click the **Start** button and move the pointer to the **Programs** option. A list of available programs is displayed. Your list of programs will be different from the one shown. Windows Explorer is at or near the end of the list. Launch **Windows Explorer** by moving the pointer over it and clicking the left mouse button.

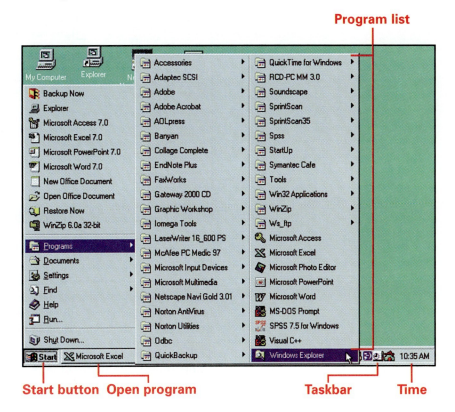

Navigate the Drives and Folders

Windows Explorer is divided into two windows. The window on the left side, labeled All Folders, displays icons for each disk drive that is accessible from your computer. Folders may be within folders to make up several layers of files. If additional folders (subfolders) are available, a plus sign (+) is placed to the left of the icon.

The All Folders section gives you an overview of the relationship between these layers, whereas the Contents window on the right displays the details of the selected drive or folder. You can choose to show details

MANAGING FILES WITH WINDOWS EXPLORER

of the files and folders or show the files and folders as icons by clicking buttons on the toolbar. Your Windows Explorer screen will look much different from the one shown, but it will contain the same elements.

To move to another disk drive, click once on the disk drive icon, such as **3 1/2 Floppy (A:)**. To open a file folder, double-click the **Folder** icon. Doing so opens the folder and displays the contents in the right-hand window.

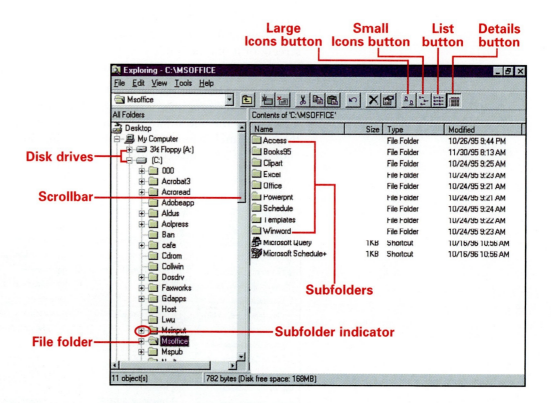

Find Files

Disk drives are capable of storing thousands of files. If you do not know which drive and folder a particular file is stored in, it could take a long time to open each one and read the list of its contents. Windows Explorer finds a file for you if you know at least part of its name.

The project files for this book all begin with the letters **Less**. In the example shown, the student files have been moved from the CD-ROM disc to the hard drive for the purposes of illustration.

To find all the files that contain the letters **Less**, click on the disk drive you want to search. Select **Tools**, **Find**, **Files or Folders** from the menu. In the **Find** window, type **Less** in the **Named** box, then click **Find Now**. All the files and file folders with those letters are listed in the bottom of the **Find** window.

After you have found a list of files, click the file you want. The location of the file is shown to the right of the filename in the In Folder column.

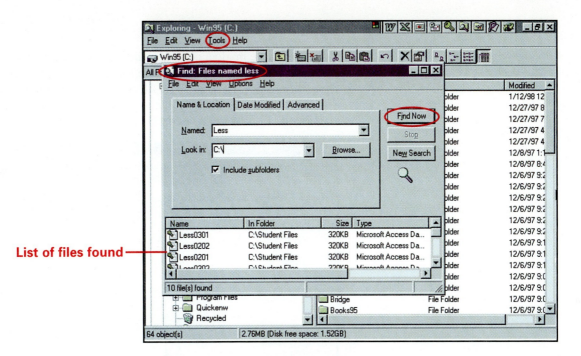

List of files found

Make Copies of Existing Files

After you have found the location of the file you need, go to the folder containing the file. Click once on the file to highlight it. Choose **Edit**, **Copy** from the menu, then choose **Edit**, **Paste**. This puts a copy of the file in the same location as the original. If you want to copy the file to another folder or disk drive, move to the new location before you perform the Paste command.

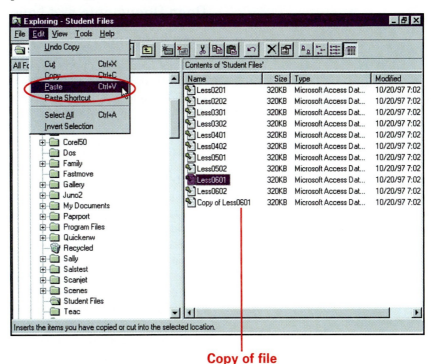

Copy of file

MANAGING FILES WITH WINDOWS EXPLORER

Rename Files

When you have made a copy of a file and pasted it into the desired location, you will often want to rename it. To rename a file, click it, and then choose **File**, **Rename**. The filename is highlighted. At this point, you can simply type a new name, or you can put the cursor in the filename and edit it as you would edit text in a word processor.

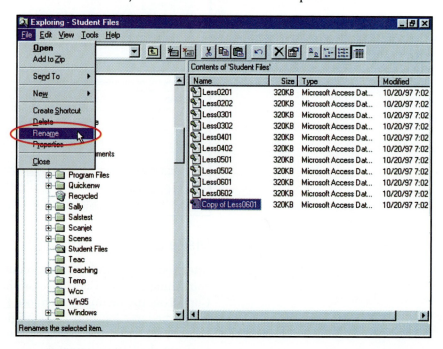

Open Documents and Launch Associated Applications Automatically

You can open a file in two ways. The first is to run the application (such as Excel), then use the **File**, **Open** commands from the menu. The second is to locate the file in Windows Explorer or My Computer and double-click on the filename.

The Concept of this Book

This book is designed for students who are new to Excel and would like to know how to use it in real-life applications. The authors have combined their many years of business experience and classroom teaching to provide a basic step-by-step approach that leads to the development of skills advanced enough to be useful in the workplace. We have designed the book so that you will be successful immediately and will create a useful document in the first lesson. In the lessons that follow, you will learn how to enter data, navigate in a worksheet, improve the appearance of the spreadsheet, write formulas and represent numbers with charts. Most lessons use one spreadsheet throughout the lesson and are designed to be completed as a unit. (Do not close your spreadsheet after a task in a lesson, but wait until the end of the lesson when you close the spreadsheet and close Excel.) Finally, we recognize that few people can remember everything that they learn in class, so we introduce the extensive Help system in the first lesson and use it in exercises throughout the book. This enables you to learn how to use the Help system to find answers to questions about using Excel 2000.

Table of Contents at a Glance

	Introduction to Excel	xvii
LESSON ONE:	**The Basics**	2
LESSON TWO:	**Formatting the Worksheet**	40
LESSON THREE:	**Editing Cell Contents**	74
LESSON FOUR:	**Filling, Copying, and Printing**	100
LESSON FIVE:	**Making the Computer Do the Math**	136
LESSON SIX:	**Understanding the Numbers Using a Chart**	184
LESSON SEVEN:	**Sorting, Grouping, and Filtering Data**	216
LESSON EIGHT:	**Creating Connections to Build Summaries, Improve Teamwork, and Work on the Web**	244

Table of Contents

	Introduction to Excel		xvii
LESSON 1	**The Basics**		2
	Task 1	Navigating a Workbook	4
	Task 2	Selecting Individual Cells	8
	Task 3	Entering Text and Numbers into Cells	11
	Task 4	Fixing Simple Typing Errors	15
	Task 5	Summing a Column of Numbers	19
	Task 6	Saving a Workbook, Printing and Closing a Worksheet	21
	Task 7	Getting Help Using the Office Assistant and Exiting Excel	25
		Comprehension Exercises	32
		True-False	32
		Identifying Parts of the Excel Screen	33
		Matching	34
		Reinforcement Exercises	34
		Challenge	36
		Discovery	38
LESSON 2	**Formatting the Worksheet**		40
	Task 1	Opening an Existing Workbook	42
	Task 2	Selecting Groups of Cells	45
	Task 3	Formatting Large Numbers, Currency, Decimal Places, and Dates	49
	Task 4	Adjusting Columns and Cells for Long Text or Numbers	53
	Task 5	Aligning Text in the Cell	56
	Task 6	Changing the Font, Size, and Emphasis of Text	60
	Task 7	Adding Lines, Borders, Colors, and Shading	61
		Comprehension Exercises	67
		True-False	67
		Identifying Parts of the Excel Screen	68
		Matching	69
		Reinforcement Exercises	69
		Challenge	71
		Discovery	72

LESSON 3		**Editing Cell Contents**	**74**
	Task 1	Changing Numbers and Editing Text	76
	Task 2	Inserting and Deleting Rows, Columns, and Sheets	78
	Task 3	Removing Cell Contents and Formatting	81
	Task 4	Undoing and Redoing Previous Steps	83
	Task 5	Automatically Correcting Common Typing Errors	85
	Task 6	Automatically Finishing Commonly Used Words or Phrases	88
	Task 7	Checking Your Spelling	90
		Comprehension Exercises	92
		True-False	92
		Identifying Parts of the Excel Screen	93
		Matching	94
		Reinforcement Exercises	94
		Challenge	96
		Discovery	98
LESSON 4		**Filling, Copying, and Printing**	**100**
	Task 1	Creating Sequential Labels	102
	Task 2	Creating a Series of Numbers	104
	Task 3	Freezing Panes and Changing Zoom	110
	Task 4	Copying Cell Contents	113
	Task 5	Selecting a Range of Cells to Print and Previewing the Printout	117
	Task 6	Improving the Printed Spreadsheet	119
	Task 7	Printing Row or Column Labels	124
		Comprehension Exercises	128
		True-False	128
		Identifying Parts of the Excel Screen	129
		Matching	130
		Reinforcement Exercises	130
		Challenge	132
		Discovery	133

LESSON 5	**Making the Computer Do the Math**		136
	Task 1	Adding, Subtracting, Multiplying, and Dividing Using Cell References and Numbers	138
	Task 2	Using Formulas with More than One Cell Reference	140
	Task 3	Combining Operations and Filling Cells with Formulas	144
	Task 4	Filling Cells with Relative and Absolute Formulas	150
	Task 5	Applying Basic Formulas to a Loan Repayment	154
	Task 6	Using Built-in Financial Formulas	156
	Task 7	Using Counting and Conditional Formulas	161
	Task 8	Using Excel to Explore Different Possibilities	168
		Comprehension Exercises	174
		True-False	174
		Identifying Parts of the Excel Screen	175
		Matching	176
		Reinforcement Exercises	176
		Challenge	179
		Discovery	181
LESSON 6	**Understanding the Numbers Using a Chart**		184
	Task 1	Creating a Chart to Show a Trend	186
	Task 2	Creating a Chart to Show Contributions to a Whole	190
	Task 3	Creating a Chart to Make Comparisons	193
	Task 4	Editing the Elements of a Chart	196
	Task 5	Changing Chart Types	200
	Task 6	Printing a Chart	204
		Comprehension Exercises	207
		True-False	207
		Identifying Parts of the Excel Screen	208
		Matching	209
		Reinforcement Exercises	209
		Challenge	211
		Discovery	214

Lesson 7		**Sorting, Grouping, and Filtering Data**	216
	Task 1	Sorting Rows by Department	218
	Task 2	Grouping and Subtotaling by Department	220
	Task 3	Displaying Totals and Subtotals Without the Details	222
	Task 4	Filtering Information to Show Specified Rows	224
	Task 5	Identifying Overdue Orders Using the Logical IF Function	228
	Task 6	Removing Filters, Totals, and Outlines	232
		Comprehension Exercises	236
		True-False	236
		Identifying Parts of the Excel Screen	237
		Matching	238
		Reinforcement Exercises	238
		Challenge	240
		Discovery	241
Lesson 8		**Creating Connections to Build Summaries, Improve Teamwork, and Work on the Web**	244
	Task 1	Inserting and Moving a New Sheet	246
	Task 2	Designing a Summary Sheet for Convenient Charting	249
	Task 3	Linking the Results of Several Sheets to a Summary Sheet	252
	Task 4	Inserting a Hyperlink to Another Worksheet	257
	Task 5	Saving a Worksheet as a Web Page	262
	Task 6	Using a Worksheet on the Web	265
		Comprehension Exercises	271
		True-False	271
		Identifying Parts of the Excel Screen	272
		Matching	273
		Reinforcement Exercises	273
		Challenge	275
		Discovery	277
	Glossary		280
	Index		282

Introduction to Excel

Microsoft Excel is an electronic spreadsheet application program. A tabular form that is divided into vertical columns and horizontal rows has been used for centuries to track numerical data. An electronic spreadsheet enables the user to quickly enter numbers and formulas that perform various bookkeeping functions such as computing totals and subtotals. While most people use a spreadsheet program for simple tasks, such programs also have built-in, automatic features that are capable of very sophisticated financial analysis.

How Spreadsheets Work

Spreadsheets are divided up into individual cells. A cell is designated by a column letter and a row number. Formulas that use numbers in the cells obey traditional mathematical rules, but instead of referring to value in a cell with a single letter such as X and Y, the cell's row and column designations are used. For example, a formula that is designed to add together the contents of cells C2 and B2 starts with an equal sign and looks like this: =C2+B2

One of the main advantages of an electronic spreadsheet is its ability to recalculate any formulas that need to be changed if the content of any cell is changed. As a spreadsheet designer, your job is to set up the formulas and cell arrangements so that the values entered into the cells will be acted upon as you direct. Then, if you make any changes to the values in the cells, the dependent formulas will be automatically recalculated.

Another feature of the electronic spreadsheet is its use of relative formulas. A relative formula might be used to add the numbers in the column of cells above it. If a formula is copied to other cells, each of those formulas will add the values in the cells above them. Using this feature, you can rapidly design large spreadsheets that repeat the same kind of formula. For example, if you had 20 columns of numbers, you could write one formula to add the numbers in the first column and then copy that formula into the cells at the bottom of the other 19 columns.

Excel is also very good at displaying numbers as charts. It is far easier to understand relationships and trends when numbers are represented in graphical form.

The third main function of an electronic spreadsheet is to perform "what if" analysis. Excel has some sophisticated tools that enable to you find a number, such as a break-even point, based on other data. You can use this tool to project trends, prepare budgets, and predict changes in projected profits based on changes in sales volume, expenses, or other factors.

How to Launch Excel

The Excel program may be initiated (launched) in several ways. When the Excel program was installed on your computer, its name was added to the list of programs that may be found when you click the **Start** button on the Windows taskbar and then click **Programs**. The Excel program may be listed by itself or you may have to open a folder such as Microsoft Office to find the icon that represents the program. When you find it, click on it and the program will launch. There may be other shortcut methods of launching Excel on your computer, but this method is the one that will work on most machines.

There are several faster ways to launch Excel. It is possible to add the Excel program icon to the list of commonly used programs that appears immediately when you click **Start**. The Excel icon could be placed on the desktop or it could be part of a small toolbar at the top of the screen. In general, if you see the Excel icon you can click or double-click on it to launch Excel.

If you are using the Windows Explorer or My Computer program to search for files, you may notice that the Excel files have a small Excel icon displayed next to their names. When this is the case, you can double-click on the filename and Excel will launch automatically and then open the file as well.

How to Identify Parts of the Excel Worksheet

There are two methods that you can use to quickly identify parts of the Excel worksheet. They are ScreenTips and What's This?. A ScreenTip displays when you place the mouse pointer on a toolbar button and leave it there for a moment. The ScreenTip displays the name of the button. (If this feature does not work on your computer, you may turn it on by selecting **Tools**, **Customize** from the menu. Then click the **Options** tab and click the **Show ScreenTips on toolbars** check box.)

If you would like a more detailed description, you may choose **Help**, **What's This?** from the menu. After you select this Help option, the pointer has a question mark attached to it until you click on part of the screen, at which time a more detailed paragraph is displayed, describing the function of the object you clicked.

Parts of the Excel Worksheet Window

The worksheet window has several components that you will learn how to use in this book. For a brief overview of the layout of the window and its parts, see the following figure.

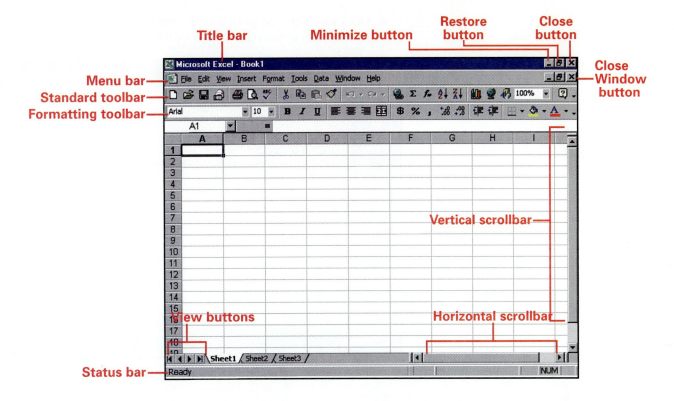

Assumptions About the Setup of Excel

We assume that the application has been fully installed, including any wizards, Help, or clip art components. You may have only one toolbar displayed instead of the two that are shown in the figures in this book. Your work area may also look different due to the display setting for your monitor.

The authors used the settings that follow when writing this book. Instructions on how to change to these settings have been included where we felt it would make a material difference in what you see on your screen. Compare your screen to the sample screen. If there is a difference, follow the steps listed to change the settings.

Settings in the Windows Operating System

■ Display Setting is 640x480 256 color.

This setting displays larger dimensions for icons, dialog boxes, and cells, as shown in the following figure.

To change to this setting, follow these steps:

1. Click the **Start** button and choose **Settings**, **Control Panel**.
2. In the Control Panel window, double-click the **Display** icon.
3. Click the **Settings** tab at the top of the window.
4. Under **Colors**, click the down arrow and select **256 Colors**.
5. In the **Screen** area, click and drag the range indicator to the far left until 640 by 480 pixels is displayed.

6. Click the **Close** (**X**) button in the upper-right corner of the **Display** window and upper-right corner of the **Control Panel** window.

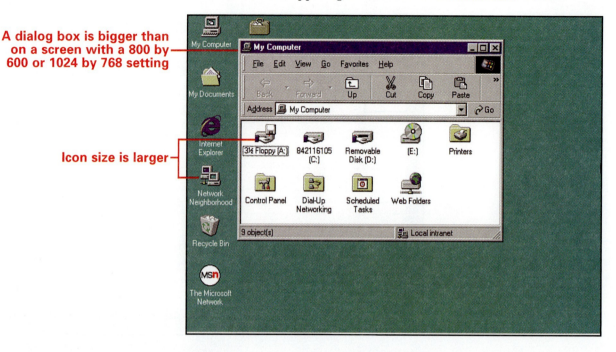

A dialog box is bigger than on a screen with a 800 by 600 or 1024 by 768 setting

Icon size is larger

■ File extensions in Windows have been turned off.

File extensions identify the type of program that was used to create a file. An Excel file uses the extension .xls. When these are turned off, your filenames will display as shown in the following figure. The program icon and the file type can be used to identify the type of file rather than the file extension. In Windows Explorer, or in the Open dialog box, if you see .xls after the name of an Excel file, the extensions need to be turned off.

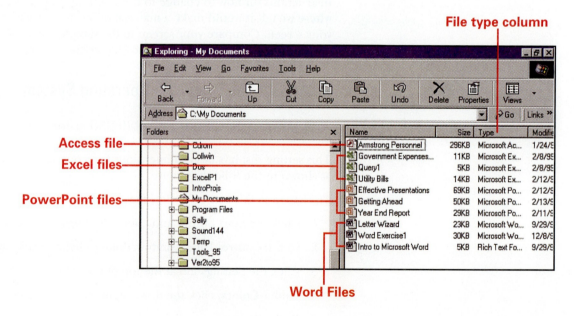

File type column

Access file
Excel files
PowerPoint files
Word Files

LEARN EXCEL 2000

To change to this setting, follow these steps:

1. Click the **Start** button and choose **Programs**, **Windows Explorer**.
2. Click **View**, **Folder Options** from the menu bar.
3. Click the **View** tab at the top of the **Folder Options** window.
4. On the list of **Advanced Settings**, make sure there is a check mark in the square box next to **Hide file extensions for known file types**. If necessary, click the box to add a check mark.
5. Click **OK** to apply the setting and close the window.

■ The Windows taskbar at the bottom of the screen is hidden in the figures.

No change is necessary. You will see the taskbar at the bottom of your screen. The authors did not show the taskbar in the figures.

Settings in Excel

There are just a few settings in Excel that may have been changed by another user. Launch Excel and compare your screen to the following figure. Make sure each of the elements highlighted is shown on your screen. If you find a discrepancy between your screen and the figure, follow the appropriate steps to modify your setup. If you need assistance, consult your instructor.

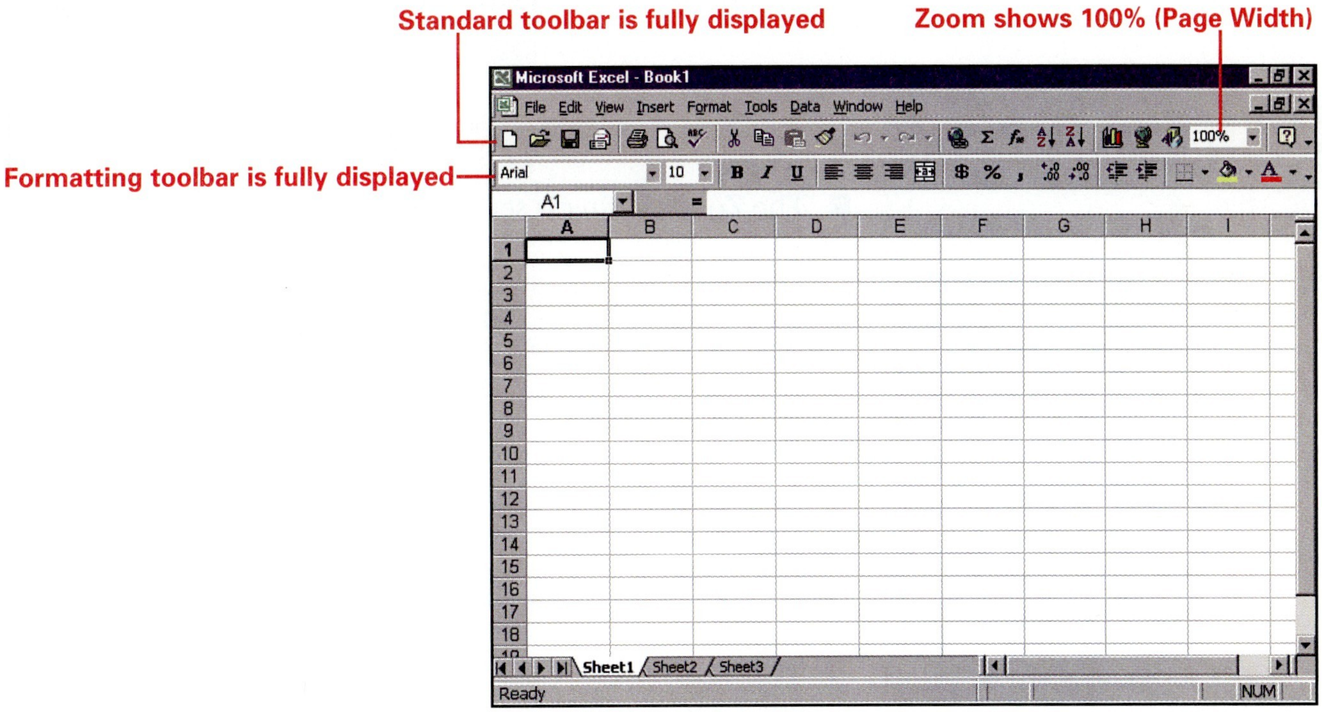

Standard toolbar is fully displayed   **Zoom shows 100% (Page Width)**

Formatting toolbar is fully displayed

■ The Standard and Formatting toolbars are fully displayed rather than docked side by side.

INTRODUCTION TO EXCEL

A new feature in Office 2000 is personalized menus and toolbars where the things you use most often are displayed and things you don't use are hidden. This includes having the Standard and Formatting toolbars share one row. While this can be an advantage because you can see more of your screen, it is cumbersome when teaching the software. This is the default setting, so you will most likely need to change it on your computer, unless it has already been done.

To Fully Display Both Toolbars:

1. Choose **Tools**, **Customize** from the menu.
2. Click the **Options** tab at the top of the dialog box.
3. Remove the check mark next to **Standard and Formatting toolbars share one row** by clicking the check box.

Click here to remove the check mark

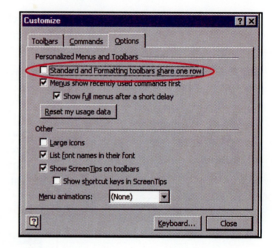

4. Click the **Close** (**X**) button on the dialog box.

■ The Zoom setting is set to 100%.

To Set Zoom to 100%:

1. On the Standard toolbar, click the arrow at the right side of the Zoom box and select **100%**.

■ The Office Assistant should be hidden when it displays unless otherwise mentioned.

To Hide the Office Assistant:

1. When the assistant displays on the screen, click **Help** on the menu and choose **Hide the Office Assistant**.

■ Default settings are used as originally installed, unless otherwise stated.

Most of the default settings are found under **Tools**, **Options**. There are numerous options that can be turned on or off in this dialog box. If we think a default setting may affect a lesson, we mention at that time.

Exit Excel

When you are done with the Excel program, you should close it before you turn off the computer. To do this, you may click the **Close** button on the title bar. If you have not saved your most recent changes to the spreadsheet, you will be asked if you wish to do so before the program closes. You may also close Excel by using the **File**, **Close** options from the menu.

Lesson: 1

The Basics

Task 1 Navigating a Workbook

Task 2 Selecting Individual Cells

Task 3 Entering Text and Numbers into Cells

Task 4 Fixing Simple Typing Errors

Task 5 Summing a Column of Numbers

Task 6 Saving a Workbook, Printing and Closing a Worksheet

Task 7 Getting Help Using the Office Assistant and Exiting Excel

Introduction

Spreadsheets are used for a variety of information that benefits from being displayed in a grid of columns and rows. Traditionally, spreadsheets have been used for financial information, but they can also be used for schedules, inventories, and other data.

This lesson is designed to provide you with the basic skills that you need to create a simple spreadsheet, print it, and save it. You will also learn how to use the Help features.

In Excel, spreadsheets are called worksheets. A workbook may contain several worksheets.

Visual Summary

When you have completed this lesson, you will have created a worksheet like the one below and you will have learned to use Help.

Furniture					<First Name Last Name>
	Desks	Tables	Chairs	Lamps	Files
Miami	150	75	275	200	100
Chicago	85	23	97	50	200
Dallas	25	200	400	40	25
Seattle	35	15	35	25	15
Portland	25	55	64	85	74
Total	320	368	871	400	414

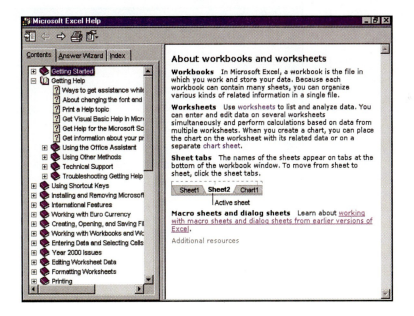

TASK 1

Navigating a Workbook

Why would I do this?

To understand how to use Excel, you first need to have a basic understanding of how Excel is structured. An Excel file is a *workbook* that consists of several *worksheets* identified by tabs at the bottom of the window. Each of these worksheets is divided into rows and columns; their intersections form a grid of cells. There are many more rows and columns available than will show in the window. To work in Excel you need to know how to navigate in a worksheet to see different rows and columns.

In this task, you will learn how to select a *sheet* and scroll it to display additional rows and columns.

1 Launch **Excel**. The program displays a set of empty worksheets. The sheets are designated with tabs near the bottom of the window.

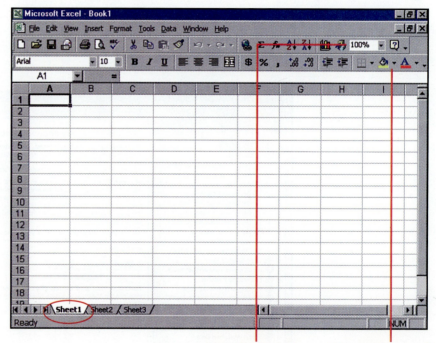

Standard toolbar   **Formatting toolbar**

In Depth: A new feature of Office 2000 places the two most commonly used toolbars on the same line. The buttons showing on that line change, depending on recent use. To provide a consistent set of instructional images, we have disabled this feature. If the toolbars on your screen do not match the figures shown, see the introduction for a description of how to disable this feature.

4 LEARN EXCEL 2000

2 Move the pointer to the tab labeled **Sheet2** at the bottom of the window. Click on the tab. A second empty sheet is displayed.

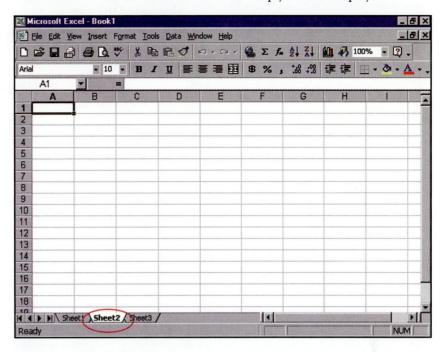

3 Click the **Sheet1** tab to return to the *default* sheet.

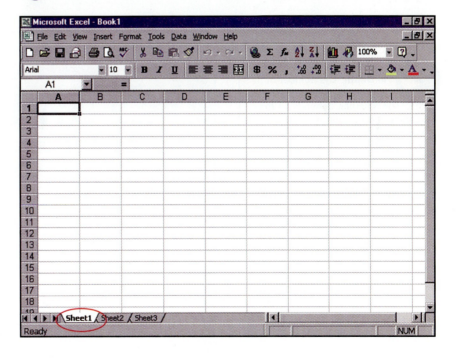

LESSON 1   THE BASICS   5

4 Click once on the down arrow at the bottom of the *vertical scrollbar*. Row 1 disappears, and a previously hidden row appears at the bottom of the screen.

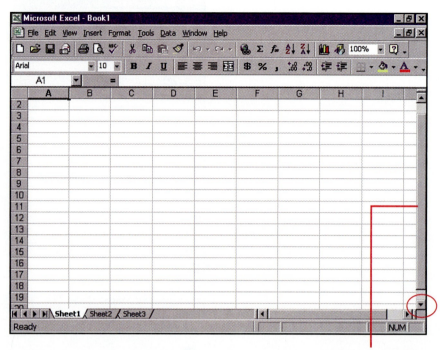

Vertical scrollbar

5 Click the same down arrow and hold down the mouse button. The rows will scroll by rapidly. Release the mouse button.

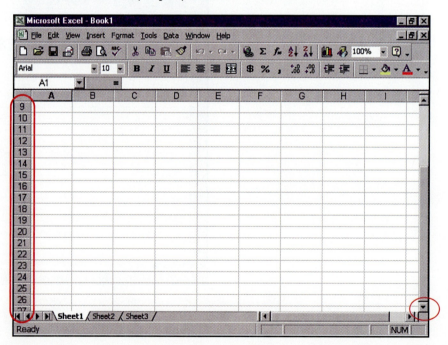

In Depth: The number of columns and rows shown on a screen depends on the *display settings* and the *Zoom*. If your screen displays more rows and columns than the illustrations in this book, do not be concerned.

In general, the left mouse button is used for more operations than the right mouse button. Unless otherwise stated, all mouse operations will assume the use of the left mouse button.

LEARN EXCEL 2000

6 Click the up arrow at the top of the vertical scrollbar and hold down the button until row **1** appears. Release the button.

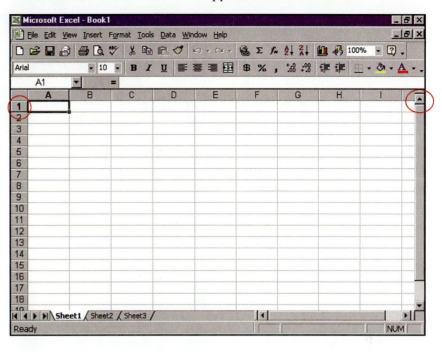

7 Click once on the right arrow on the *horizontal scrollbar*. Column A will scroll off the screen, and the next column to the right will appear.

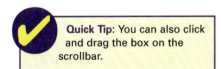

Quick Tip: You can also click and drag the box on the scrollbar.

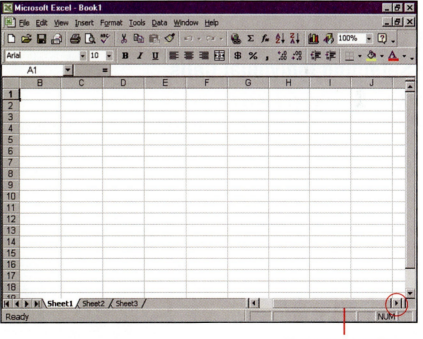

Horizontal scrollbar

LESSON 1 THE BASICS 7

8 Click once on the left arrow on the horizontal scrollbar. The sheet will scroll to the right, and column A will reappear.

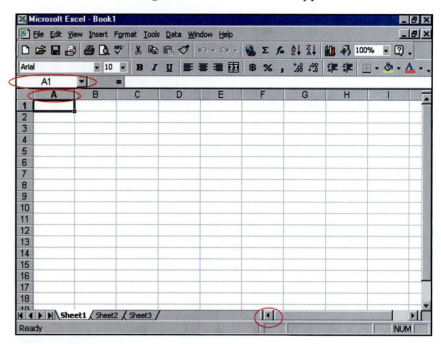

TASK 2

Selecting Individual Cells

Why would I do this?

You must *select a cell* before you can enter text, numbers, or formulas. If a cell is selected, it will have a dark border around it.

In this task, you learn how to move the selection from one cell to another on a worksheet.

1 Use the mouse to move the pointer to the cell that is in column **B** and row **2** (this cell can be referred to as cell B2). Notice that the cell selection does not move with the pointer.

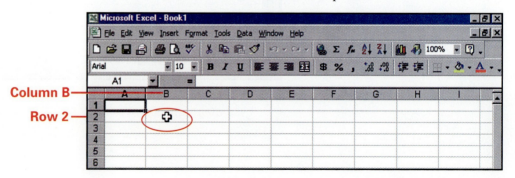

LEARN EXCEL 2000

2 Click the left mouse button. Notice that the border of the cell changes to a darker line. The column and row headers become boldface and the address of the cell (B2) appears in the Name box.

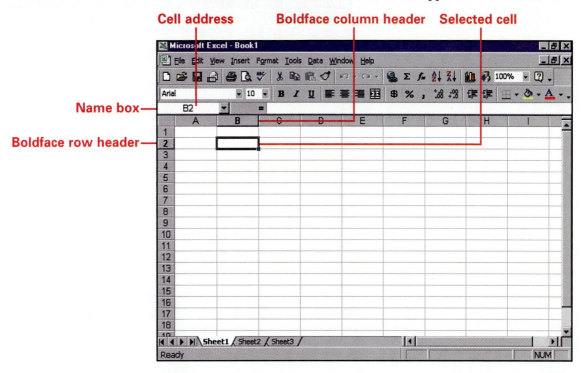

3 Press the up arrow on your keyboard once. Notice that the selection moves to cell B1.

> **Caution:** Moving the pointer to a cell does not select it. If you start typing without actually moving the selection, your text or number will be placed in whatever cell is currently selected.

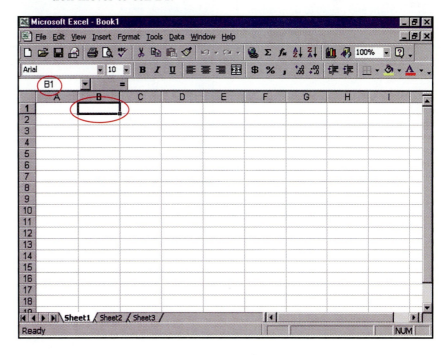

4 Press `Tab` three times. The selection moves one cell to the right each time you press this key.

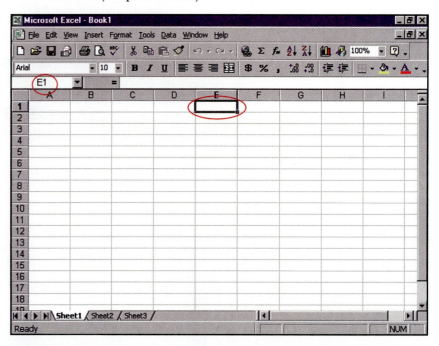

5 Press `Enter`. The selection drops to the next row and returns to the cell below B1.

In Depth: Using `Tab` to move the selection to the right and `Enter` to drop down a row and return to the original column makes it easier to enter multiple rows of data.

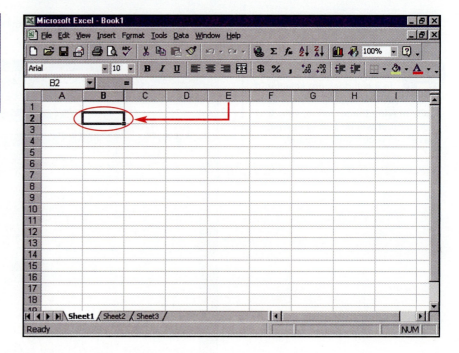

TASK 3

Entering Text and Numbers into Cells

Why would I do this?

Text is entered into cells to provide labels and other information for users of the sheet. Numbers are used in calculations and formulas. A cell may contain text or numbers, but not both. Once the numbers have been entered into the cells, you can manipulate the numbers, perform calculations, and use the numbers to visually portray a trend by creating a chart.

In this task, you learn how to enter text and numbers in cells.

1 Move the pointer to cell **A1** and click the left mouse button to select the cell.

> **In Depth:** If numbers are used as labels or mixed with text, as in a street address, they are treated as text.

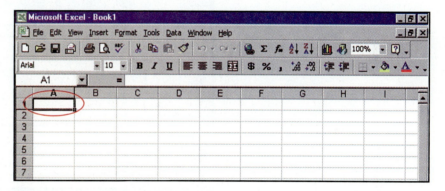

2 Type the word **Stock** and press ⏎Enter.

> **In Depth:** The direction that the selection moves when you press ⏎Enter can be changed. The setting is found under **Tools, Options, Edit, Move selection after Enter**.

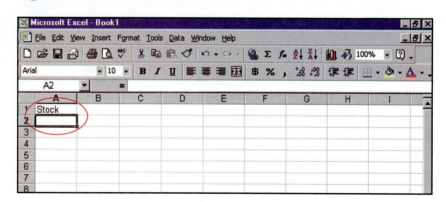

LESSON 1   THE BASICS   **11**

3 Select cell **A3**. This will be the upper-left corner of the table of data. It is left blank.

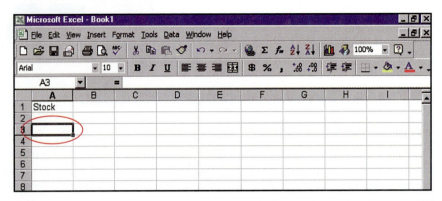

4 Press `Tab`. This moves the selection to cell B3.

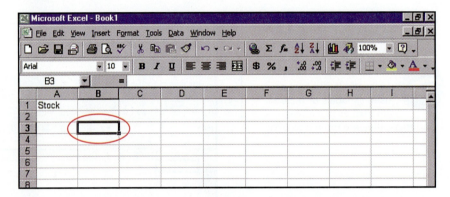

5 Type **Desks** and press `Tab`. The text is entered and the selection moves to cell C3.

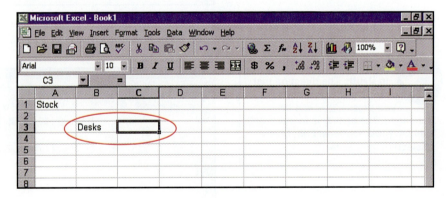

6 Type **Tables**, then press `Tab`. Repeat this process to enter **Chairs** and **Lamps** in cells **D3** and **E3**.

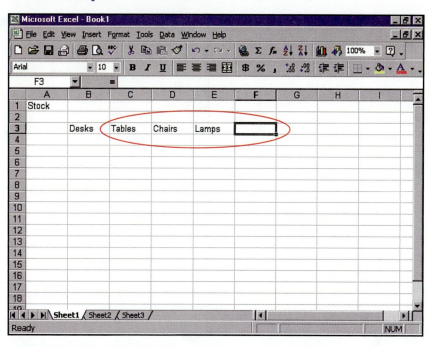

7 Type **Files** in **F3**, but press `Enter` instead of `Tab`. The selection automatically returns to cell A4 to start the next row.

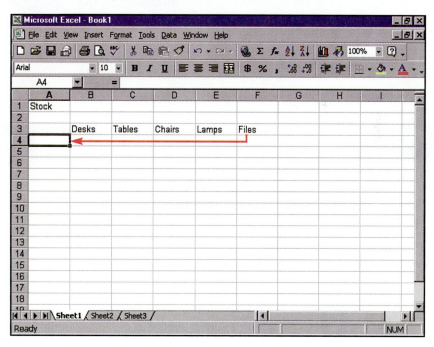

LESSON 1   THE BASICS

8 Type **Miami** in cell **A4** and press Tab.

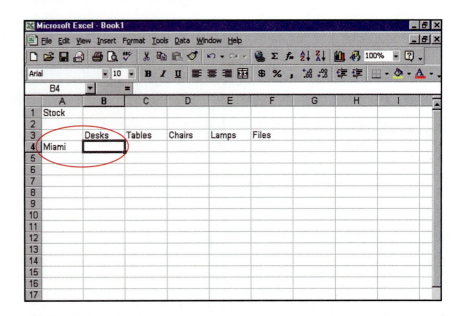

9 Refer to the figure and use this method to fill out the table with the following information:

	Desks	Tables	Chairs	Lamps	Files
Miami	150	75	275	200	100
Chicago	85	23	97	50	200
Dallas	25	200	400	40	25
Seattle	35	15	35	25	15
Portland	25	55	64	85	74

Caution: When you use Tab to enter values in adjacent cells, Excel remembers the starting point of the series and returns to that column when you press Enter. But interrupting the pattern, for instance to correct an error, sets a new starting point. Therefore, if you make mistakes entering the text or numbers, leave them for now. You will learn how to fix mistakes in the next task.

10 Select cell **F1** and type your last name. Press ⏎Enter. If your name is too long to fit in the cell, enter it anyway. You will learn how to deal with this in Lesson 2.

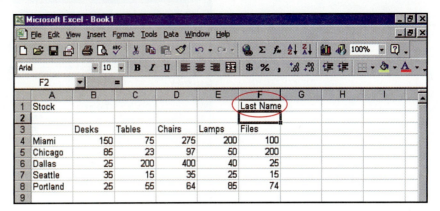

Fixing Simple Typing Errors

Why would I do this?

It is possible to make mistakes when entering data. Also, information may change and need to be adjusted. The power of using an electronic spreadsheet is in the capability to easily change information and have formulas recalculated.

In this task, you learn how to edit the contents of the cells.

1 Select cell **A9** and type the incorrectly spelled word **Totle** in the cell. Do not press the ⏎Enter or Tab⇄ key yet. Notice that a vertical line marks the position where text is entered. This line is called the *insertion point*.

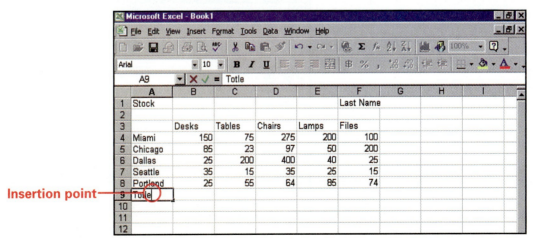

LESSON 1   THE BASICS   **15**

2 Press ⌫Backspace twice. The insertion point moves to the left, erasing the last two letters.

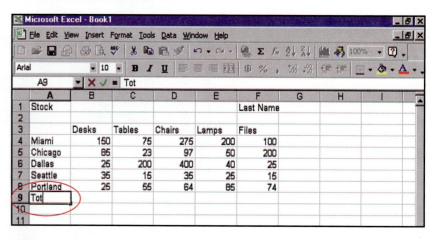

3 Type **al** and press Tab⇥.

> **In Depth:** You can move the insertion point within the text by using the right and left arrow keys on the keyboard. ⌫Backspace deletes characters to the left of the insertion point, and Del deletes letters to the right of the insertion point.

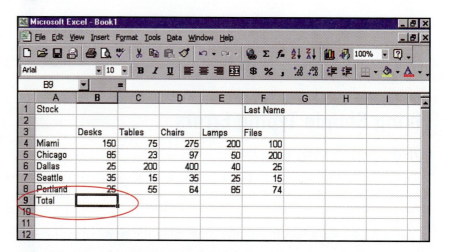

4 To replace an entire entry, just type over it. Select cell **A1**, type **Furniture** and press ↵Enter. The word "Stock" is replaced with "Furniture."

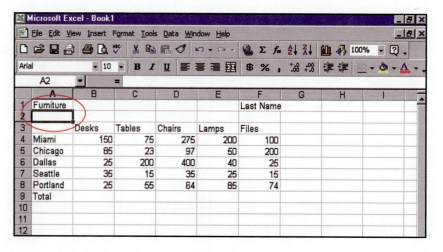

16 LEARN EXCEL 2000

5 If you change your mind, you may undo your action. Click the **Undo** button on the Standard toolbar.

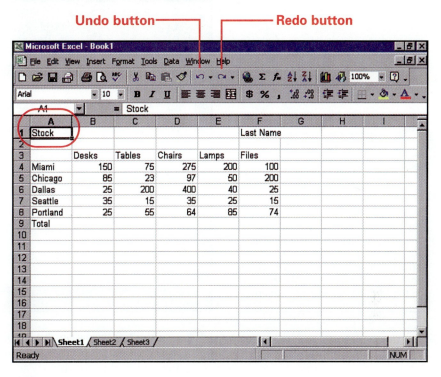

6 Click the **Redo** button to change the cell back to **Furniture**.

> **Caution:** If you are using the feature that places the Standard and Formatting toolbars on the same line, you may not see the Undo button if it has not been used recently. If that is the case, locate the **More buttons** button for the Standard toolbar and click it to display the rest of the buttons on the Standard toolbar. Do not use the More buttons button at the far right. That one refers to the additional buttons on the Formatting toolbar.

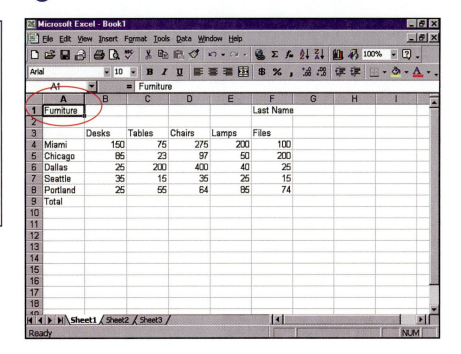

LESSON 1   THE BASICS

7 You can also edit the contents of a cell. Move the pointer to cell **F1**. Double-click the left mouse button to place the insertion point in the text within the cell.

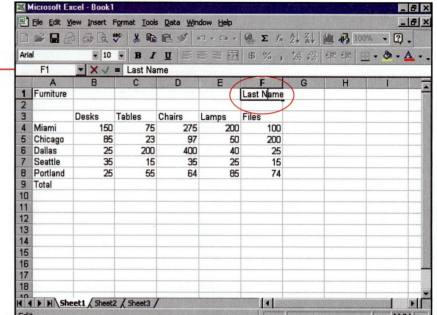

Formula bar

Caution: You may have trouble double-clicking. The most common problem is caused by the mouse rolling slightly between clicks. Rest the heel of your hand on the table so the mouse is less likely to roll. It may take a little practice. If this is frustrating you, click the cell once and the contents will appear in the *formula bar*. Click once on the text in the formula bar and edit it there.

8 Use the left arrow on the keyboard to position the insertion point to the left of your last name and type your first name and a space. Press ⏎Enter to finish.

Add your first name

TASK 5

Summing a Column of Numbers

Why would I do this?

The purpose of most worksheets is to make *calculations* based on the data you have entered. The simplest and most commonly used calculation is the sum calculation. It is used so often, in fact, that Excel has a built-in AutoSum button.

In this task, you learn how to sum columns of numbers using AutoSum.

1 Select cell **B9**.

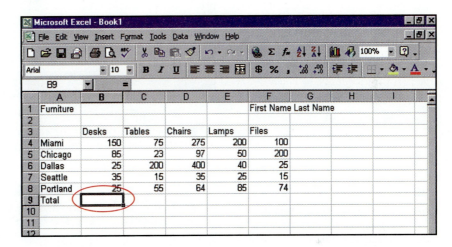

2 Click the **AutoSum** button located in the Standard toolbar. Several things will happen. A formula, =SUM(B4:B8), will appear in cell B9 and in the formula bar. Also, a moving dashed line called a *marquee* will surround the group of cells being summed.

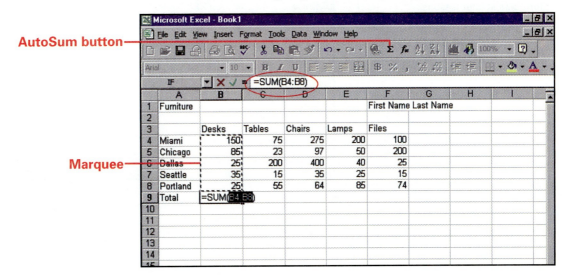

LESSON 1 THE BASICS 19

3 Press `Tab` to activate the formula. The sum is the total number of desks on hand in the various locations.

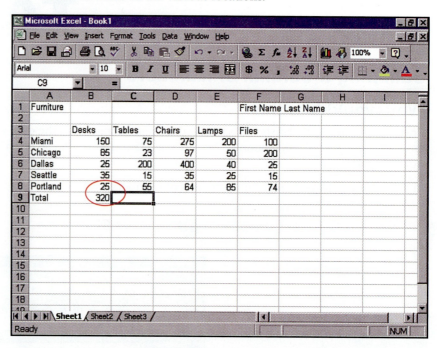

4 Repeat this process for each of the remaining columns. If the Office Assistant appears, right-click on it and choose **Hide** from the **Shortcut menu**.

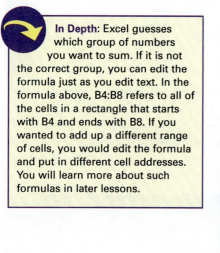

In Depth: Excel guesses which group of numbers you want to sum. If it is not the correct group, you can edit the formula just as you edit text. In the formula above, B4:B8 refers to all of the cells in a rectangle that starts with B4 and ends with B8. If you wanted to add up a different range of cells, you would edit the formula and put in different cell addresses. You will learn more about such formulas in later lessons.

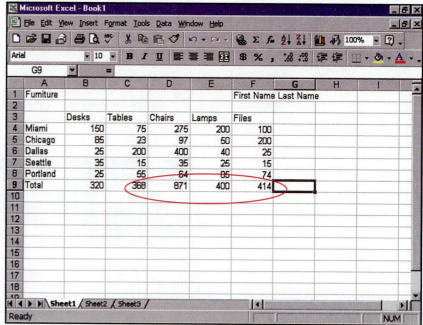

TASK 6

Saving a Workbook, Printing and Closing a Worksheet

Why would I do this?

A computer has a short-term memory that forgets when the power is turned off or interrupted. In order to record your spreadsheet for later use, you will need to make a more permanent copy of it. One way to do this is to save a copy magnetically on a disk.

Even in an age of digital communications, there are still advantages to recording data on paper. A paper copy is lightweight, portable, and compatible with older storage systems. It is often easier to review several pages of data simultaneously and share the information with others who do not have a computer.

In this task, you will learn how to print a worksheet and save the workbook on disk.

1 Click the **Save** button on the Standard toolbar. The Save As dialog box will appear with a suggested filename already highlighted in the **File name** box.

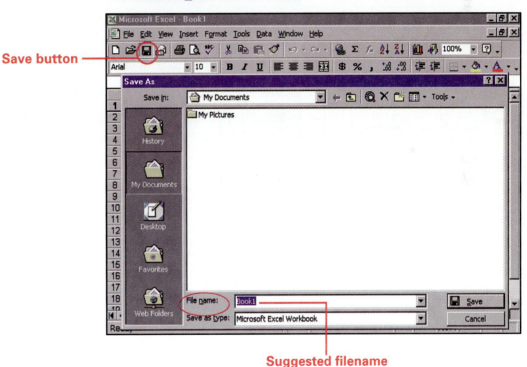

LESSON 1 THE BASICS 21

2 Type **Basic Skills** and Excel will replace the highlighted text in the **File name** box. Do not press ⏎Enter yet.

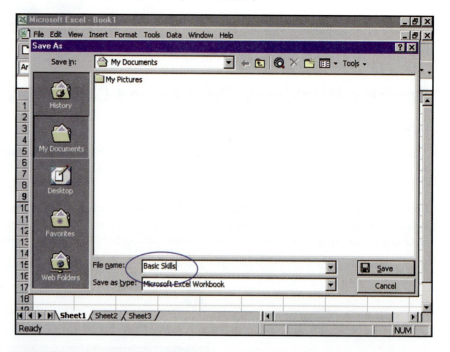

In Depth: The conventions of this book assume that the file extensions for *registered programs* have been hidden. If this is not the case in your computer setup, you will see an .xls extension added to your Excel filenames. File extensions can be turned on or off in Windows Explorer under **View**, **Options**.

3 Place a 3 1/2 inch floppy disk in drive A (A:). Ask your instructor for assistance if necessary. Click the down arrow at the right side of the **Save in** box. A diagram of your computer's disk drives will appear.

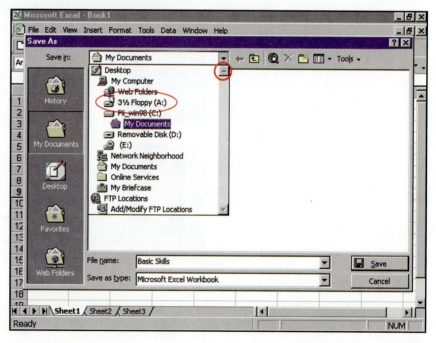

Caution: A dialog box has buttons that you can click to produce certain actions. Often, one of the buttons is indicated as the default choice by a darker and thicker border. In this case, the **Save** button is the default. If you press ⏎Enter after typing in the name of the file, Excel will save the file in whatever folder or disk is currently selected. If you do this by mistake, click **File** and **Save As**. This will open the Save As dialog box and you can now select the folder where this file should be saved.

❹ Click the **3 1/2 Floppy (A:)** drive. If your class is using another disk drive, follow your instructor's directions.

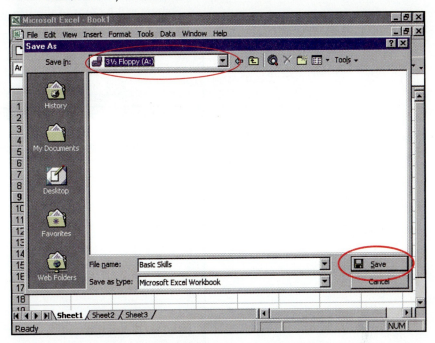

❺ Click **Save**. A copy of the workbook will be saved on your floppy disk. The pointer will turn into an hourglass while the file is being saved, and a progress indicator displays in the status bar.

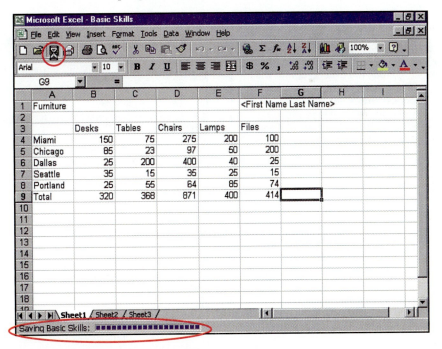

LESSON 1   THE BASICS

6 Check to make sure that your printer is connected and turned on. Click the **Print** button on the Standard toolbar. The current worksheet will be sent to the printer.

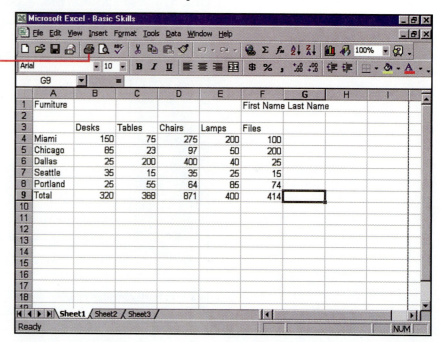

Print button

7 Move the pointer onto the **Close Window** button on the menu bar.

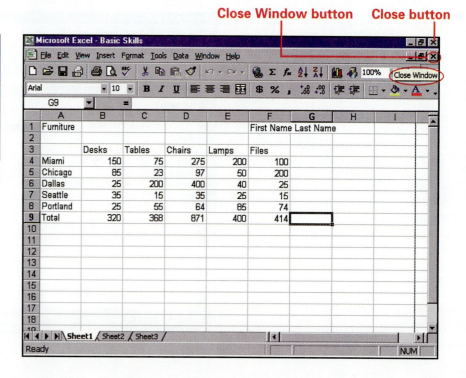

Close Window button   Close button

Caution: If you click the **Close** button on the Title bar, the Excel program will close, along with any open workbooks. This is not a big problem since you will not lose your work. Simply launch Excel again if you intended to leave it open.

8 Click the **Close Window** button on the menu bar. The workbook closes, but Excel stays open. If you have made any changes to the workbook since the last time it was saved, you will be prompted to save it.

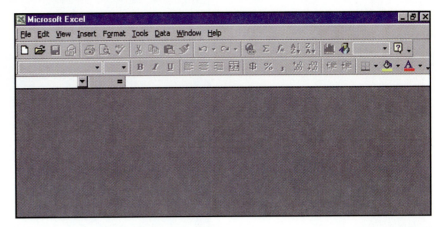

Getting Help Using the Office Assistant and Exiting Excel

Why would I do this?

This book introduces many Excel topics, but Excel has many more features than those covered here. Fortunately, there are many powerful tools at your disposal to help you expand your working knowledge of Excel and to answer your specific application questions. An entire Help manual that you can search electronically comes with Excel.

In this task, you learn how to use the Office Assistant to find out more about saving documents.

1 Choose **Help, Microsoft Excel Help,** if necessary, to display the Office Assistant.

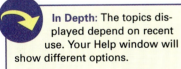

In Depth: The topics displayed depend on recent use. Your Help window will show different options.

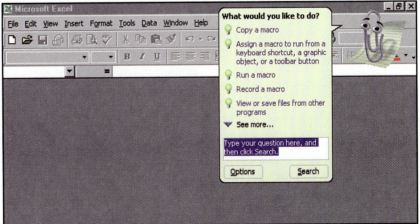

LESSON 1 THE BASICS **25**

2 Enter the following question: **What is a workbook?**

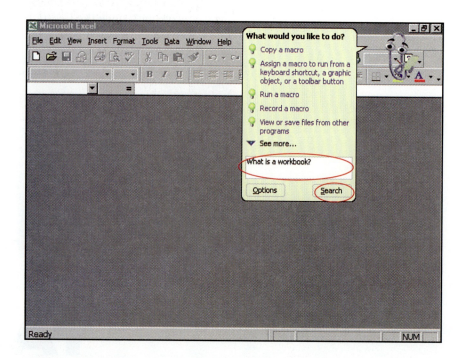

3 Click <u>S</u>earch. A menu of possible choices is displayed.

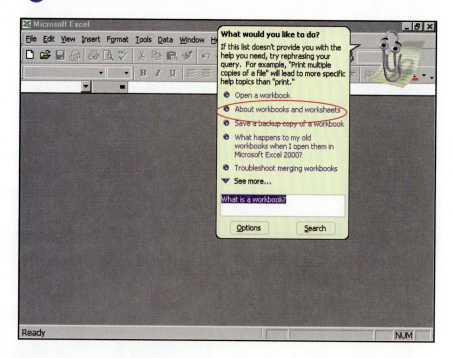

4 Click **About workbooks and worksheets**. A Help window opens. Maximize the window if necessary. Right-click on the Office Assistant and choose **Hide**.

> **Caution:** The Help window may minimize when you hide the Office Assistant. Click the **Microsoft Excel Help** button on the taskbar to restore the Help window, if necessary.

Click to display definition

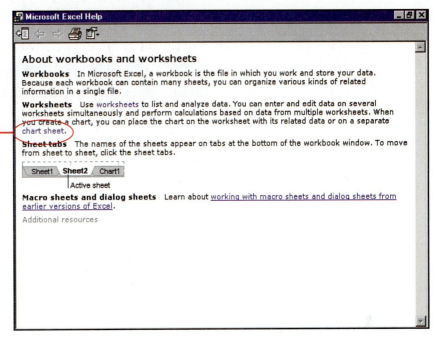

5 Click **chart sheet**. Words in blue that are not underlined have definitions that may be viewed in a pop-up window when you click them.

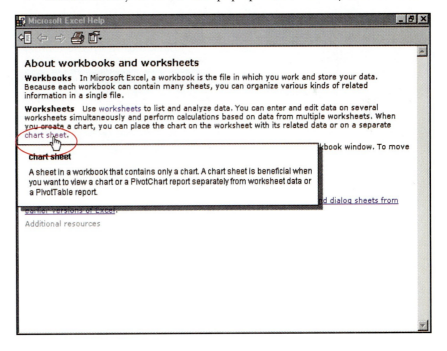

LESSON 1   THE BASICS

6 Click a blank portion of the window to close the pop-up window. Move the pointer onto the phrase **working with macro sheets and dialog sheets from earlier versions of Excel**. Notice that the text is underlined, indicating that this is a *hyperlink* to another page in the Help manual. Hyperlinks are indicated by colored text that is underlined.

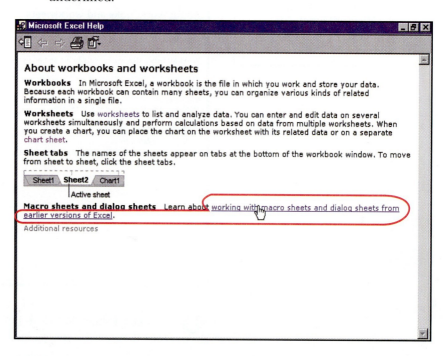

7 Click the hyperlinked text. A Help sheet on that topic displays. The Back button on the toolbar becomes active.

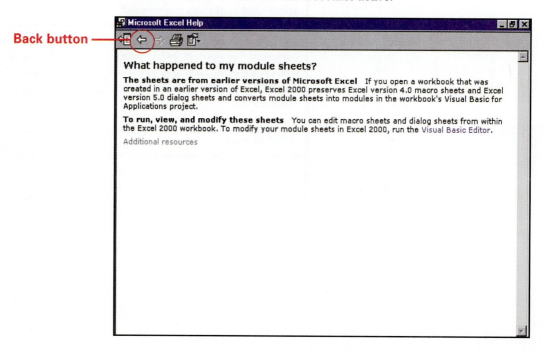

Back button

8 Click the **Back** button. The previous Help page is displayed.

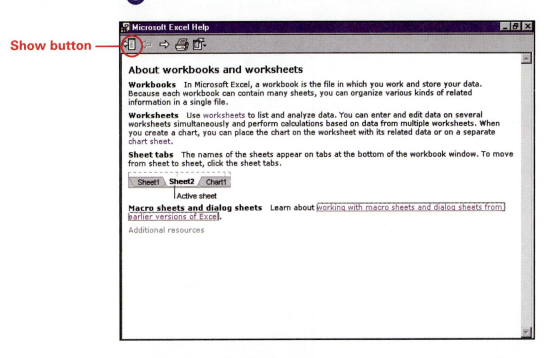

Show button

9 Click the **Show** button on the toolbar. An additional pane displays three methods of searching the Help manual. Click the **Answer Wizard** tab if necessary. The Answer Wizard recognizes keywords that you use when you type a question as a sentence.

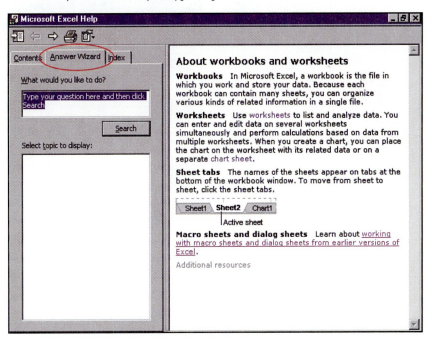

10 Click the **Contents** tab. Click the small box with a ⊞ next to the **Getting Help** topic. This pane organizes the display of related subjects in the same way as the table of contents of a book.

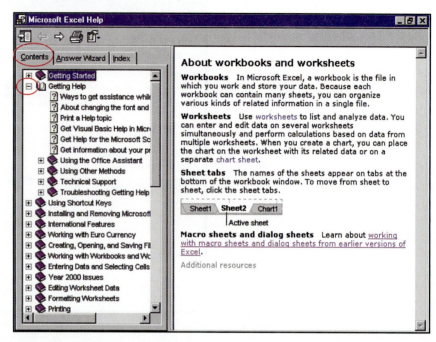

11 Click the **Index** tab. This pane allows you to search for help on specific keywords.

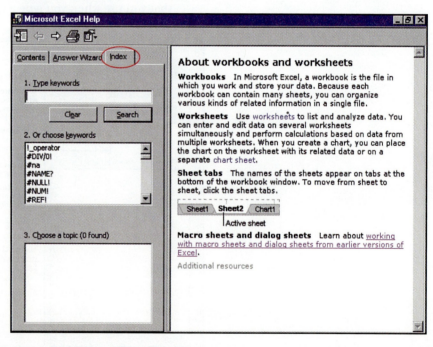

In Depth: Some people like the Office Assistant and others find it distracting. You can hide the Assistant by right-clicking it and choosing the **Hide** option from the shortcut menu.

12 Confirm that the pane on the right side is displaying the topic **About workbooks and worksheets.** Click the **Print** button on the toolbar. Confirm that the correct printer is selected and click **OK** to print a copy of this Help page.

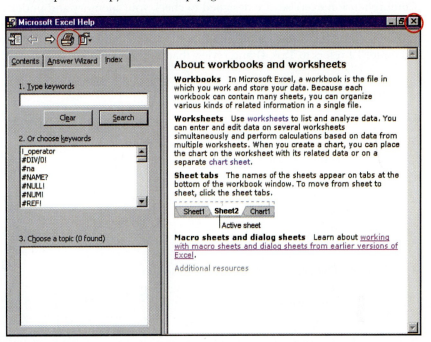

13 Click the **Close** button on the title bar to close the Help window. Click the **Close** window button on the title bar of the Excel window to close the Excel program.

LESSON 1   THE BASICS   31

Comprehension Exercises

Comprehension exercises are designed to check your memory and understanding of the basic concepts in this lesson. You distinguish between true and false statements, identify new screen elements, and match terms with related statements. If you are uncertain of the correct answer, refer to the task number following each item (for example, T4 refers to Task 4) and review that task until you are confident that you can provide a correct response.

True-False

Circle either T or F.

T F **1.** The scrollbar at the right of the screen is the vertical scrollbar. **(T1)**

T F **2.** Workbook and worksheet are the same thing. The words may be used interchangeably. **(T1)**

T F **3.** The cells that are visible on the screen when you first open Excel are the only ones available. **(T1)**

T F **4.** The vertical scrollbar and its arrows can be used to rapidly scroll through the sheet or scroll one row at a time. **(T1)**

T F **5.** A cell that is in column C and row 2 would be referred to as cell 2C. **(T2)**

T F **6.** A selected cell has a darker border than the other cells. **(T2)**

T F **7.** When you press ⏎Enter the selection will always move to the cell below it. This is a basic feature of Excel that cannot be changed. **(T3)**

T F **8.** Text and numbers should be placed in the same cell together to save space. **(T3)**

T F **9.** Clicking on the **AutoSum** button will place a formula in the currently selected cell that will automatically add the nearest row or column of numbers. **(T5)**

T F **10.** The Help feature can recognize keywords in questions you enter and display a list of Help topics that may answer that question. **(T7)**

Identifying Parts of the Excel Screen

Refer to the figure and identify the numbered parts of the screen. Write the letter of the correct label in the space next to the number.

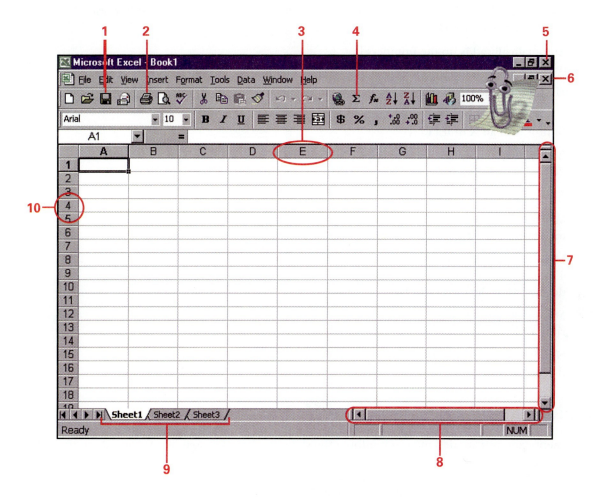

1. __F__
2. __G__
3. __B__
4. __J__
5. __H__
6. __I__
7. __D__
8. __E__
9. __A__
10. __C__

A. Tabs to identify sheets (**T1**)
B. Column header (**T2**)
C. Row header (**T2**)
D. Vertical scrollbar (**T1**)
E. Horizontal scrollbar (**T1**)
F. Save button (**T6**)
G. Print button (**T6**)
H. Close button for Excel (**T7**)
I. Close Window button for the workbook (**T7**)
J. AutoSum button (**T5**)

Matching

Match the statements below to the word or phrase that is the best match from the list. Write the letter of the matching word or phrase in the space provided next to the number.

1. ___ A tab at the bottom of the second worksheet in a workbook (T1)
2. ___ Automatically adds up the numbers in nearby cells (T5)
3. ___ Method used to begin editing existing text or numbers in a cell (T4)
4. ___ Button with an X in it (T7)
5. ___ Button that looks like a 3 1/2" floppy disk (T6)
6. ___ The cell in row 3, column D (T2)
7. ___ May be used to erase to the left of the insertion point (T4)
8. ___ May be used to finish the process of placing a number or text into a cell and move downward to the next cell (T3)
9. ___ May be used to move the selection to the right (T2)
10. ___ Numbers that appear along the left side of the sheet (T2)

A. Move pointer to cell and double-click
B. Save
C. 3D
D. ↵Enter
E. The AutoSum button
F. ←Backspace
G. Tab
H. Sheet2
I. Close
J. D3
K. Row headers

Reinforcement Exercises

Reinforcement exercises are designed to reinforce the skills you have learned by applying them to a new situation. Detailed instructions are provided along with a figure, where appropriate, to illustrate the final result. The Reinforcement exercises that follow should be completed sequentially. Leave the workbook open at the end of each exercise for use in the next exercise until you are specifically directed to close it.

R1—Creating a Worksheet to Show Income for January

1. Launch Excel.
2. Enter **January** in cell **A1**.
3. Enter your name in cell **F1**.
4. Enter the following data in the cells as shown in the figure:

	Gas	Water	Electric	Phone
East Side	185	55	550	120
West Side	100	35	450	67
Downtown	384	120	980	520
North Side	200	85	350	250
Total				

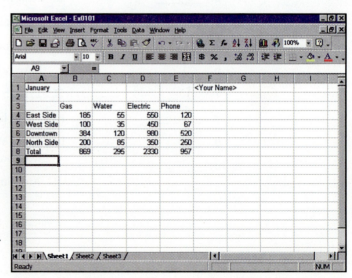

34 LEARN EXCEL 2000

5. Use the **AutoSum** button at the bottom of each column.
6. Print **Sheet1**.
7. Save the workbook on your floppy disk. Use **Ex0101** for its name.
8. Leave the workbook open for use in the next exercise.

R2—Using Another Sheet

1. Click the **Sheet2** tab to select the second sheet of the Ex0101 workbook.
2. Enter **February** in cell **A1**.
3. Place your name in cell **E1**.
4. Enter the following text and numbers as shown in the figure:

	Gas	Water	Electric	Phone
East Side	168	57	500	130
West Side	95	38	480	85
Downtown	350	115	900	650
North Side	185	80	360	300
Total				

5. Use the **AutoSum** button to calculate the sum of the column of numbers.
6. Print the sheet.
7. Click the **Save** button on the Standard toolbar to save your changes. (You will not need to give it a name again. It will automatically update the existing file on your disk.)
8. Leave the workbook open for use in the next exercise.

R3—Editing a Worksheet

1. Click the **Sheet1** tab to select Sheet1.
2. Edit cell **B4** to read **2400**. (If you have used the AutoSum button correctly, the sum of column B will be automatically updated.)
3. Click the **Save** button to save the change.
4. Print **Sheet1**.
5. Leave the workbook open for use in the next exercise.

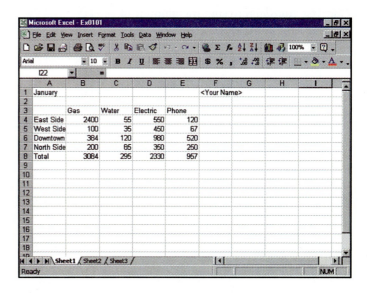

R4—Closing and Exiting Excel

1. Click the **Close Window** button to close the workbook. (If you have any unsaved work, the program will always prompt you to save your changes before it closes the workbook.)

2. Click the **Close** button to close the Excel program.

Challenge

Challenge exercises are designed to test your ability to apply your skills to new situations with less detailed instruction. These exercises also challenge you to expand your repertoire of skills by using Excel commands that are similar to those you have already learned. The desired outcome is clearly defined, but you have more freedom to choose the steps needed to achieve the required result.

C1—Create a Monthly Income and Expense sheet

Sometimes it is not obvious where your money is going. You can use Excel to take a look at the amount of money coming in and compare it to your expenses. Since many expenses occur on a monthly basis, it is useful to compare them to monthly income.

Goal: Create a worksheet that looks like the figure. Use the **AutoSum** feature to add the income and expenses, and then print the worksheet.

Use the following guidelines:

1. Launch Excel. Place your name in cell **A1**.

2. Refer to the figure and set up two columns to list the type and amount of monthly income you have and two more columns to list the type and amount of monthly expenses. Fill in all four columns with types and amounts of income and expenses. Use your own numbers. Change the types of income or expenses as needed to match your income and expenses.

3. Use **AutoSum** to sum the amount of income in the cells at the bottom of the column of income amounts and the amount of expenses at the bottom of the column of expenses.

4. Save the workbook on your disk as **Ex0102**.

5. Print the worksheet. Leave the workbook open for use in the next exercise.

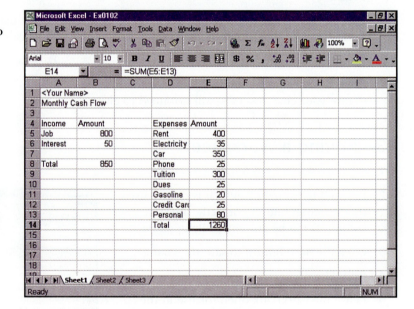

C2—Find Present Balance of a Checkbook

If the total income exceeds or matches the total expenses for a month, you may still run out of money in your checking account, depending on when the deposits are made and the checks are written.

Goal: Create a worksheet that resembles a check register as shown in the figure. Enter the deposits as positive numbers and check amounts as negative numbers. Sum the starting balance, deposits, and check amounts using the **AutoSum** feature.

1. Select **Sheet2**. Set up a three-column system for calculating your checkbook balance as shown in the figure.

2. Enter your own starting deposits and check amounts. The deposits should be positive numbers and the check amounts should be negative numbers (there are two negative signs on most keyboards, one at the upper-right corner of the number keypad, and the other two keys to the left of (←Backspace)).

3. Use the **AutoSum** feature to display the balance at the bottom of the column.

4. Look at the deposits and the check amounts. Estimate what the balance should be to within ten dollars. Does the final balance agree with your estimate? If so, it is probably right. Always do a quick check of your spreadsheet to make sure that it makes sense.

5. Save the workbook. Print **Sheet2**.

6. Close the workbook, but do not close Excel.

C3—Open a New Workbook and Close It Without Saving Changes

Excel will open a new workbook when it is launched. If you want to open a new workbook without closing and re-launching Excel, you can do so by clicking the **New** button.

Goal: Open a workbook without closing and re-launching Excel.

1. Click the **New** button on the Standard toolbar.
2. Enter your name in cell **A1** of **Sheet1**.
3. Print the sheet.
4. Close the workbook. Do not save the changes.

C4—Turn the Office Assistant On and Off

Some people love the Office Assistant and others find it to be distracting.

Goal: Open the Office Assistant and find out how to turn it off and on. Print the directions. Turn the Assistant on and off, but leave it in the mode in which you found it.

1. Click the **Office Assistant** or click the **Microsoft Excel Help** button to open the Assistant's dialog box.
2. Type the following question: **How do I turn the Office Assistant on or off?** and click the **Search** button.
3. Click **show, Hide, or turn off the Office Assistant**. The Microsoft Excel Help window opens.
4. Click the **Print** button to print the directions.
5. Follow the directions to turn the Office Assistant on and off. If you are working on a computer that is shared with others, be sure to leave the Assistant the way you found it.
6. Close the workbook.

Discovery

Discovery exercises are designed to help you learn how to teach yourself a new skill. In each exercise, you discover something new that is related to the topic taught in this lesson. You may be directed to use built-in wizards or some of the extensive Help features provided in Excel to discover new features and learn new skills with minimum assistance from books or instructors. The required outcome demonstrates your ability to apply the new skill. You determine the choice of topic, worksheet design, and steps of execution. The first three exercises use Microsoft Web pages. These pages, and the features therein, change often. You will probably need to modify the steps or the goals of these exercises. Consult with your instructor if you need to modify the goals.

D1—Register with Microsoft Online Support

Microsoft provides a free support service for users of Microsoft products. They require that you provide a valid email address and fill out some information about yourself. You may select that no unsolicited email or other form of contact is made based on this information. To contact this support service, you must have a connection to the Internet, an Internet browser, and a valid email address.

Goal: Find Microsoft's support page and register for free access. Obtain and record a password for future use. Open and print Microsoft's Support Online Web page as shown in the figure. (This page changes often, so it may have a somewhat different appearance when you view it.)

1. Choose **Help, Office on the Web**.
2. Look for a link to the Support page.
3. Pick a description of your user status and follow the directions for registering.
4. Proceed to the Online Support Web page.
5. Use the browser's print option to print the page.
6. Leave the page open for use in the next Discovery exercise.

D2—Get Help from Microsoft by Asking a Specific Question Online

Now that you are registered and have found the Online Support page, you will notice that you have several options. You can choose a product (Excel) and ask a specific question, look at frequently asked questions, view articles on popular subjects, or contact Microsoft Technical support. Leave the site open for use in the next exercise.

Goal: Select the product **Excel for Windows** and pose a specific question. Read some of the questions and responses. Print one of them.

D3—Get Help from a Microsoft Technical Support Engineer

Individualized help is available from Microsoft. Some types of support are free and others are available for a fee. Find out what your options are and how much it would cost to contact a Microsoft Engineer via the Web and ask a specific question.

Goal: Find out what your support options are if you have purchased Excel as part of the Office suite and want to ask a question using the Internet. Print out the Web response page that links to those options (see the previous figure). Print one page each from the no-charge, pay-per-incident, and Priority Contract pages. These are multipage sites, so just pick a representative page. Do not establish an account that will incur charges.

1. Select **Microsoft Technical Support** from the Support Online page.

2. Select **Contact Microsoft Technical Support** from the menu at the left side of the page.

3. Look for the option that lets you contact an engineer via the Web, and select it.

4. Print the Web response page.

5. Read each of the sections on no-charge, pay-per-incident, and Priority Contracts and print a page from each. Do not subscribe or commit to any financial obligation.

6. Close the Web browser.

D4—Use Pre-written Spreadsheet Templates

If you use the menu option for opening a new workbook, you will have the opportunity to open one of several pre-written spreadsheets that have been set up to accomplish specific tasks.

Goal: Explore the available pre-written spreadsheets.

1. Click **File** on the menu bar. Hold down the mouse button on this selection for several seconds until the complete menu displays.

2. Click **New**. The New dialog box appears.

3. Click the **Spreadsheet Solutions** tab.

4. Select one of the solutions listed. If they have not been installed, check with your instructor. If you have a set of Office 2000 CD-ROM discs, you will be prompted to insert the first CD.

5. These workbooks contain automated features called *macros* and are fairly complex. Your objective at this time is to just take a look to see what is available.

6. Close the workbook(s) and close Excel.

Lesson: 2

Formatting the Worksheet

Task 1 Opening an Existing Workbook

Task 2 Selecting Groups of Cells

Task 3 Formatting Large Numbers, Currency, Decimal Places, and Dates

Task 4 Adjusting Columns and Cells for Long Text or Numbers

Task 5 Aligning Text in a Cell

Task 6 Changing the Font, Size, and Emphasis of Text

Task 7 Adding Lines, Borders, Colors, and Shading

Introduction

A variety of formatting techniques can be used to improve the appearance of a worksheet. Formatting your worksheet can also make it easier to read. This is especially important for worksheets that are used by others. In this lesson, you learn how to work with existing worksheets to improve their appearance, make them easier to read, and give them a professional look.

Visual Summary

When you have completed this lesson, you will have a worksheet that looks like this:

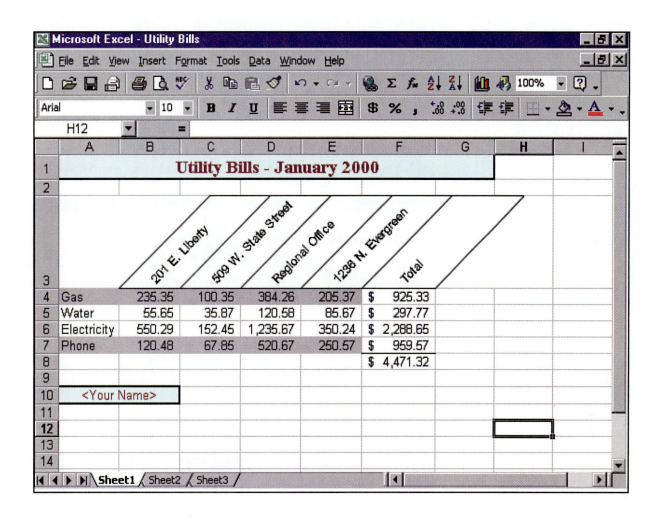

TASK 1

Opening an Existing Workbook

Why would I do this?

Launching Excel opens a blank workbook. There are times, however, when you would like to use a workbook that you previously created. The Open procedure allows you to load a file that you have stored on a floppy disk, a hard disk, or a *network file server*. If you don't remember where the file is stored, the Open procedure also allows you to search for the desired file.

In this task, you learn how to locate and open an existing workbook.

1 Launch **Excel**. Excel opens and displays an empty workbook.

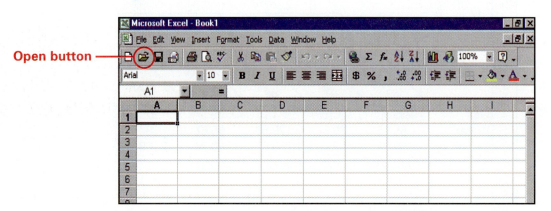

Open button

2 Place the CD-ROM disc that came with this book in your computer and click the **Open** button. The Open dialog box appears.

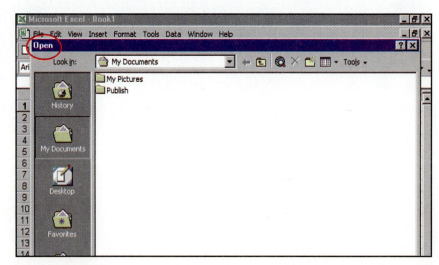

Caution: When you place the CD-ROM disc in your computer, a program may launch automatically that can be used to install the student files to your hard disk. It is not necessary to do so. Click the Exit button.

42 LEARN EXCEL 2000

3 Click the arrow on the right of the **Look in** list and click the CD-ROM drive where you have placed your book's disc. The program displays the folders that are on that disc. Double-click the **Student** folder. Double-click the **Lesson02** folder.

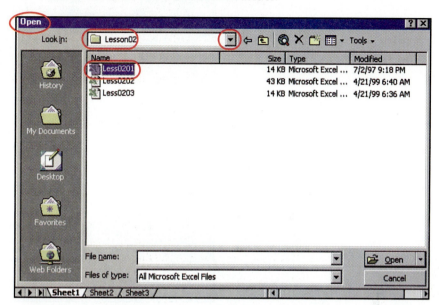

4 Click the **Less0201** file and click **Open**. Excel opens the file. The name of the file is shown in the title bar, and the selected cell is the one that was selected when the file was last saved.

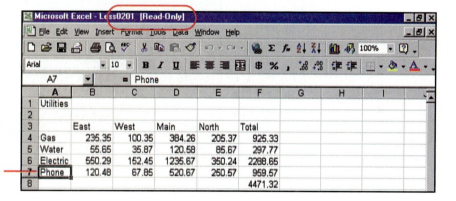

Selected cell

5 Place a floppy disk in drive **A:**. Click **File, Save As**. The Save As dialog box appears.

> **In Depth:** The compact disc (CD) is not made to be changed. It is a type of Read Only Memory (ROM). When you open a file from the CD-ROM disc, the program displays a reminder that you cannot change this file. If you save the file to another location, you can make changes to that copy of the file.

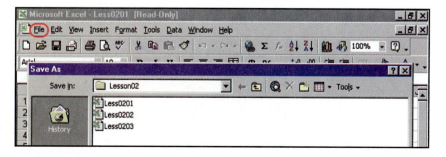

LESSON 2 FORMATTING THE WORKSHEET   **43**

6 Change the **File name** to **Utility Bills**. Click the down arrow next to the **Save in** box and select the **3 1/2 Floppy (A:)** drive.

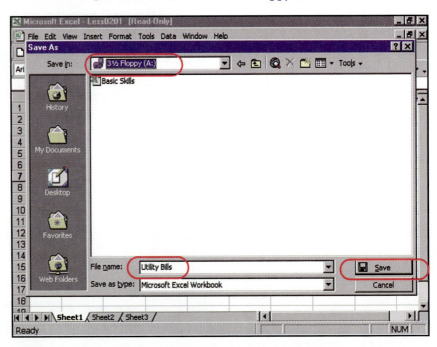

7 Click the **Save** button. The workbook is saved on the floppy disk, and the new name appears at the top of the window.

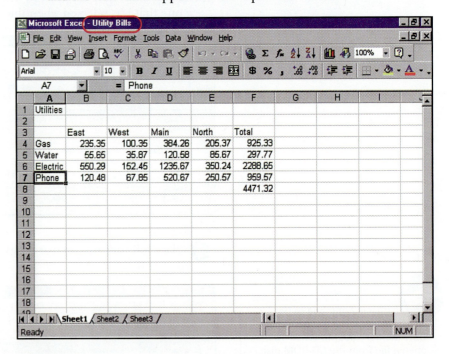

TASK 2

Selecting Groups of Cells

Why would I do this?

To change the formatting of a cell, it must be selected. It is common to want to change the formatting of groups of cells, so it is preferable to select the entire group and format all of them at the same time. You can select the entire sheet, an entire row or column, a rectangle of cells, or unconnected groups of cells. By formatting the entire group of cells, you help ensure that the same formatting is applied.

In this task, you learn different techniques for selecting a group of cells.

1 Click the **Select All** button in the upper-left corner of the sheet. The entire worksheet is selected.

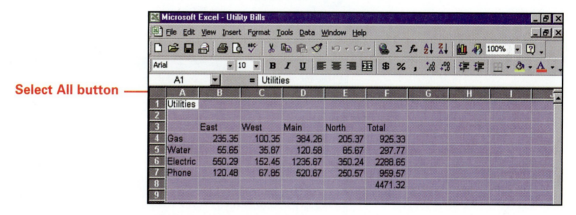

2 Click the heading of column **F**. The entire column of totals is selected.

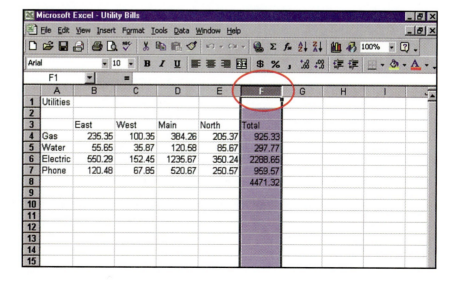

LESSON 2   FORMATTING THE WORKSHEET   **45**

3 Click the heading for row **5**. The entire row pertaining to water bills is selected.

Notice that the first cell of the group is always the opposite highlight of the rest of the selected cells. It is still one of the selected group.

> **Caution:** All of the cells in the row, including those that are not visible, are selected. Be careful when you select an entire sheet, row, or column. You may make changes to cells that are not on the screen.

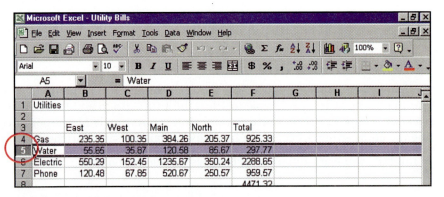

4 Position the pointer over cell **B4**. Click and drag a rectangular selection area to cell **E7,** then release the mouse button. This selects the actual bills.

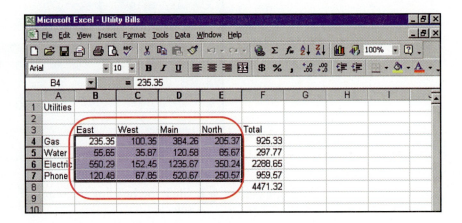

5 Selecting two groups of cells that are not next to each other is a two-step process. First, select cells **B4** through **B7** and release the mouse button.

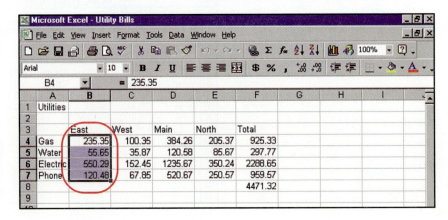

6 Hold down Ctrl and select cells **E4** through **E7**. Release the mouse button and Ctrl. Both sets of cells are selected.

This is a useful skill that can be applied in a later lesson when you chart content of cells that are not next to each other.

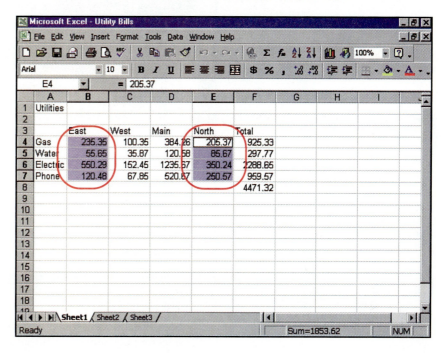

7 Click cell **B1** to select it. Use the vertical scrollbar to scroll down so that you can see cell **B30**.

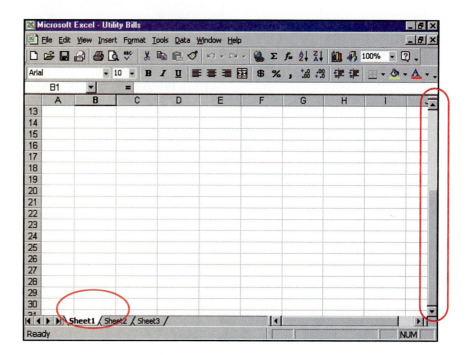

LESSON 2 FORMATTING THE WORKSHEET

8 Hold down ⇧Shift and click cell **B30**. This selects all of the cells between B1 and B30.

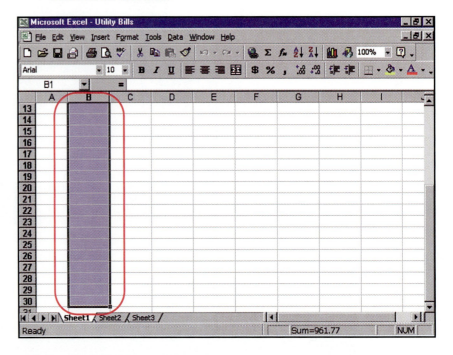

Caution: If you try to select a large group of cells that extends beyond the edge of the screen by using the click and drag method, you may find that the screen scrolls by so fast that you are hundreds of rows or columns beyond your intended destination. Scroll back to the beginning of the group and try it again using ⇧Shift as described in steps 7-9.

9 Scroll back to the top of the sheet. This method is useful when selecting a group of cells that are so far apart that you have to use the scrollbar to find the other end of the group.

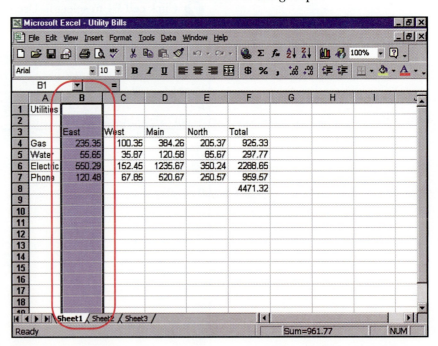

Quick Tip: If you want to select a long range of cells without taking your hands off the keyboard, select the first cell, hold down ⇧Shift, and use the arrow keys on the keyboard to select the range.

48　LEARN EXCEL 2000

TASK 3

Formatting Large Numbers, Currency, Decimal Places, and Dates

Why would I do this?

Most numbers greater than 999 should have commas inserted to make them easier to read. In some cases, numbers represent money and should have commas, decimal points, and dollar signs. Many numbers have decimal components, and you must decide how many places to display. Excel allows you to format numbers the way you want them to be displayed. You also need to know how to handle dates.

In this task, you learn how to apply different types of numerical formats.

1 Select the cells from **B4** through **E7** and click the **Comma Style** button. Notice the electricity bill for the Main office in cell D6 is now displayed with a comma.

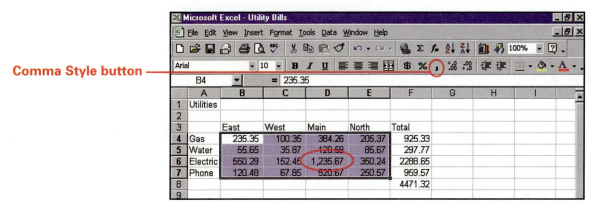

2 Select cells from **F4** through **F8** and click the **Currency Style** button. A dollar sign is added to the left side of the cell, and commas are inserted in numbers that are greater than 999. Leave this range selected for the next step.

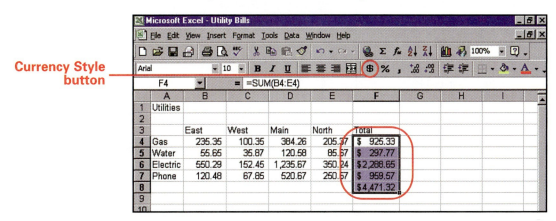

LESSON 2 FORMATTING THE WORKSHEET **49**

3 Click once on the **Decrease Decimal** button. Notice that the numbers are displayed with one less decimal place.

Decrease Decimal button

Display rounded down

Display rounded up

4 Click the **Increase Decimal** button once to display two decimal places.

Increase Decimal button

In Depth: The display of a number in a cell may be rounded off; however, Excel shows the full number in the formula bar and uses it in calculations. If the number that needs to be rounded ends in a 5, Excel rounds up. Numbers 0 through 4 are rounded down, and numbers 5 through 9 are rounded up.

Caution: Rounding the display does not change the actual number in the cell or any cell that depends upon it. If you use the Decrease Decimal button to change the display so that it does not show any of the decimal places in cells F4 through F8, the rounded numbers do not appear to add correctly to the sum in cell F8.

5 Select cell **C1**, type **1/30/00**, and press ↵Enter.

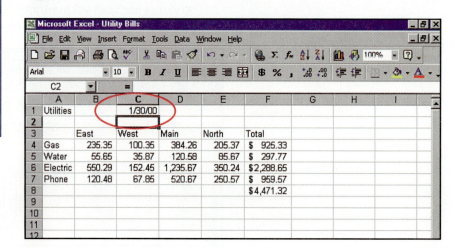

50 LEARN EXCEL 2000

Quick Tip: Commonly used menu items can be accessed quickly by clicking on an object with the right mouse button. A shortcut menu opens containing options that are relevant to the object. At step 6 you could have right-clicked cell **C1** and chosen **Format cells** from the shortcut menu.

6 Select cell **C1** again. Choose **Format** from the menu, then choose **Cells**. The Format Cells dialog box opens. Click the **Number** tab if necessary.

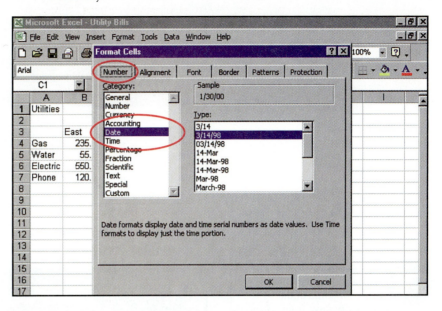

7 Click **Date** if necessary to select it. Click the example **Mar-98** in the **Type** box.

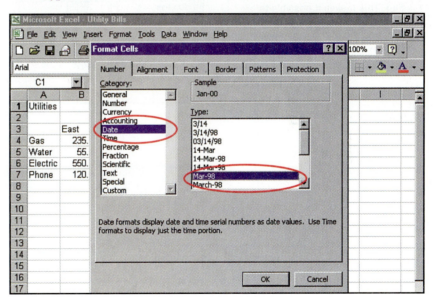

LESSON 2　FORMATTING THE WORKSHEET　51

8 Click **OK**. The date displays showing just the month and year. Notice the actual content of the cell is displayed in the formula bar.

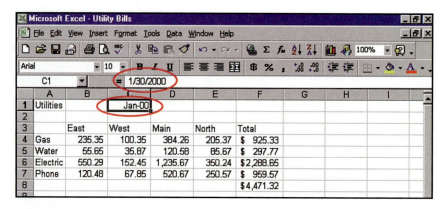

9 With cell **C1** still selected, choose **Edit**, **Clear**, **Formats**. The number 36555 appears.

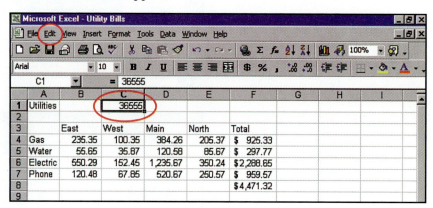

> **In Depth:** Excel thinks of dates in terms of the number of days from a fixed date in the past. When you remove the formatting from the cell, it displays the number that it actually is using. This makes it possible to subtract one date from another to determine the number of days between two dates.

10 Choose **Edit**, **Clear**, **All**. The date is removed.

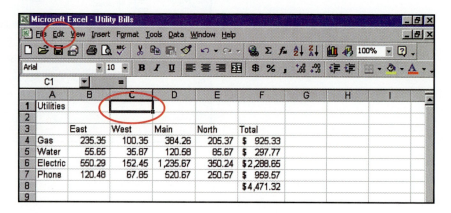

LEARN EXCEL 2000

TASK 4

Adjusting Columns and Cells for Long Text or Numbers

Why would I do this?

Text and numbers entered into a cell are often longer than the cell width. If the cell to the right contains an entry, the text in the left cell is cut off. If a number is too long, Excel displays a string of # signs.

In this task, you learn how to change column widths to accommodate entries, wrap text onto several lines within a cell, and center titles across several columns.

1 Select cell **A6** and type **Electricity**. Press ⏎Enter. Notice that word is cut off.

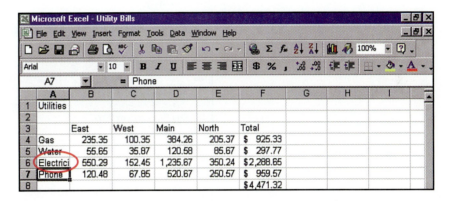

2 Move the pointer to the line that separates the headings for columns **A** and **B**. The mouse pointer turns into a double-sided black arrow.

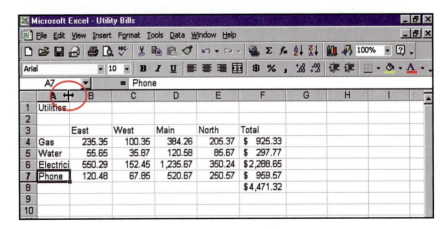

LESSON 2   FORMATTING THE WORKSHEET   **53**

3 Double-click and the column width automatically adjusts to fit the longest word in any of the cells in column A.

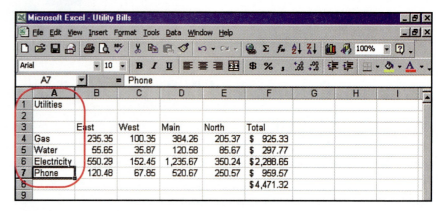

4 Select cell **A1** and type **Utility Bills - January 2000**. Press ⏎Enter. Notice that the text overlaps the cells to the right because they are empty.

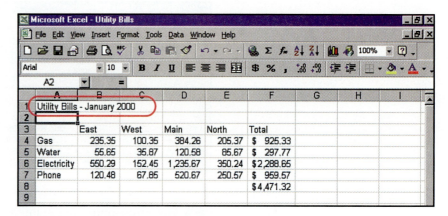

5 Select cells **A1** through **G1**. Click the **Merge and Center** button. The selected cells display the text as if they were one cell, and the long title is centered. The text is centered across one more column than necessary to accomodate a change that will be made in Task 7.

Merge and Center button

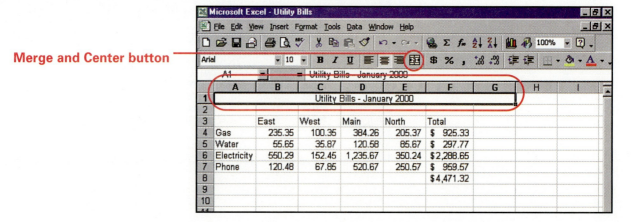

6. Select cell **D6**, type **7000** and press ↵Enter. Notice that the size of the final total in cell F8 exceeds the available cell space. A series of # signs is displayed.

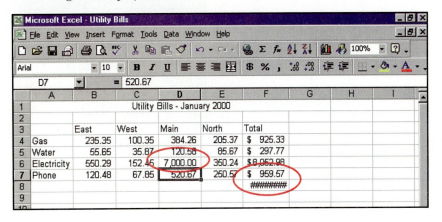

7. Double-click the line between the headings for columns **F** and **G**. The width of column F adjusts to display the larger number.

In Depth: If you want to make sure that the column is wide enough to handle future entries, there is another way that you can make the column wider. You can click and drag the line between the headings to the right to widen the column.

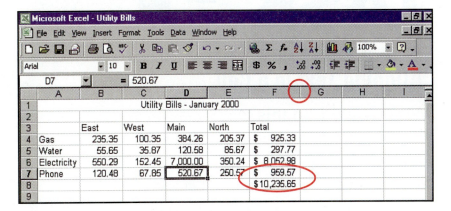

8. Select cell **D6**, type **1235.67** and press ↵Enter to replace the entry with a more realistic number.

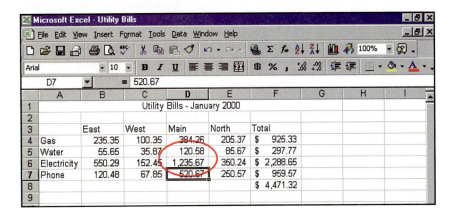

LESSON 2 FORMATTING THE WORKSHEET

9 Click the **Save** button to save the changes made up to this point.

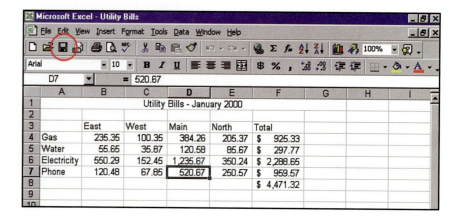

TASK 5

Aligning Text in a Cell

Why would I do this?

If text is used to label a row or column, you may find that it looks better if the text is centered in or aligned with the right side of the cell. If the text used as a column label is much longer than the numbers in the column, you may want to increase the height of the row and wrap the text in the cell. Another way to handle long column labels is to slant the cells at an angle.

In this task, you learn how to align long text labels.

1 Select cell **B3** and type **201 E. Liberty**. Press Tab and type **509 W. State Street**. Press Tab and type **Regional Office**. Press Tab and type **1236 N. Evergreen**. Press Enter.

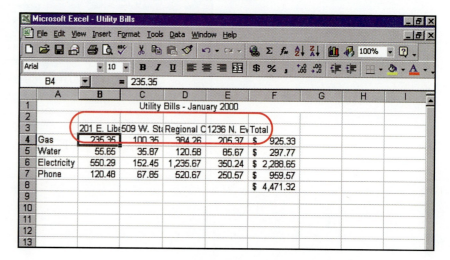

56 LEARN EXCEL 2000

❷ Select cells **B3** through **F3**. Click **Format**, **Cells**. The Format Cells dialog box appears. Click the **Alignment** tab, if it is not already selected.

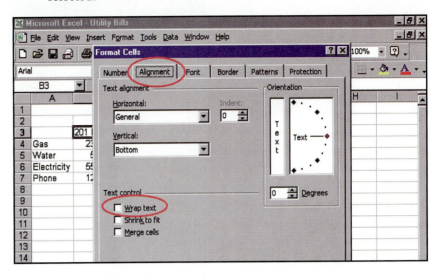

❸ Click the **Wrap text** check box. Click **OK**. The height of the row increases, and the text wraps within the cells just as if it were a word processing document.

> ⚠ **Caution:** Excel's word wrapping feature does not have an automatic hyphenation feature and is not as smart as a word processor when it comes to estimating where to break words. Check your work when you use the **W**rap text feature.

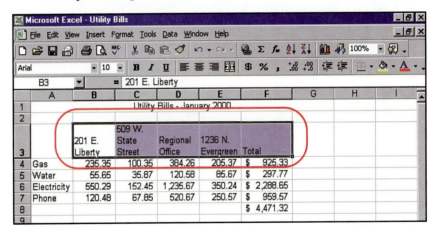

❹ Click the **Undo** button to remove the **Wrap text** feature. There is another way to handle this type of column label.

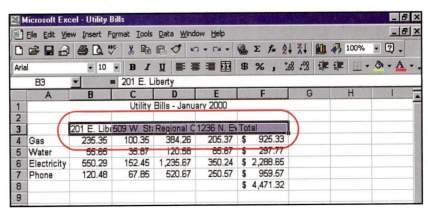

LESSON 2 FORMATTING THE WORKSHEET   57

5 Make sure that cells **B3** to **F3** are still selected and click **F**o**rmat**, **C**e**lls**. The Format Cells dialog box appears.

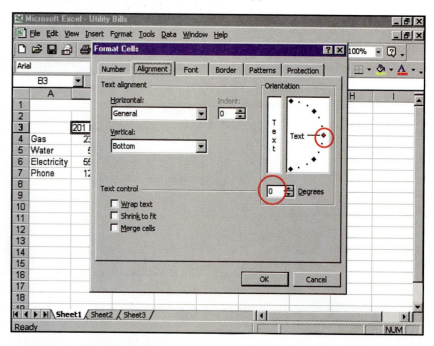

6 Click and drag the small red diamond in the **Orientation** window upward until the **Degrees** box reads **45**.

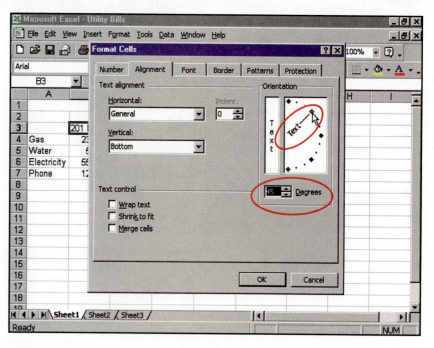

LEARN EXCEL 2000

7 Click the down arrow next to the **Horizontal** box. Click **Center**. This centers the text in the cell.

✓ **Quick Tip:** You can also type the angle in the **Degrees** box or use the small arrows in the **Degrees** box to change the angle.

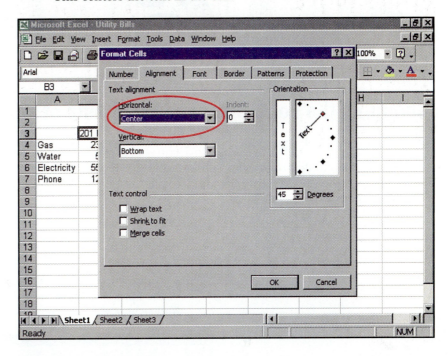

8 Click **OK**. The text in cells B3 to F3 is displayed at an angle.

✓ **Quick Tip:** A faster way to change horizontal alignment is to use one of the three buttons on the Formatting toolbar: **Align Left**, **Center**, or **Align Right**.

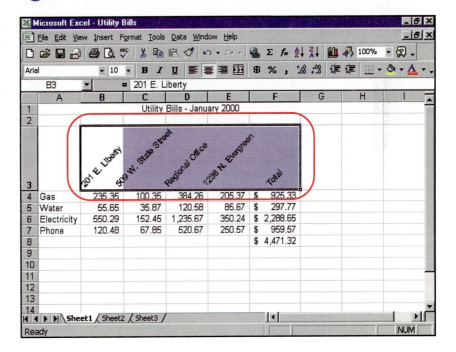

LESSON 2 FORMATTING THE WORKSHEET   59

TASK 6

Changing the Font, Size, and Emphasis of Text

Why would I do this?

You may want to emphasize titles and important words by making them larger and by using a different *font*. This helps improve the overall appearance of your worksheet. You can draw attention to key numbers by adding emphasis to those numbers.

In this task, you learn how to change the *point size* of a title and change a font from *Arial* to *Times New Roman*. You also add emphasis by using boldface or italicized versions of the font.

1 Click anywhere on the title to select it. Click the down arrow next to the **Font** box. Scroll down and click **Times New Roman**. The font style of the title changes.

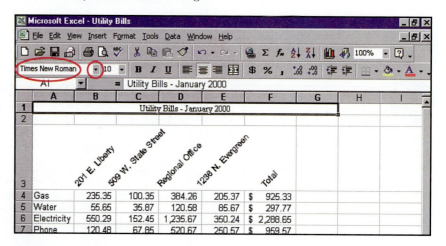

2 Click the down arrow next to the **Font Size** box. Click **14**. The title changes to 14 point.

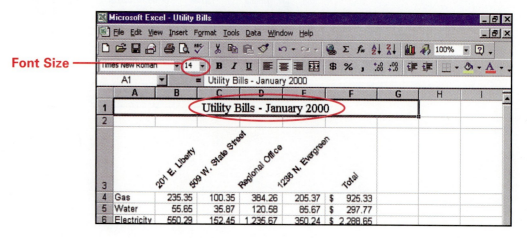

Font Size

3 Click the **Bold** button.

> **In Depth:** In addition to Bold, you also can change the emphasis of text or numbers by using the Underline or Italic buttons. Simply select the cells you want to change and click the appropriate button on the Formatting toolbar. Numerous other options may be found by using **F**ormat, **C**ells, and selecting the **Font** tab.

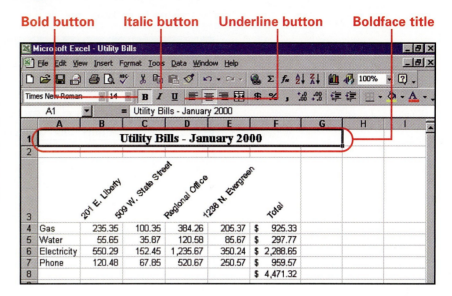

Adding Lines, Borders, Colors, and Shading

Why would I do this?

You may want to separate a column's total from the preceding numbers or add shading and borders to assist the reader in following a row of numbers across a complex page. Color, if used carefully, can add a special emphasis. Unless you have a color printer, use of colors on printed documents can be a hindrance rather than a help. It is important to use colors judiciously.

In this task, you learn how to add borders and shading to various parts of the worksheet.

1 Make sure that the title is still selected from the previous task. Click the down arrow next to the **Borders** button.

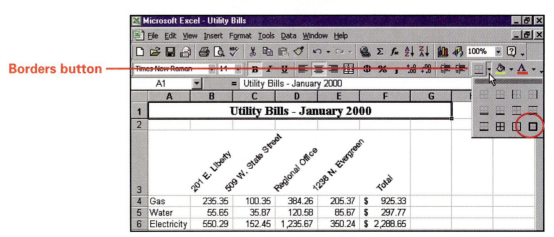

LESSON 2 FORMATTING THE WORKSHEET   61

2 Click the **Thick Box Border** option at the right side of the bottom row. Select cells **B3** to **F3**. Click the down arrow next to the **Borders** button.

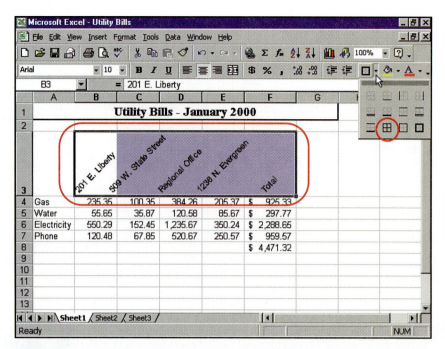

3 Click the **All Borders** option, which is the second box from the left in the bottom row that looks like a window with four panes. Select cell **F7**. Click the down arrow next to the **Borders** button.

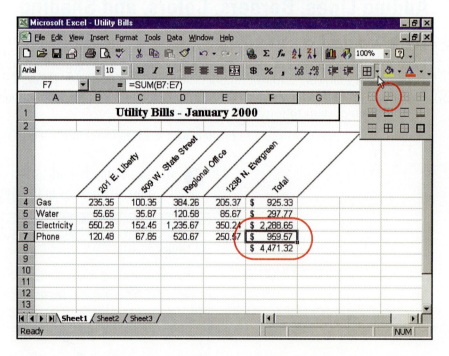

4 Click the **Bottom Border** option, which is second from the left in the top row. Select cells **A4** through **E4** and cells **A7** through **E7** (remember to use Ctrl to select the second group of cells). Click the down arrow next to the **Fill Color** button.

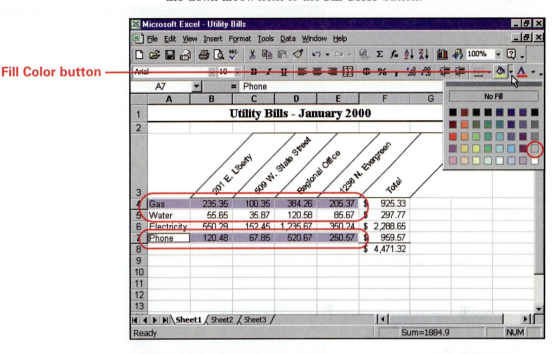

Fill Color button

5 Click the **Gray-25%** button. The selected cells are shaded. (To see the gray, deselect the shaded cells by clicking in any other cell.)

In Depth: If you are unsure of the name of a color, allow the pointer to remain stationary on one of the colors for a few seconds and a ScreenTip displays the name.

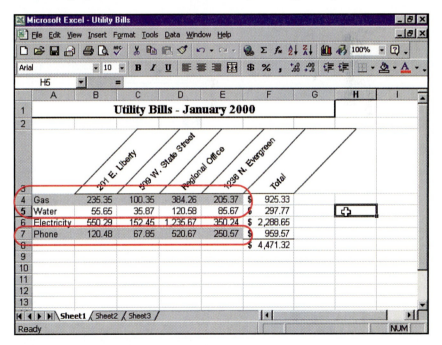

LESSON 2   FORMATTING THE WORKSHEET

6 Select the title again. Click the down arrow next to the **Fill Color** button and click the **Light Turquoise** option. This changes the background (fill color) to a light turquoise color on the screen.

> **Caution:** If you do not have a color printer, the program assigns different shades of gray to different colors. If you pick two colors for your text and background that are assigned to the same shade of gray, the printout may be unreadable.

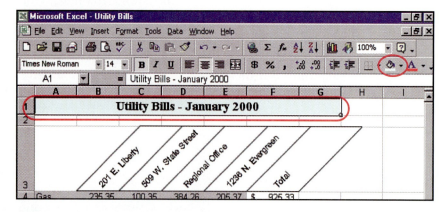

7 With the title still selected, click the down arrow next to the **Font Color** button.

Font Color button

8 Click the **Dark Red** option.

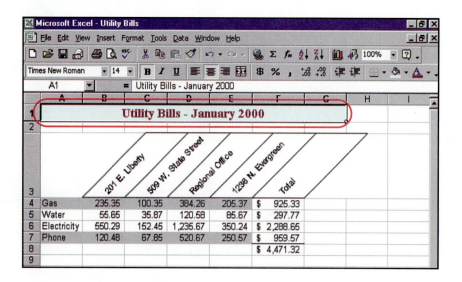

64   LEARN EXCEL 2000

9 Select cell **A10** and type your name. Change the font, font size, border, background color, and font color to something you like. Merge across two or more cells if your name exceeds the current column width.

> ✓ **Quick Tip:** The Font Color, Fill Color, and Borders buttons on the Formatting toolbar display the most recent choice, respectively. If you want to use the type of emphasis that is displayed on the button, you can apply it by clicking once on the button without using the drop-down menu.

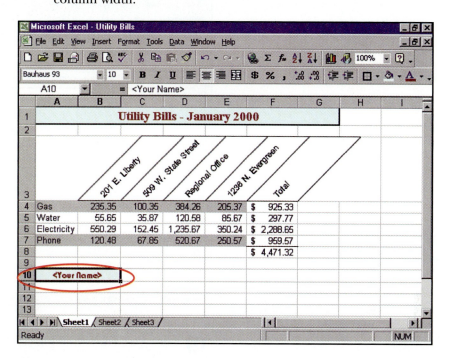

10 Click the **Print** button to print a copy.

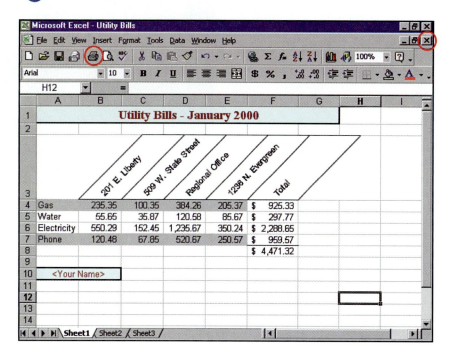

LESSON 2　FORMATTING THE WORKSHEET　65

11 Click the **Close Window** button to close the workbook. A dialog box warns you that you have not saved the changes you have made.

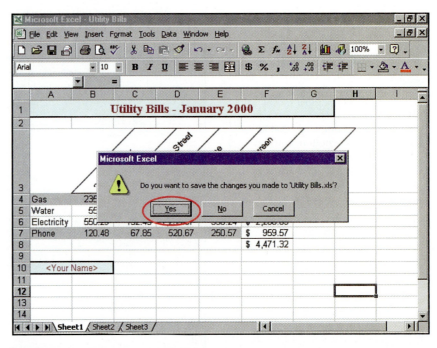

12 Click **Yes**. The workbook closes, leaving the Excel program active.

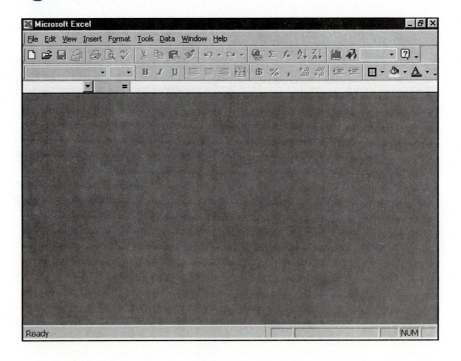

Comprehension Exercises

Comprehension exercises are designed to check your memory and understanding of the basic concepts in this lesson. You distinguish between true and false statements, identify new screen elements, and match terms with related statements. If you are uncertain of the correct answer, refer to the task number following each item (for example, T4 refers to Task 4) and review that task until you are confident that you can provide a correct response.

True-False

Circle either T or F.

T F **1.** The way to open an existing workbook is to use the **Insert**, **File** options from the menu. **(T1)**

T F **2.** You can select all of the cells in a row by clicking on the row heading. **(T2)**

T F **3.** All the cells in a selection must be touching each other; separate groups of cells cannot be selected at the same time. **(T2)**

T F **4.** If you select a group of cells and click the **Comma Style** button, all of the numbers in those cells will have a comma placed between every two numbers. **(T3)**

T F **5.** If a selected cell contains the number 5.25 and you click the **Decrease Decimal** button, the number 5.2 is displayed. **(T3)**

T F **6.** If a cell displays a row of # signs, it means that you made a mistake in writing a formula. **(T4)**

T F **7.** One way to handle long labels is to use the **Wrap text** option. **(T5)**

T F **8.** A 16-point character is larger than an 8-point character. **(T6)**

T F **9.** If you have a printer with only one color of ink, it does not matter what colors you choose for text and background. **(T7)**

T F **10.** It is possible to print long column labels at an angle. **(T5)**

Identifying Parts of the Excel Screen

Refer to the figure and identify the numbered parts of the screen. Write the letter of the correct label in the space next to the number.

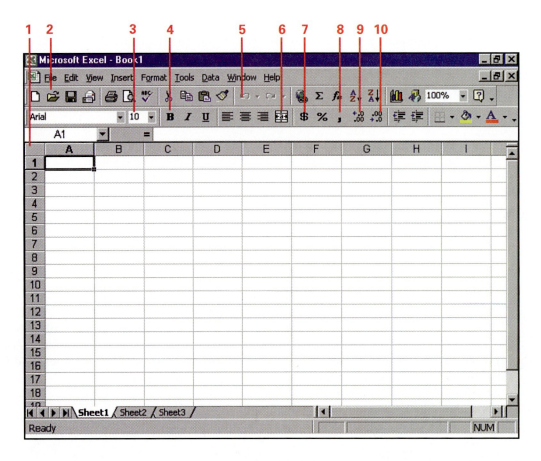

1. _____
2. _____
3. _____
4. _____
5. _____
6. _____
7. _____
8. _____
9. _____
10. _____

A. Open button (T1)
B. Bold button (T6)
C. Select All button (T2)
D. Comma Style button (T3)
E. Currency Style button (T3)
F. Decrease Decimal button (T3)
G. Increase Decimal button (T3)
H. Merge and Center button (T4)
I. Borders button (T7)
J. Font Size (T6)

LEARN WORD 2000

Matching

Match the statements below to the word or phrase that is the best match from the list. Write the letter of the matching word or phrase in the space provided next to the number.

1. ___ Used to open an existing Excel workbook (T1)
2. ___ Used to select a group of cells that is not touching the first group (T2)
3. ___ Method used to automatically adjust the width of a column to accommodate the widest cell entry (T4)
4. ___ Method used to manually change the width of a column (T4)
5. ___ Button that inserts dollar signs (T3)
6. ___ Symbols that indicate that a number is too long to fit in a cell (T4)
7. ___ Method for displaying column labels at a slant (T5)
8. ___ Setting that forces long text entries to fit within the available column width by increasing the row height and displaying the text on several lines within the cell (T5)
9. ___ A font (T6)
10. ___ A border style (T6)

A. Move pointer to the line between column headings and double-click
B. Save
C. Currency Style
D.
E. #######
F. Click and drag the small red diamond in the **O**rientation window to the desired angle of slant
G. Click and drag the line between column headings
H. Wrap text
I. Open
J. Arial
K. Thick box

Reinforcement Exercises

Reinforcement exercises are designed to reinforce the skills you have learned by applying them to a new situation. Detailed instructions are provided along with a figure, where appropriate, to illustrate the final result. The Reinforcement exercises that follow should be completed sequentially. Leave the workbook open at the end of each exercise for use in the next exercise until you are specifically directed to close it.

Open **Less0202** from the **Student\Lesson02** folder on the CD-ROM disc and save it as **Comparison** on your floppy disk for use in the following exercises.

R1—Apply Formats to an Existing Worksheet

1. Select **Sheet1**.
2. Type your name in cell **F17**.
3. Format **Sheet1** to match the figure. See the steps below for more detail.
4. Use the **Merge and Center** feature to center the main title across columns **A** through **F**. Center the subtitle **All Metal** across cells **C2** and **D2** and the subtitle **Glass and Metal** across cells **E2** and **F2**.
5. Center and wrap the text in cells **B3** through **F3**.
6. Center data in all cells from **B4** through **F13**.

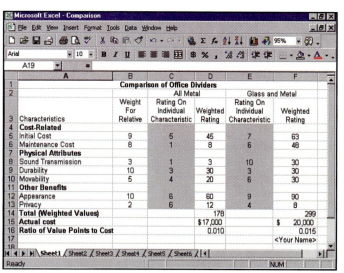

7. Select both groups of shaded cells and choose a background of **Gray-25%**.

8. Select cells **A1**, **A4**, **A7**, **A11**, **A14**, **A15**, and **A16**. Make them **Bold**.

9. Select **D15** and **F15** and format the numbers to display currency with no decimals.

10. Select **D16** and **F16** and format the numbers to display only three decimal places.

11. Adjust the column widths, print the sheet, and save the workbook.

R2—Add Border Lines and Colors

1. Select **Sheet2**. Type your name in cell **F19**.

2. Add border lines and colors to match the figure. (The Status bar has been turned off to display the entire sheet in the figure—you may have to scroll to see the last line on your screen.) See the steps below for more information.

3. Place a **Thick Box Border** around the title and the two ratio numbers in cells **D15** and **F15**.

4. Add a **Bottom Border** to the cells in rows **3**, **6**, and **10** in columns **A** through **F** only. (Do not use the row heading to select the row).

5. Add a **Bottom Double Border** to the bottom of cells **D12** and **F12**.

6. Change the **Fill Color** of the title to **Turquoise** and change the **Font Color** to **Dark Red**.

7. Change the orientation of the column labels to a 45 degree angle. Select the **All Borders** option that shows all lines. (Your text may wrap differently than what is shown in the figure).

8. Drag the line between the row headings for rows **2** and **3** to increase the height of row **2** to show the labels correctly.

9. Adjust the column widths, print the sheet, and save the workbook.

R3—Edit a Worksheet

1. Select **Sheet3**.

2. Type your name in cell **A16**.

3. Format the sheet to match the figure. Make sure you change font size and style, merge and center, center text, fill color, align text, and add borders. Remember to adjust the columns to fit the data.

4. Save the workbook and print the sheet.

Challenge

Challenge exercises are designed to test your ability to apply your skills to new situations with less detailed instruction. These exercises also challenge you to expand your repertoire of skills by using Excel commands that are similar to those you have already learned. The desired outcome is clearly defined, but you have more freedom to choose the steps needed to achieve the required result.

C1—Use Borders and Gridlines to Format a Table

If a table of data is to be distributed to several people, it is useful to use formatting tools to organize the cells into functional groups. In this example, several people in the office have been asked to evaluate and compare two room divider systems using a weighted scale.

Goal: Format the worksheet that is provided to look like the example in the figure.

Use the following guidelines:

1. Use the Comparison file created in the Reinforcement exercises or open **Less0202** from the **Student\Lesson02** folder on the CD-ROM disc and save it on your floppy disk as **Comparison**. Select Sheet 4.

2. Center the text in cells **B2** through **F2**.

3. Use **Tools**, **Options**, **View**, **Gridlines** to turn off the gridlines on the screen.

4. Use borders to add the lines shown.

5. Print the worksheet. Leave the workbook open for use in the next Challenge exercise.

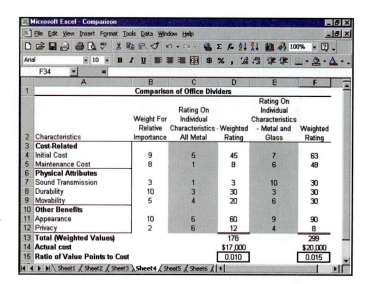

C2— Learn About Alignment of Text that Is Displayed at an Angle

When you display a column heading at a 45-degree angle, it is unclear which direction is indicated by the horizontal or vertical controls. Use Sheet 5 of the Comparison workbook.

Goal: Change the column headings of the comparison sheet to align at a 45-degree angle. Adjust the height of the row so that the text wraps as shown. Add borders and set the vertical and horizontal alignments to match the figure.

1. Select cells **B2** through **F2** and align the text at 45 degrees.

2. Use the **All Borders** option.

3. Drag the line between row headers 2 and 3 to adjust the height of the row so that none of the text wraps to more than two lines and no words are wrapped incorrectly.

4. Experiment with the **Horizontal** and **Vertical** alignment options to find the combination that matches the figure. Observe what the effect of each option is on the placement of the text in the cell.

5. Save the workbook. Print the sheet.

C3—Learn How Excel Works with Dates

Computers work with dates and times as if they were numbers, which allows you to subtract one date (or time) from another.

Goal: Open the Office Assistant and use it to find out how Excel works with dates. Print the Help page. Experiment with sample figures.

1. Click the **Office Assistant** or click the **Microsoft Excel Help** button to open the Assistant's dialog box.

2. Type the following question: **How does Excel subtract one date from another?** and click the **Search** button.

3. Click **How Microsoft Excel stores dates and times**. The Microsoft Excel Help window opens.

4. Read the topic and print a copy.

5. Close the workbook.

Discovery

Discovery exercises are designed to help you learn how to teach yourself a new skill. In each exercise, you discover something new that is related to the topic taught in this lesson. You may be directed to use built-in wizards or some of the extensive Help features provided in Excel to discover new features and learn new skills with minimum assistance from books or instructors. The required outcome demonstrates your ability to apply the new skill. You determine the choice of topic, worksheet design, and steps of execution.

D1—Explore Some Effects of the Year 2000 Problem

Representing the year in a date with only two digits creates problems because the computer is forced to guess the century in which it belongs.

Goal: Determine how to work with the century assumptions built into Excel 2000 so that you know when you must use four digits to represent the year in a date.

1. Open **Less0203** from the **Student\Lesson02** folder on the CD-ROM disc and save it on your floppy disk as **Year2000**. Place your name in cell **A1**.

2. In cell B3, type a date of birth from the Twenties, such as 5/20/28. In cell C3, type today's date. Notice the calculation in cell **D3** displays a negative number because it assumed you meant 2028 rather than 1928.

3. Type the date again, but specify the year using four digits.

4. Refer to Excel's Help on this matter and write a directive that you might send out to your staff telling them when to use four digits for the year when entering numbers into Excel worksheets. Enter the message in cell **A6**.

5. Widen column **A** to about four times its current width and format the text in cell **A6** to wrap.

6. Leave the page open for use in the next Discovery exercise.

D2—Learn How to Use Conditional Formatting

You can use formatting to draw attention to errors or unusual results. Use the **Year2000** file that was created in the previous exercise or open **Less0203** and save it as **Year2000** on your floppy disk.

Goal: Use Help to learn about Conditional Formatting. Format cell **D3** in the **Year2000** worksheet so that the number is displayed in red, boldface type whenever the number is negative.

1. Search Help for information about Conditional Formatting.

2. Format cell **D3** as described above.

3. Enter the date **1/1/25** in cell **B3** that is supposed to be from the year 1925. The value in cell **D3** should be a negative number, displayed as described.

4. Print the page.

5. Leave the page open for use in the next Discovery exercise.

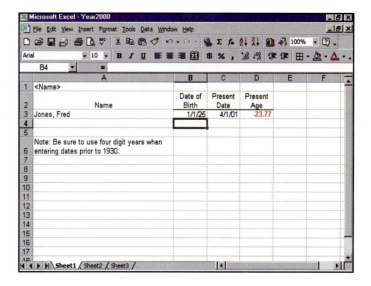

D3—Protect Cells from Unintentional Change

The formula in cell D3 will be lost if someone accidentally enters a value in the cell. Similarly, you do not want others to change the column headings or message you have chosen. To prevent users from overwriting formulas or making unauthorized changes, you can limit the cells they can write in by unlocking those cells and protecting the rest of the sheet. Use the year 2000 file that was created in the previous exercise, or open **Less0203** and save it as Year 2000 on your floppy disk.

Goal: Unlock cells **B3** and **C3** and protect the rest of the sheet so that users can only change values in cells **B3** and **C3**.

1. Select cells **B3** and **C3**. Choose **Format**, **Cells**, **Protection**. Remove the check mark from the **Locked** option.

2. Use the **Tools** menu to protect the sheet. Do not use a password.

3. Try to make changes to any other part of the sheet and observe the error message.

4. Save the changes you have made.

5. Close the workbook and close Excel.

LESSON 2   FORMATTING THE WORKSHEET

Lesson: 3

Editing Cell Contents

Task 1 Changing Numbers and Editing Text

Task 2 Inserting and Deleting Rows, Columns, and Sheets

Task 3 Removing Cell Contents and Formatting

Task 4 Undoing and Redoing Previous Steps

Task 5 Automatically Correcting Common Typing Errors

Task 6 Automatically Finishing Commonly Used Words or Phrases

Task 7 Checking Your Spelling

Introduction

In Lesson 1, you learned some simple rules about editing cells and making corrections. In this lesson, you will expand on those basic skills by learning other techniques for editing cells. You will also learn how to insert and delete rows and columns in your worksheet. There are a number of automated features that come with Excel 2000, and you will learn how to use these tools. To use a worksheet effectively and easily, not only do you need to know how to edit cells, but you can benefit from knowing how to take advantage of the automated features to help you work more efficiently.

Visual Summary

When you have completed this lesson, you will have edited a worksheet to add a column, and add and remove rows.

Location	Region	Pool Size					
		15'	18'	24'	27'	15'x30'	18'x33'
Albuquerque	Southwest	11	16	18	17	10	4
Ann Arbor	Midwest	25	22	35	12	15	16
Bangor	Northeast						
Boise	Mountain	3	3	4	2	1	0
Boston	Northeast	12	15	18	11	14	21
Chicago	Midwest	31	37	56	23	25	11
Denver	Mountain	16	18	31	15	17	19
Durham	Southeast	21	26	44	18	27	22
Indianapolis	Midwest	16	15	18	9	9	8
Los Angeles	Pacific	46	65	89	37	42	41
Phoenix	Southwest	8	18	37	39	27	22
Santa Fe	Southwest	7	11	12	11	12	8
Tacoma	Pacific	5	6	8	8	4	1
Tallahassee	Southeast	23	40	65	61	41	37
	Total Units	224	292	435	263	244	210

The Armstrong Pool, Spa, and Sauna Co.

Location	Region	Swimming Pool Size					
		15'	18'	24'	27'	12'X24'	15'x30'
Albuquerque	Southwest	11	16	18	17	3	10
Ann Arbor	Midwest	25	22	35	12	7	15
Boise	Mountain	3	3	4	2	0	1
Boston	Northeast	12	15	18	11	1	14
Charleston	Southeast	8	10	15	22	5	7
Chicago	Midwest	31	37	56	33	6	25
Denver	Mountain	16	18	31	15	5	17
Durham	Southeast	21	26	44	18	6	27
Indianapolis	Midwest	16	15	18	9	7	9
Toledo	Midwest	12	22	43	34	3	15
Los Angeles	Pacific	46	65	89	37	25	42
Phoenix	Southwest	8	18	37	39	12	27
Santa Fe	Southwest	7	11	12	11	2	12
Tacoma	Pacific	5	6	8	8	1	4
Tallahassee	Southeast	23	40	65	61	4	41
Total Units		244	324	493	329	87	266

New column → (12'X24')

<Your Name>

TASK 1

Changing Numbers and Editing Text

Why would I do this?

When you enter a lot of data into a worksheet, you will sometimes make errors. There will also be times when you enter data or labels correctly, but decide to change them later. In either case, you will need to edit the contents of a cell.

In this task, you change data in one cell and edit text in another.

1 Launch **Excel**, open **Less0301** from the **Student\Lesson 03** Lesson 03 folder on your CD-ROM disc, and save the file on your floppy disk as **Pool and Spa**. The new title will appear in the title bar. Maximize the window if necessary.

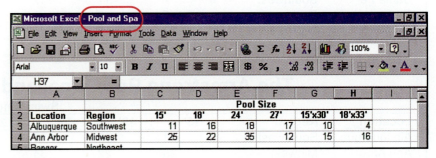

2 Select cell **F8**, type **33** and press **←Enter**. The new number replaces the old one, and the sum at the bottom of the column is recalculated.

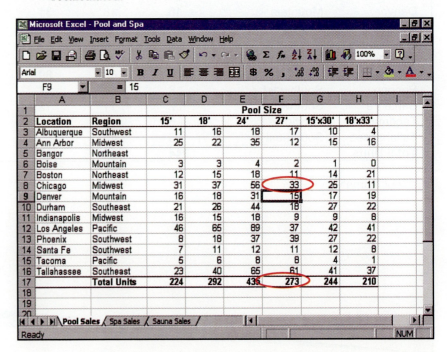

76 LEARN EXCEL 2000

3 Select cell **C1**, which has been merged and centered over six columns. Notice that the contents of the cell are shown both in the cell and in the formula bar. The cell location is also shown in the Name box.

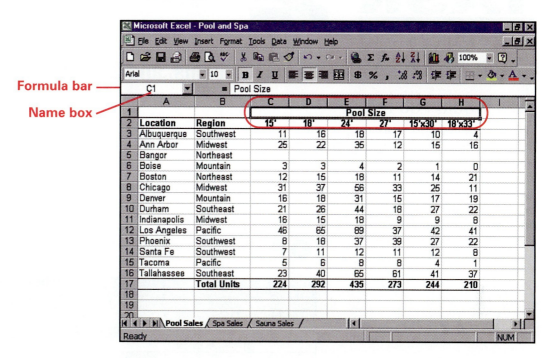

4 Move the pointer to the left of the word "Pool" in the formula bar and click to position the insertion point. Type in **Swimming**, then press Spacebar, Enter. The contents of cell C1 reflect the change you made.

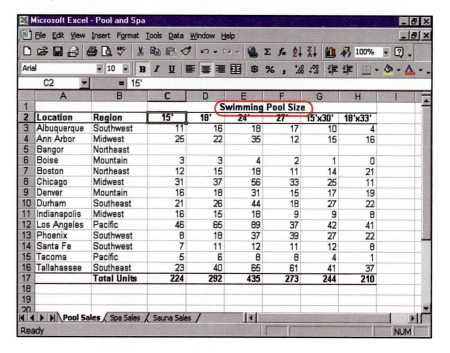

LESSON 3   EDITING CELL CONTENTS   77

TASK 2

Inserting and Deleting Rows, Columns, and Sheets

Why would I do this?

If your worksheet lists items in a particular order, it would not be ideal to add a new item at the bottom of the list if it did not belong there. Similarly, if you deleted the contents of a row or column, it would not look right to leave the row or column empty. Excel can insert or delete rows or columns in a worksheet and automatically move the rest of the data. It will also revise any formulas that are affected by the change. Your workbook contains several sheets, but you may need to have a workbook with several more sheets to analyze data by individual month or week. Excel allows you to add additional sheets to your workbook. In this task, you insert and delete rows, columns, and sheets.

1. Click on the heading for row **5** to select the entire row.

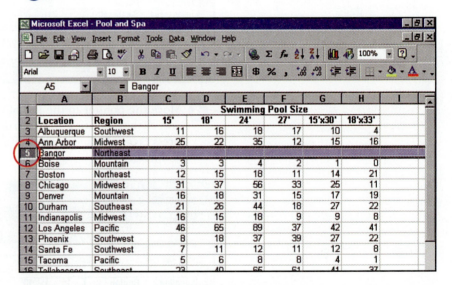

2. Choose **Edit**, **Delete**. The entry for "Bangor" disappears and the entry for "Boise" has now moved up to row 5.

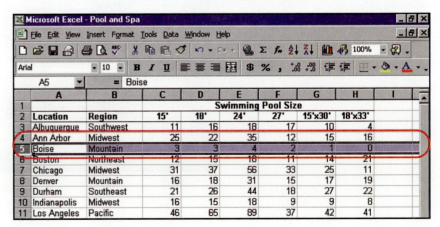

78 LEARN EXCEL 2000

Caution: It would seem that you should be able to delete a row by highlighting it and pressing the Del key. This will remove the contents of the cells, but will not delete the row.

3 Select any cell in row **7**, then choose **I**nsert, **R**ows. The contents of row 7, and all the rows below it, moves.

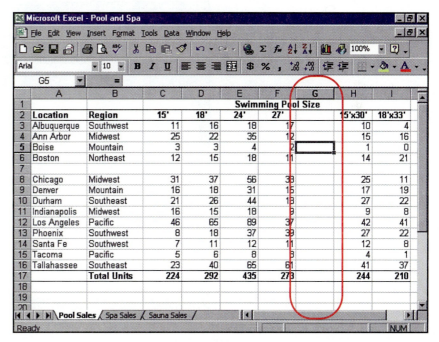

4 Select any cell in column **G**, then choose **I**nsert, **C**olumns. The contents of column G, and all the columns to the right of it, are moved to the right.

In Depth: To insert more than one row at a time, select more than one cell vertically, then choose **I**nsert, **R**ows. The number of new rows equals the number of cells selected. You may also insert or delete rows using Ctrl and the + or − keys.

LESSON 3 EDITING CELL CONTENTS 79

5 Choose **Insert**, **Worksheet**. A new worksheet will appear named **Sheet1**.

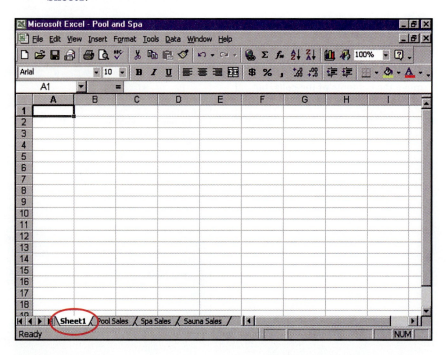

6 Double-click the **Sheet1** tab, then type **Grill Sales** and press ⏎Enter. The *sheet tab* is now renamed.

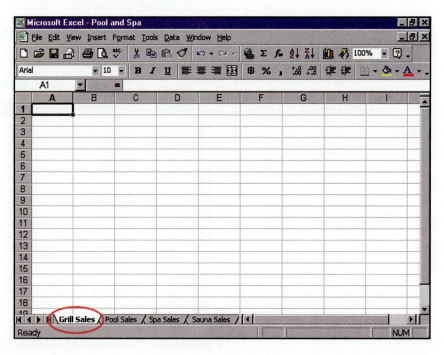

TASK 3

Removing Cell Contents and Formatting

Why would I do this?

When you use Del to delete the contents of a cell, the contents are removed. Any formatting that has been added, such as decimal places, currency, and character formatting, remains. If you enter data into what appears to be a blank cell, you will find that the formatting will be applied. Sometimes this is beneficial and sometimes it is not. There are ways you can delete the content, the formatting of cells, or both at the same time.

In this task, you delete the contents of a cell and remove the formatting.

1 Click the **Pool Sales** sheet tab to move back to the worksheet you have been working on. Select cell **A17**, type **Total Units** and press ↵Enter. Notice that the text is bold, even though you did not format it.

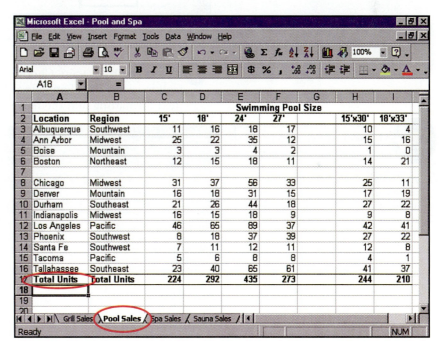

LESSON 3   EDITING CELL CONTENTS   81

2 Select cell **B17** and press Del. Select another cell so that you can see cell B17 when it is not selected. The contents of the cell are deleted, but the top and bottom border lines remain.

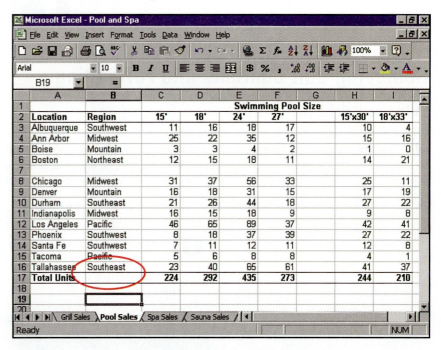

3 Select cell **B17** again. Choose **Edit**, **Clear**, **Formats**. Select another cell to reveal the change to cell B17. The formatting, including the text formatting and the border lines, is gone.

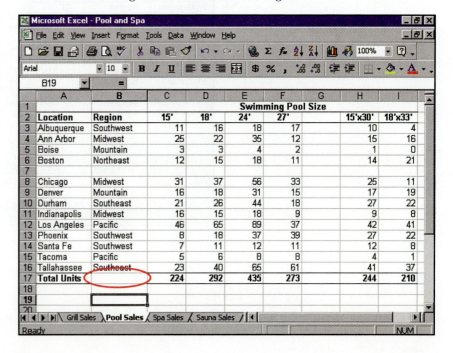

In Depth: A cell can be formatted without having any numbers or text in it. If you are editing a worksheet that someone else created, the formatting that is in place when you enter values into empty cells may surprise you.

TASK 4

Undoing and Redoing Previous Steps

Why would I do this?

Occasionally you will begin a procedure and decide that you want to do it differently. You may also make major changes to a worksheet by mistake. Excel gives you a way to undo and redo previous procedures.

In this task, you learn to use the Undo and Redo buttons to change a sequence of actions.

1 Select cell **A19**, type your name, and press ⏎Enter. Click the **Undo** button. The program removes your name, undoing the last action you took.

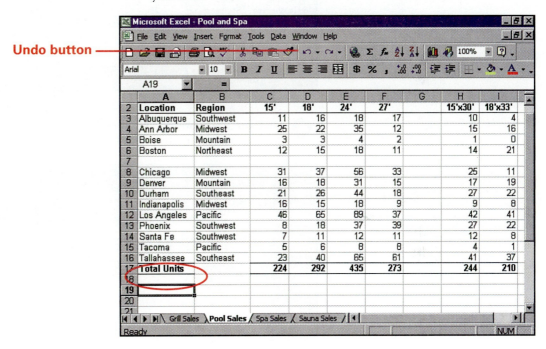

Undo button

LESSON 3   EDITING CELL CONTENTS   83

2 Click the **Undo** button three times to undo the last few steps of the previous task. Stop when cell B17 has its formatting restored and the text replaced.

3 Click the **Redo** button. This reverses the last undo, removing the text, but leaving the top and bottom border lines.

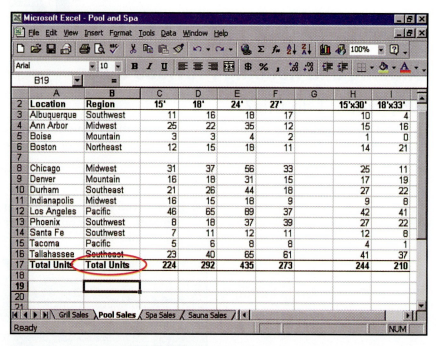

Redo button

In Depth: If you click the drop-down arrow next to the Undo or Redo button, a list of the previous actions will display. If you select one of the actions from the list, it will have the same effect as clicking the button repeatedly to get down to that item on the list. You cannot undo a single item from the list except the one at the top of the list.

4 Enter your name into cell **A19**.

TASK 5

Automatically Correcting Common Typing Errors

Why would I do this?

There are certain words that many people type incorrectly time after time, such as teh for the, or managment for management. Excel has a built-in feature called *AutoCorrect* that anticipates hundreds of these possible mistakes and corrects them automatically. AutoCorrect also allows you to create shortcuts for longer words or phrases that you use frequently.

In this task, you learn to use the AutoCorrect feature.

1 Choose **Tools**. Click the double arrow at the bottom of the menu to display the AutoCorrect choice, if necessary. Click **AutoCorrect**. The AutoCorrect dialog box appears.

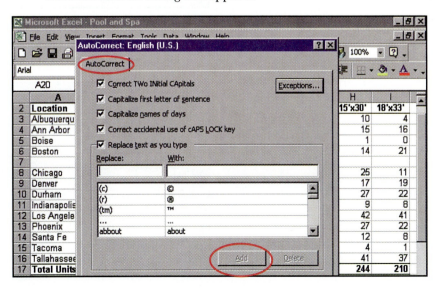

LESSON 3 EDITING CELL CONTENTS 85

2 Type **apss** in the **Replace** box. Press `Tab` and type **Armstrong Pool, Spa, and Sauna Co.** in the **With** box. Click **Add**. The Add button turns into a Replace button.

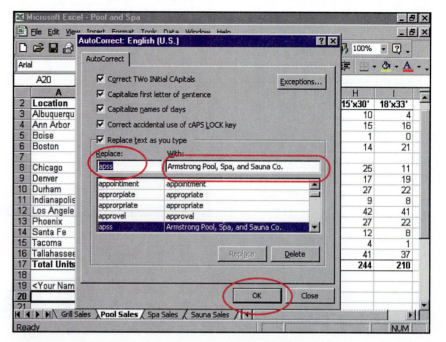

Caution: If someone has already added this abbreviation, you will see the Replace button instead of the Add button. Click the **Delete** button to remove the existing version of apss, then enter your own.

3 Click **OK**. Click cell **A1** and insert a blank row **1**. Select cell **A1**, if it is not already selected.

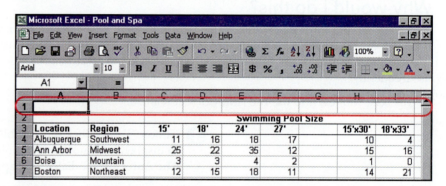

4 Type the word **Teh** and watch cell A1 as you press `Spacebar`. Notice that the AutoCorrect feature automatically corrects the spelling.

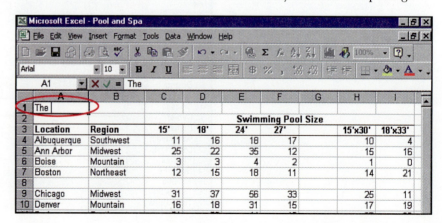

86 LEARN EXCEL 2000

5 Now type **apss**, the shortcut you added to AutoCorrect in Step 2, and press [Enter]. Notice that the name of the company is displayed.

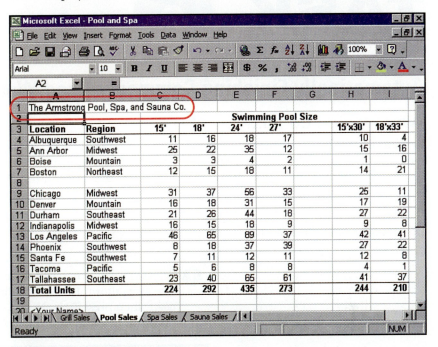

6 Select cells **A1** through **I1** and click the **Merge and Center** button. Boldface the title and change the font size to **16**.

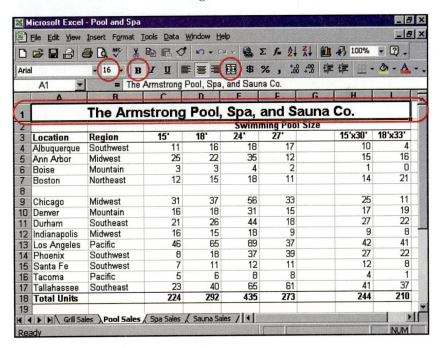

LESSON 3   EDITING CELL CONTENTS   87

TASK 6

Automatically Finishing Commonly Used Words or Phrases

Why would I do this?

In many worksheets, you enter the same word or phrase many times in the same column. The Excel program looks in the column above and below the cell in which you are entering data, and if it finds a word or phrase beginning with the same letters, it automatically places that word in the cell. If you do not want to accept the word, you can continue typing. This feature can be a great timesaver, particularly in a worksheet with a lot of redundant data.

In this task, you learn about Excel's automatic entry feature.

1 Select cell **A8**. Watch cell A8 as you type each character of **Charlston** exactly as shown (the misspelling will be taken care of in the next task), then press Tab. Notice that Excel put "Chicago" in the cell until you typed the third letter.

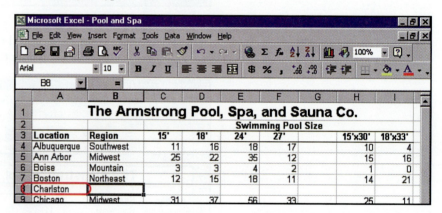

2 Insert a new row **13**. Select cell **A13**. Watch cell A13 while you type **Toledo** and press Tab.

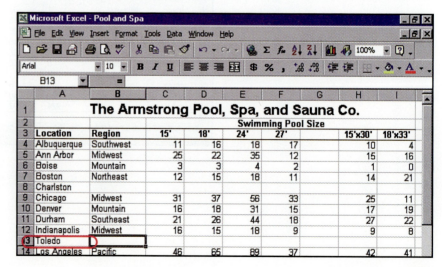

3 In cell **B13**, type **Mi** to produce **Midwest**. Since there are two words in that column beginning with the letter M, you needed to type a second letter for the automatic entry to work.

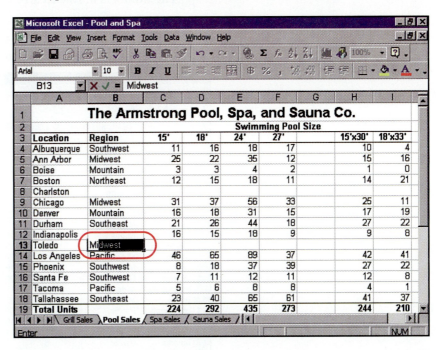

4 Press Tab. Select cell **B8**. Start typing **Southeast**. Notice that the word is not filled in until you type the sixth letter, since "Southeast" and "Southwest" are identical through the first five letters.

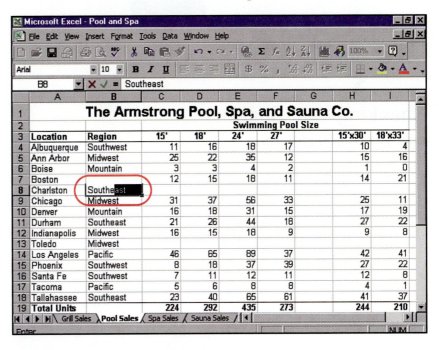

5 Press `Tab`. Finish filling out the worksheet as shown in the illustration. The numbers in row **8** are: **8,10,15,22,5,7**, and **12**.

The numbers in row **13** are: **12**, **22**, **43**, **34**, **3**, **15**, and **22**.

The values in column **G** (starting in cell G3) are: **12'X24'**, **3**, **7**, **0**, **1**, **5**, **6**, **5**, **6**, **7**, **3**, **25**, **12**, **2**, **1**, **4**. Use the **AutoSum** button in cell **G19** to add the column showing the 12'x24' pool sales.

TASK 7

Checking Your Spelling

Why would I do this?

The spelling checker program, which is so useful in some of the other Microsoft Office applications, can be of limited use in worksheets, particularly those that are number-based. Some worksheets, on the other hand, use quite a bit of text. In those cases, Excel has an extensive dictionary available. The dictionary even includes the names of most of the larger cities in the U.S. Your worksheet may not have many words, but it is still important to avoid an embarrassing mistake.

In this task, you use the spelling checker program to find a misspelled city name.

1 Select cell **A1**, then click the **Spelling** button. The Spelling dialog box displays. The unrecognized word (Charlston) appears in the Not in Dictionary list, and suggestions appear in the Suggestions box.

LEARN EXCEL 2000

2 Look at the list of suggested alternatives. Click **Charleston** to select the first suggestion.

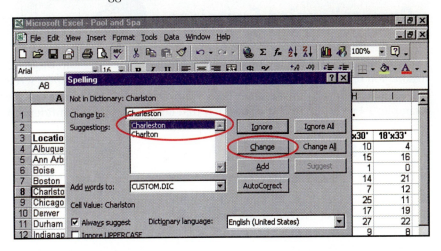

3 Click the **Change** button. The correct word appears in cell A8 and a message box displays to inform you that the spelling check is complete.

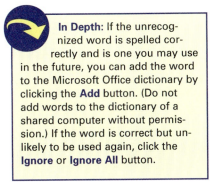

In Depth: The Office Assistant may appear. You may close it and continue.

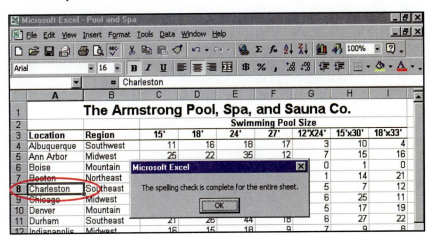

4 Click **OK**. Save your workbook and print the worksheet. Close the workbook when you are done.

In Depth: If the unrecognized word is spelled correctly and is one you may use in the future, you can add the word to the Microsoft Office dictionary by clicking the **Add** button. (Do not add words to the dictionary of a shared computer without permission.) If the word is correct but unlikely to be used again, click the **Ignore** or **Ignore All** button.

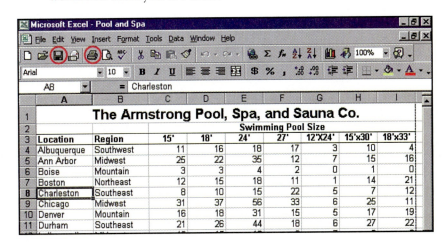

LESSON 3 EDITING CELL CONTENTS

Comprehension Exercises

Comprehension exercises are designed to check your memory and understanding of the basic concepts in this lesson. You distinguish between true and false statements, identify new screen elements, and match terms with related statements. If you are uncertain of the correct answer, refer to the task number following each item (for example, T4 refers to Task 4) and review that task until you are confident that you can provide a correct response.

True-False

Circle either T or F.

T F 1. One way to edit a number in a cell is to select the cell and type the new number. **(T1)**

T F 2. The only way to insert a row is to select the entire row by clicking on the row heading and then inserting a row. **(T2)**

T F 3. When you select a cell, the contents are shown both in the cell and in a box called the Formula bar near the top of the screen. **(T1)**

T F 4. The cell location is shown in the Name box. **(T1)**

T F 5. To rename a sheet tab, double-click the tab and type the new name. **(T2)**

T F 6. When you use Del to remove the contents of a cell, you remove both the contents and the formatting. **(T3)**

T F 7. You can only undo one previous step. **(T4)**

T F 8. The AutoCorrect feature allows you to enter shortcuts for commonly used words and phrases. **(T5)**

T F 9. With the automatic entry feature, if two words begin with the same first two letters, the entry will appear when you type the third letter of the word. **(T6)**

T F 10. To add a word to the Microsoft Office dictionary, click the **Add** button in the Spelling dialog box. **(T7)**

Identifying Parts of the Excel Screen

Refer to the figure and identify the numbered parts of the screen. Write the letter of the correct label in the space next to the number.

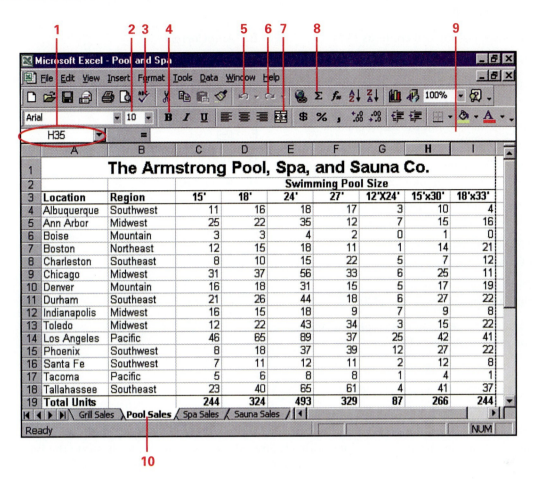

1. _____   A. Sheet tab (**T2**)
2. _____   B. Bold button (**T5**)
3. _____   C. Spelling button (**T7**)
4. _____   D. AutoSum button (**T6**)
5. _____   E. Redo button (**T4**)
6. _____   F. Name box (**T1**)
7. _____   G. Formula bar (**T1**)
8. _____   H. Merge and Center button (**T5**)
9. _____   I. Undo button (**T4**)
10. _____ J. Font size (**T5**)

LESSON 3   EDITING CELL CONTENTS   93

Matching

Match the statements below to the word or phrase that is the best match from the list. Write the letter of the matching word or phrase in the space provided next to the number.

1. ___ Shows the cell that is selected (**T1**)
2. ___ Removes just the cell contents (**T3**)
3. ___ Reverses the last action (**T4**)
4. ___ Allows you to type shortcuts for long words or phrases (**T6**)
5. ___ A quick way to sum the numbers in a column (**T5**)
6. ___ Shows the names of the worksheets available in the workbook (**T2**)
7. ___ The second place, besides the cell itself, where the cell contents are shown (**T1**)
8. ___ Lets you remove both contents and formatting of a cell (**T3**)
9. ___ Directs the spelling checker to skip a word that it does not recognize (**T7**)
10. ___ The place where you can create shortcuts for words or phrases (**T5**)

A. Sheet tabs
B. AutoCorrect
C. Ignore button
D. Formula bar
E. Edit, Clear, All
F. Del
G. AutoSum button
H. Name box
I. Font Size box
J. Undo
K. AutoCorrect dialog box

Reinforcement Exercises

Reinforcement exercises are designed to reinforce the skills you have learned by applying them to a new situation. Detailed instructions are provided along with a figure, where appropriate, to illustrate the final result. The Reinforcement exercises that follow should be completed sequentially. Leave the workbook open at the end of each exercise for use in the next exercise until you are specifically directed to close it.

Open **Less0302** from the **Student/Lesson 03** folder on your CD-ROM disc and save it as **Ex0301** on your floppy disk for use in the following exercises.

R1—Editing Text and Numbers and Using Automatic Entries

1. Select **Sheet1**.
2. Enter your name in cell **A17**.
3. Change the sheet tab name to **Books**.
4. Modify the Books worksheet to match the figure. See the steps below for more detail.
5. Change the year in cell **C7** to **1910**.
6. Edit the authors' names in cells **A7** and **A9**. In cell **A7**, replace Richard H. Davis's middle initial with **Harding**. In cell **A9**, add a middle name of **Salisbury** to Edward Fields's name.

7. Center and boldface the column headings in row 1. Choose a background of **Grey-25%**, and put a thin line border on the bottom of the row.

8. Click on another cell to deselect the heading cells. Run the spelling checker and correct the misspelled words. Don't worry about unrecognized author or publisher names. You may need to move the spelling checker window to see the word it has found.

9. Print the worksheet and save the workbook.

R2—Adding Columns and Rows

1. Select **Sheet2**.

2. Enter your name in cell **F19**.

3. Change the sheet tab name to **Occupations**.

4. Modify the Occupations worksheet to match the figure. See the steps below for more detail.

5. Insert a new row 1. Type **Alcona County, Michigan Occupations** into cell **A1**.

6. Merge and center the title between cells A1 and D1. Boldface the title and increase the font size to 14 point.

7. Add a bottom border to cells B2 through D2.

8. Insert a new column B. Adjust the column width to match columns C through E.

9. Add the year 1860 to cell B2. Make sure the formatting of the new year matches the other three years. Fill in the numbers in column B to match the figure. They are Farming, 6; General Labor, 18; Lumbering, 4; Skilled Trades, 2; and Fishing, 47.

10. Save the workbook and print the worksheet.

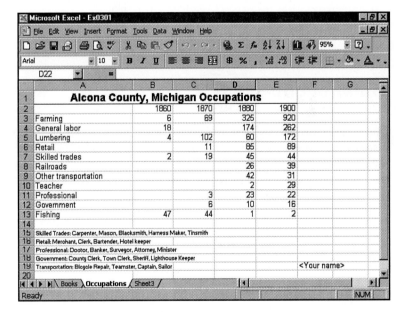

LESSON 3 EDITING CELL CONTENTS

R3—Adding Columns, Totals, and Formatting

1. Select **Sheet3**.
2. Enter your name in cell **A18**.
3. Change the sheet tab name to **Oil Production**.
4. Modify the Oil Production worksheet to match the figure. See the steps below for more detail.
5. Merge and center the titles in row **1** and row **2**.
6. Boldface the main title in row **1** and change the font size to 14 point. Change the title in row **2** to 11 point.
7. Center and boldface the column labels, then add a bottom border.
8. Add a new column between the USSR and the USA. Add the Saudi Arabia data from the figure. Make sure the column label is formatted the same as the other column labels. The numbers are: **7.60**, **8.48**, **7.08**, **8.58**, **9.25**, **8.30**, **9.53**, **9.90**, **9.81**, **6.47**, **5.09**, and **4.67**.
9. Center the row labels (the years in column **A**).
10. Add totals to the columns as shown in the figure. Add a bottom border to cells **B15** through **E15**. Also, give the totals row a label: **Totals**. Boldface the totals.
11. Format all of the numbers (except the years) so they show two decimal places.
12. Save the workbook, leave the workbook and Excel open for use in the following exercises.

Challenge

Challenge exercises are designed to test your ability to apply your skills to new situations with less detailed instruction. These exercises also challenge you to expand your repertoire of skills by using Excel commands that are similar to those you have already learned. The desired outcome is clearly defined, but you have more freedom to choose the steps needed to achieve the required result.

The following challenge exercises use the file EX0301 that was created in the previous reinforcement exercises. If you have not done those exercises, open **Less0302** from the **Student/Lesson 03** folder on your CD-ROM disc and save it as **Ex0301** on your floppy disk.

C1—Copy a Sheet and Move it

To manage a workbook effectively, you need to be able to add, delete, rename, and rearrange the sheets.

Goal: Make a copy of the Books sheet and place it at the end of the list of sheets. Rename the sheet and then move it to second place in the list.

Use the following guidelines:

1. Open **Ex0301** and right-click the **Books** sheet tab.
2. Use the shortcut menu to create a copy.
3. Double-click the name of the new sheet to select it and change the name to **Columns**.
4. Point at the **Columns** tab. Click and drag the tab to a position between the Books and Occupations tabs.
5. Save the workbook. Leave the workbook open for use in the next exercise.

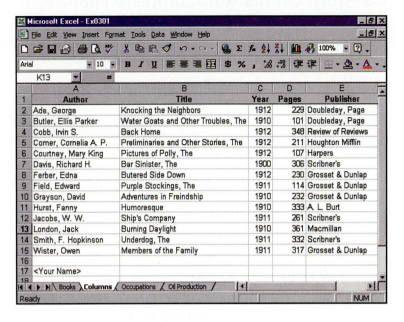

C2—Hide and Unhide Columns

Use the Columns sheet created in Challenge exercise 1.

If your worksheet has numerous columns, it is difficult to manage the display and printouts. It is often useful to hide certain columns so that printouts only display the needed columns.

Goal: Learn how to hide selected columns so that they do not display on the screen or on a printout. Also, learn how to unhide columns.

1. Select columns **C** and **D**.
2. Use the **Format** menu to hide the columns.
3. Select the columns on either side of the hidden column(s), Columns B and E, and use the **Format** menu to unhide the columns.
4. Select columns **C** and **E** (hold Ctrl before you click the second column heading).
5. Hide both columns.
6. Print the worksheet.
7. Save the workbook. Leave the workbook open for use in the next exercise.

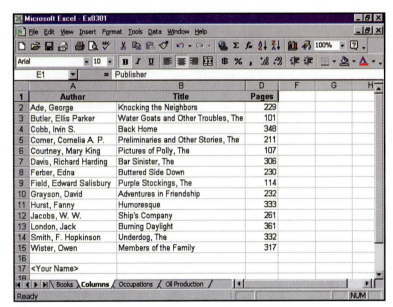

LESSON 3 EDITING CELL CONTENTS 97

C3—Turn Off the AutoComplete Feature

The AutoComplete feature can be distracting and can occasionally cause errors. You can turn this feature off if you have permission to make such changes to the computer you are using. If you share a computer with others, make sure you turn this feature back on when you finish.

Goal: Disable the AutoComplete feature.

1. Open the **Ex0301** file and choose the columns sheet that was created in Challenge exercise 1 (or use the Books sheet if you have not done the previous Challenge exercises).

2. Select the cell at the bottom of the Title column and type the letter **K**. The AutoComplete feature suggests the title Knocking the Neighbors. Press Esc to remove the entry.

3. Select **Tools, Options**, and the **Edit** tab. Deselect **Enable AutoComplete for cell values**. Click **OK**.

4. Type the letter **K** in the cell. This time, no suggestion will be made.

5. Turn the feature back on.

6. Leave the workbook open for use in the Discovery exercises.

Discovery

Discovery exercises are designed to help you learn how to teach yourself a new skill. In each exercise, you discover something new that is related to the topic taught in this lesson. You may be directed to use built-in wizards or some of the extensive Help features provided in Excel to discover new features and learn new skills with minimum assistance from books or instructors. The required outcome demonstrates your ability to apply the new skill. You determine the choice of topic, worksheet design, and steps of execution.

D1—Using Named Ranges

Cell references are hard to remember or relate to specific totals or ranges. You can apply your own names to cells or cell ranges. These names may be used to find the desired cell or range, or they may be used in formulas as substitutes for cell references.

Goal: Name the cells that contain oil production totals and name the range of OPEC production from 1980 to 1984.

1. Open **EX0301** and select the **Oil Production** sheet (if you have not yet created this file, open **Less0302** and save it on your floppy disk as **EX0301**).

2. Select cell **B16** (total USSR oil production).

3. Locate the Name box. It is at the left end of the Formula bar and displays the name of the currently selected cell. Click the name of the cell, **B16**, to select it.

4. Type the following cell name, **USSR_total**. (Spaces are not allowed in range names, so an underline character has been used to simulate the appearance of a space.)

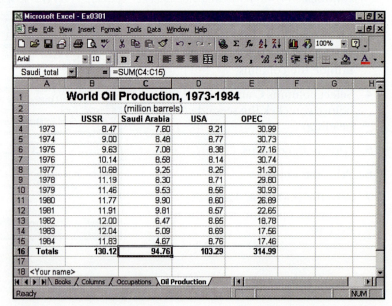

5. Use this method to name the totals in cells **C16**, **D16**, and **E16** as **Saudi_total**, **USA_total**, and **OPEC_total**, respectively.

6. Select cells **E11** through **E15**. Use the same method to name this range of cells **OPEC_in_the_early_80s**.

7. Click the list arrow next to the Name box. Pick a name from the list. Notice the selection is moved to that cell. This method may be used as a fast way to move around large worksheets.

8. Leave the workbook open for use in the next Discovery exercise.

D2—Insert Comments

You can communicate thoughts or comments to yourself or others by inserting comments into the cells. Excel allows you to create a pop-up comment and attach it to a cell so that it appears when you move the pointer onto the cell. Cells with comments are denoted by a small red triangle in the corner that does not print.

Goal: Insert comments into cells.

1. Open **EX0301** if necessary, and select the **Oil Production** sheet.

2. Search for Help on how to add a comment to a cell. Read the instructions.

3. Add the comment **Notice the dramatic decrease** to cell **C13**.

4. Move your pointer onto the cell. Notice the user name is included. This name is taken from the Office registration.

5. Use the **Tools**, **Options** menu to find the user name and change it to your own.

6. Insert a second comment. Notice the name displayed reflects the new user name. Change the user name back if you are not the sole operator of the computer.

7. Save the workbook and close it.

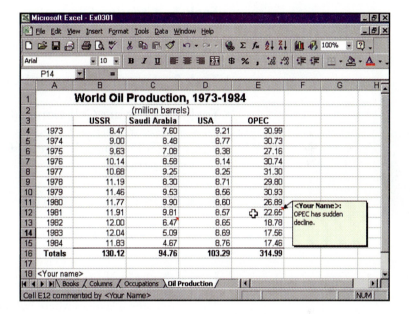

Lesson: 4

Filling, Copying, and Printing

Task 1 Creating Sequential Labels

Task 2 Creating a Series of Numbers

Task 3 Freezing Panes and Changing Zoom

Task 4 Copying Cell Contents

Task 5 Selecting a Range of Cells to Print and Previewing the Printout

Task 6 Improving the Printed Worksheet

Task 7 Printing Row or Column Labels

Introduction

There are many instances where you need to *fill* in a series of dates or times as row or column labels. You may also find occasions where the same text must be entered into numerous cells. Excel has powerful tools that help you with these tasks and improve your efficiency. In this lesson, you learn how to fill sequences of labels and how to *copy* cell contents in order to produce a work schedule for several part-time employees. Finally, you learn how to change the orientation of the page to print out sheets that are wider than they are tall.

Visual Summary

When you have completed this lesson, you will have filled out a scheduling worksheet and printed a section of it.

<Your Name>

Schedule for Jan 6 to Jan 12							
	Monday	Tuesday	Wednesday	Thursday	Friday	Saturday	Sunday
8:00 AM	Bill	Bill	Angi	Bill	Grace	Scott	Scott
8:30 AM	Bill	Bill	Angi	Bill	Grace	Scott	Scott
9:00 AM	Bill	Bill	Angi	Bill	Grace	Scott	Scott
9:30 AM	Bill	Bill	Angi	Bill	Grace	Scott	Scott
10:00 AM	Bill	Bill	Angi	Bill	Grace	Scott	Scott
10:30 AM	Bill	Bill	Angi	Bill	Grace	Scott	Scott
11:00 AM	Bill	Bill	Angi	Bill	Grace	Scott	Scott
11:30 AM	Bill	Bill	Angi	Bill	Grace	Scott	Scott
12:00 PM	Bill	Bill	Angi	Bill	Grace	Scott	Scott
12:30 PM	Bill	Bill	Angi	Bill	Grace	Scott	Scott
1:00 PM	Bill	Bill	Angi	Bill	Grace	Scott	Scott
1:30 PM	Bill	Bill	Angi	Bill	Grace	Scott	Scott
2:00 PM	Derek	Alexis	Alexis	Grace	Derek	Angi	Scott
2:30 PM	Derek	Alexis	Alexis	Grace	Derek	Angi	Scott
3:00 PM	Derek	Alexis	Alexis	Grace	Derek	Angi	Scott
3:30 PM	Derek	Alexis	Alexis	Grace	Derek	Angi	Scott
4:00 PM	Derek	Alexis	Alexis	Grace	Derek	Angi	Scott
4:30 PM	Derek	Alexis	Alexis	Grace	Derek	Angi	Scott
5:00 PM	Derek	Alexis	Alexis	Grace	Derek	Angi	Scott
5:30 PM	Derek	Alexis	Alexis	Grace	Derek	Angi	Scott
6:00 PM	Derek	Alexis	Alexis	Grace	Derek	Angi	Scott
6:30 PM	Derek	Alexis	Alexis	Grace	Derek	Angi	Scott
7:00 PM	Derek	Alexis	Alexis	Grace	Derek	Angi	Scott
7:30 PM	Derek	Alexis	Alexis	Grace	Derek	Angi	Scott
8:00 PM	Derek	Alexis	Alexis	Grace	Derek	Angi	Scott
8:30 PM	Derek	Alexis	Alexis	Grace	Derek	Angi	Scott
9:00 PM	Derek	Alexis	Alexis	Grace	Derek	Angi	Scott

TASK 1

Creating Sequential Labels

Why would I do this?

Worksheet programs use days of the week, months of the year, fiscal quarters, or other sequences of labels as column or row labels. Excel recognizes text that begins such sequences and assists you in entering them. This feature of Excel improves your efficiency in creating a worksheet.

In this task, you learn how to create sequential labels.

1. Launch **Excel** and open **Less0401** from the **Student\Lesson 04** folder on the CD-ROM disc that came with this book. Save it as **Work Schedule** on your floppy disk.

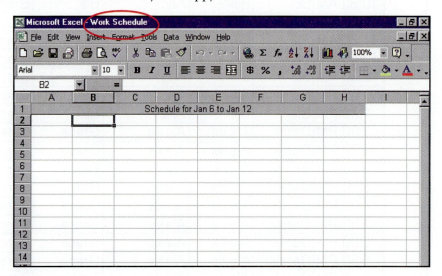

2. Select cell **B2**, if necessary type **Monday**, and press Tab.

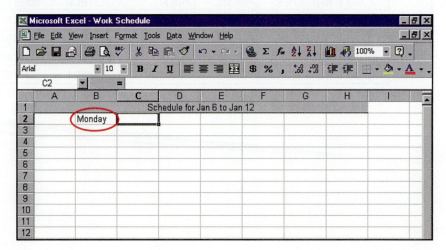

102 LEARN EXCEL 2000

3 Select cell **B2** again. Move the pointer to the small black square at the lower-right corner of the cell, called a *fill handle*. The pointer changes to a black plus sign.

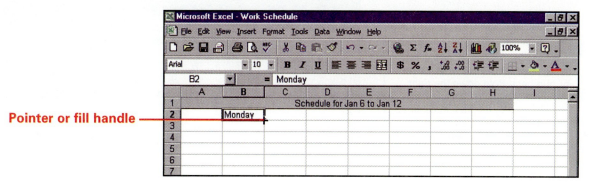

4 Click and drag the fill handle to the right to cell **H2**. Notice that the name of the next day in the sequence is displayed in a ScreenTip as you drag.

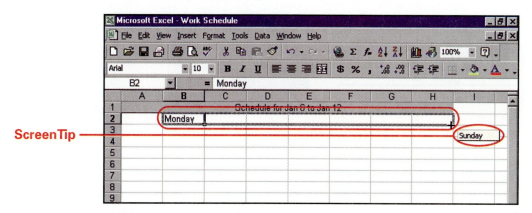

5 Release the mouse button. The sequence of days is filled in.

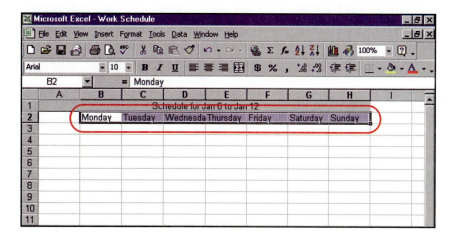

6 Click the **Save** button. The workbook is saved on your floppy disk.

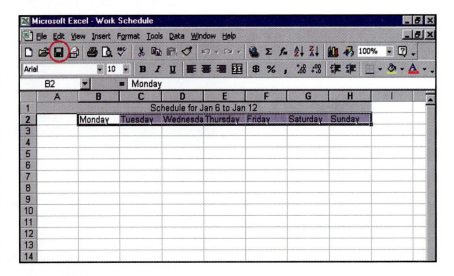

In Depth: There are several interesting options available when you fill cells with dates or numbers. Hold down the right mouse button rather than the left when you drag the fill handle and you get a shortcut menu of options. One option is to fill weekdays, excluding weekend days. Other choices include filling months or years, and numeric series using growth, linear, or specific trends. These options are explored in the end-of-lesson exercises.

TASK 2

Creating a Series of Numbers

Why would I do this?

Normally, numbers in a worksheet are entered in order to make calculations, which is why they are entered in separate cells. Sometimes you use numbers to represent dates or times as the labels for rows or columns. Excel is able to recognize when date formats such as 9/5 or 9-5-97 are entered in a cell. You can choose how to format dates or times.

In this task, you learn how to create a series of times as row labels. You also learn how to set both common and custom intervals.

1 Select cell **A3**, type **8:00**, and press ↵Enter.

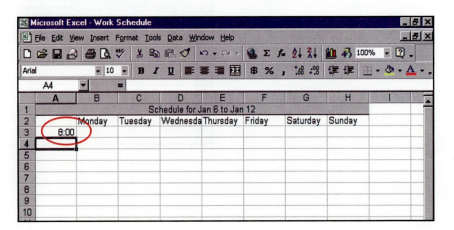

104 LEARN EXCEL 2000

2 Select cell **A3** again. Click and drag the fill handle down to cell **A10**.

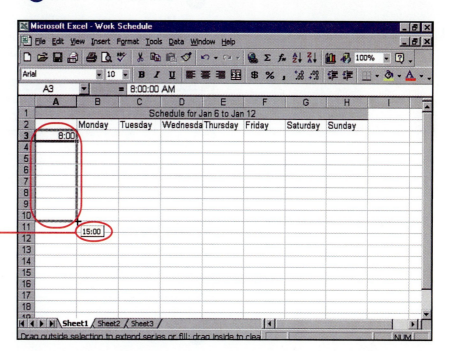

ScreenTip displays series value using a 24-hour format

3 Release the mouse button. Notice that the sequence of times increases by one hour and that each time is displayed using a 24-hour format.

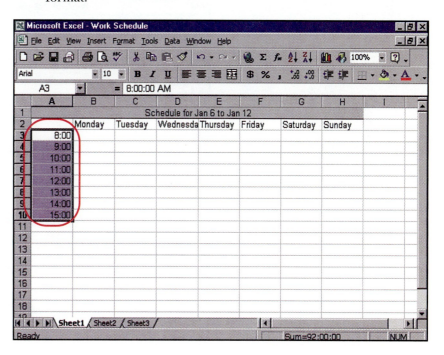

LESSON 4 FILLING, COPYING, AND PRINTING   105

4 Click the **Undo** button. The fill is undone.

This company schedules its part-time workers on the half hour. In order to establish this half-hour pattern, you need to enter data in at least two cells before applying the fill.

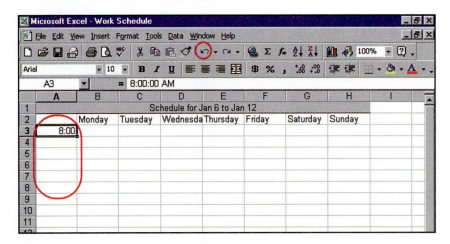

5 Select cell **A4**, type **8:30**, and press ⏎Enter.

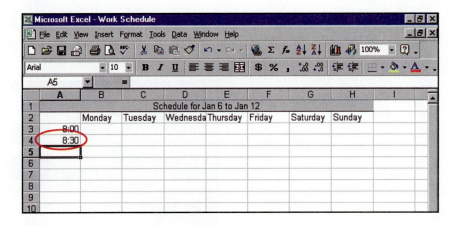

6 Select cells **A3** and **A4**.

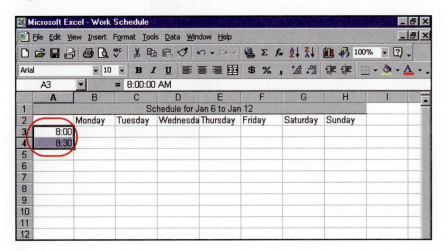

Caution: Remember, since the first cell of a selected group does not change to a background color, it may not look like cell A3 is selected. The thick line border encloses both cells if they are both selected.

It is important that both cells are selected to indicate what interval to use to create the rest of the series. It is also important that you release the mouse button after cell selection before you try to use the fill handle.

7. Click and drag the fill handle down to cell **A18**.

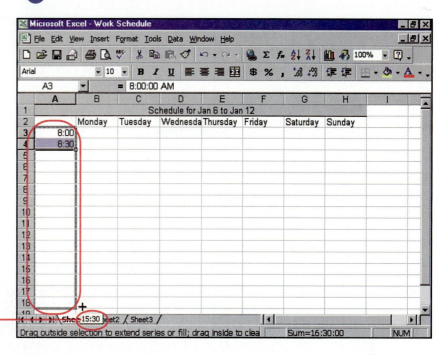

ScreenTip displays series value using a 24-hour format

8. Release the mouse button. The sequence is filled in half-hour increments.

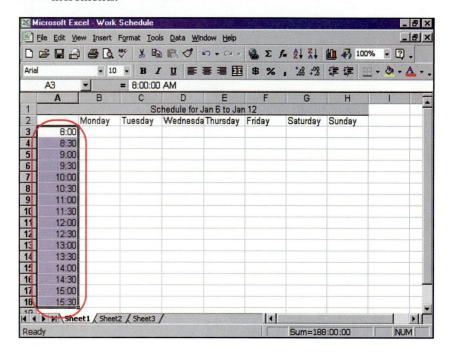

LESSON 4 FILLING, COPYING, AND PRINTING

9 Use the vertical scrollbar to scroll down to show rows **18** through **30**.

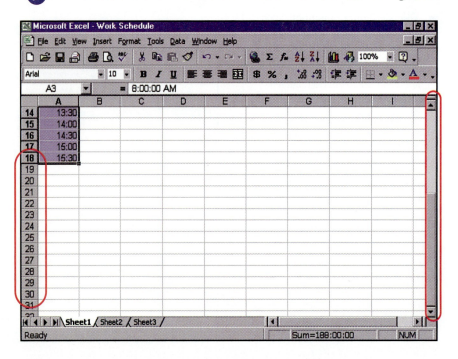

10 Click and drag the fill handle down to cell **A29**. Release the mouse and the sequence is extended.

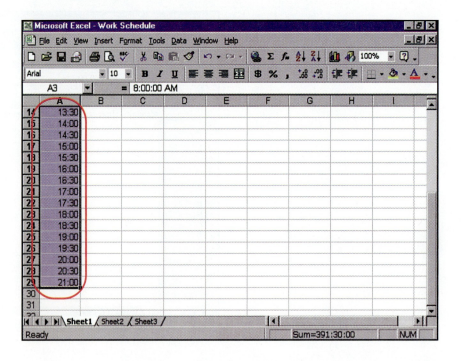

11. With cells **A3** through **A29** still selected, choose **Format**, **Cells** to open the Format Cells window. Click the **Number** tab, if necessary.

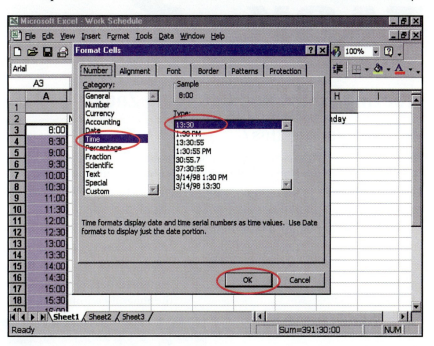

Quick Tip: Many formatting options are available from a shortcut menu that opens when you right-click on the selected cells.

12. Click the **1:30 PM** sample format and click **OK**.

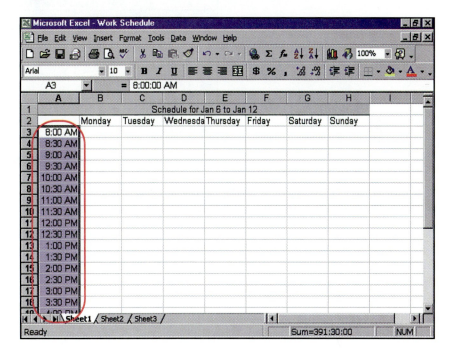

LESSON 4 FILLING, COPYING, AND PRINTING 109

TASK 3

Freezing Panes and Changing Zoom

Why would I do this?

When rows and columns are too long to be viewed on the screen in their entirety, you must scroll the window in order to see cells at the end of the row or column. Unfortunately, when you get to the cell, the row or column label is no longer visible, so you may easily mistake one row or column for another.

In this task, you learn how to change the magnification of the view so that you can see larger areas of the worksheet. You also learn how to freeze the row and/or column labels so they stay visible while you scroll.

1 Select cell **A1**. This step is not required, but ensures that the upper-left part of the sheet remains visible when you change the magnification.

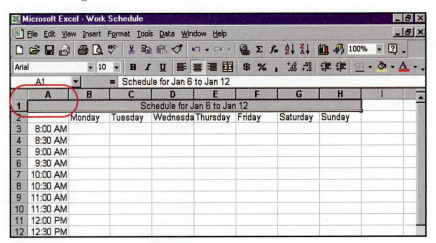

2 Click the down arrow next to the **Zoom** box on the Standard toolbar. A list of magnification percentages is displayed.

List of Zoom options

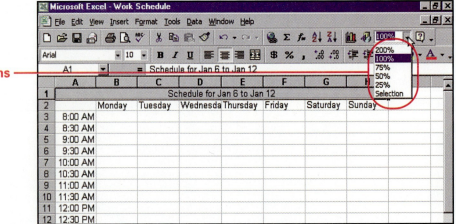

110 LEARN EXCEL 2000

In Depth: Even though the cells look smaller, a printout of this sheet looks the same at 75 percent magnification as at 100 percent magnification. You can choose any magnification you desire by typing the percentage directly into the **Zoom** box.

3 Click **75%**. All of the screen components are displayed at 3/4 size so more information fits on the screen.

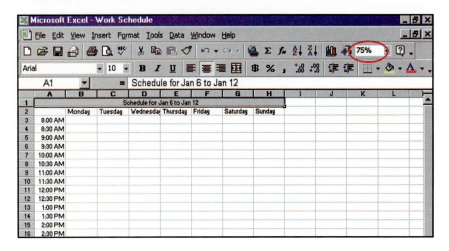

4 Click the down arrow next to the **Zoom** box and click on **100%** to return to normal magnification.

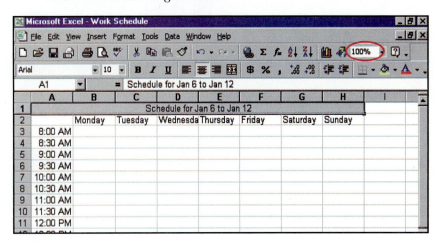

5 Click cell **B3**. Notice that this cell is below rows 1 and 2 and to the right of column A. We want to freeze the two rows above and the column to the left of cell **B3**.

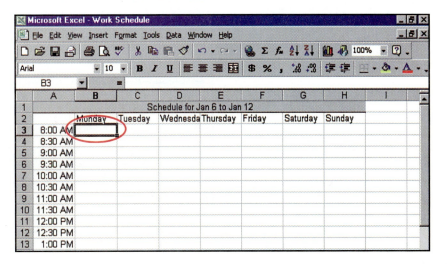

LESSON 4   FILLING, COPYING, AND PRINTING

6 Choose **Window, Freeze Panes.** The rows above the selected cell (rows 1 and 2) and the columns to the left of the selected cell (column A) remain on the screen, regardless of how far to the right or bottom you may scroll.

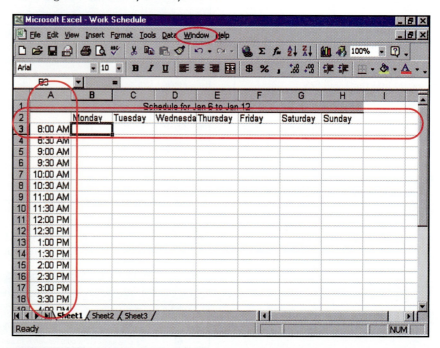

7 Scroll down until row **14** follows row **2**. Notice that rows 1 and 2 remain on the screen.

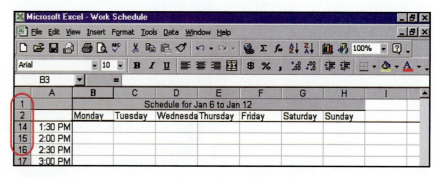

8 Scroll to the right until column **D** is next to column **A**. Notice that column A remains on the screen.

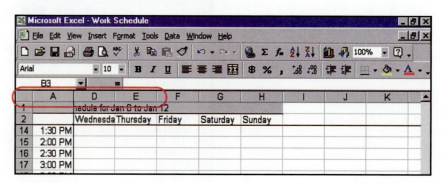

⑨ Choose **W**indow, **Un**freeze Panes. Columns B and C and rows 3 through 13 return to view.

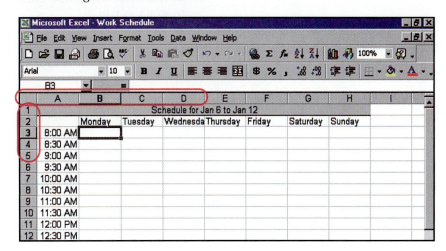

TASK 4

Copying Cell Contents

Why would I do this?

Some worksheets require the display of the same data in many cells. For example, a business that is open from 8 a.m. to 9 p.m., Monday through Sunday, uses six different part time employees. If you wanted to post this work schedule for employees, you would have to fill out a table with more than 200 cells.

In this task, you learn how to use the fill, copy, and paste techniques to fill out a form with repetitive data.

① Select cell **B3**, type **Bill**, and press ⏎Enter.

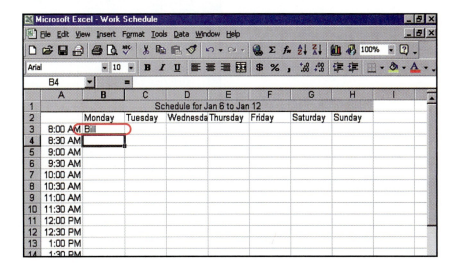

LESSON 4   FILLING, COPYING, AND PRINTING   113

2 Select cell **B3** again. Click and drag the fill handle down to cell **B14**. Release the mouse button. Bill's name is filled into the cells from B4 to B14.

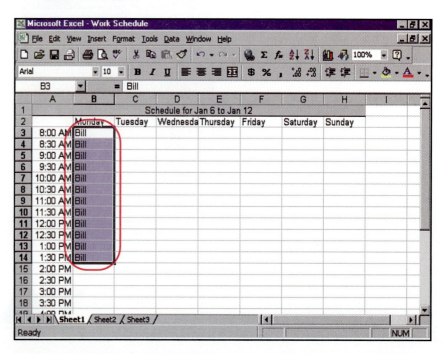

3 Click and drag the fill handle to the right to cell **C14**. Release the mouse button. The cells to the right are filled with Bill's name.

Caution: If a custom list that starts with Bill has already been created on your computer, you may see the custom list rather than Bill's name. If this occurs, you can either use the copy and paste method or delete the custom list by choosing **Tools, Options, Custom Lists**.

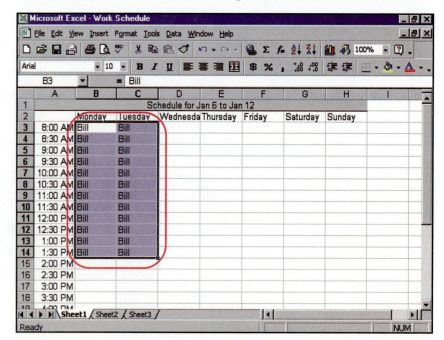

114 LEARN EXCEL 2000

4 Click cell **B3** again to select a cell that contains Bill's name. Click the **Copy** button on the Standard toolbar.

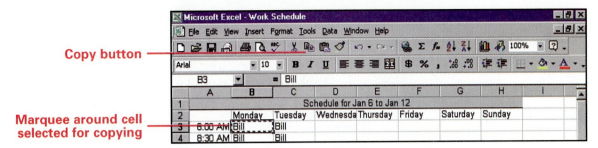

Copy button

Marquee around cell selected for copying

5 Select cells **E3** through **E14**.

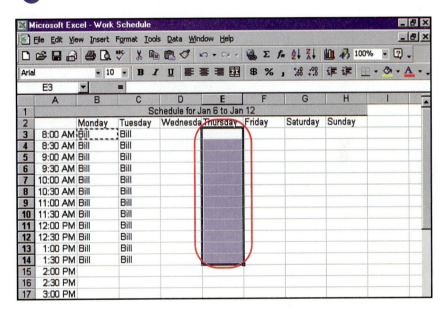

6 Click the **Paste** button on the Standard toolbar. Bill's name is filled into the entire cell range.

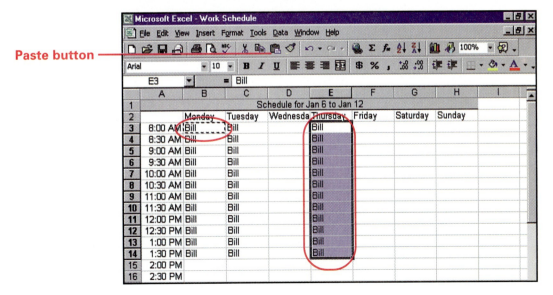

Paste button

LESSON 4 FILLING, COPYING, AND PRINTING   115

7 Use the fill and copy techniques described above to fill out the following schedule:

Angi—Wednesday 8 a.m.–2 p.m.; Saturday 2 p.m.–9 p.m.
Grace—Thursday 2 p.m.–9 p.m.; Friday 8 a.m.–2 p.m.
Scott—Saturday 8 a.m.–2 p.m.; Sunday 8 a.m.–9 p.m.
Alexis—Tuesday 2 p.m.–9 p.m.; Wednesday 2 p.m.–9 p.m.
Derek—Monday 2 p.m.–9 p.m.; Friday 2 p.m.–9 p.m.

Click the **Save** button to save your work.

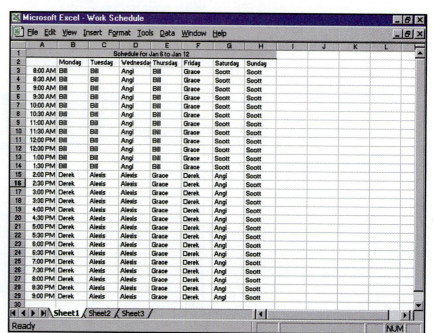

In Depth: The figure is shown at 85 percent Zoom, and the view is set to Full Screen to show the whole work schedule. You do not have to make these changes.

TASK 5

Selecting a Range of Cells to Print and Previewing the Printout

Why would I do this?

If a worksheet is too large to fit on one page, or for some other reason you do not want to print an entire sheet, you may select a portion of the sheet to print. It is useful to first preview the printout on the screen to catch errors in layout and formatting, such as one column printing on a page by itself. You can make the needed adjustments and save time and paper by not printing mistakes.

In this task, you learn how to print part of the work schedule and to preview it before printing.

1 Scroll down to display rows **15** through **29**. Select the cells from **A15** through **H29**. This includes the row labels and all of the work scheduled after 2 p.m.

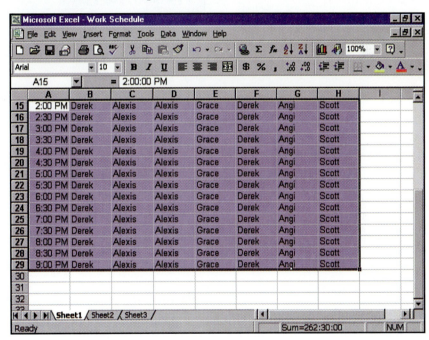

LESSON 4 FILLING, COPYING, AND PRINTING

2 Choose <u>F</u>ile, <u>P</u>rint, Selectio<u>n</u>.

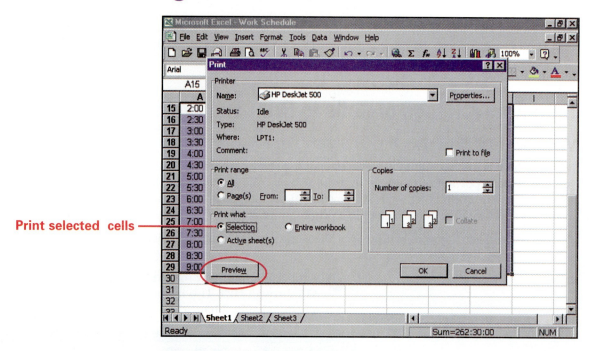

Print selected cells

3 Click the Pre<u>v</u>iew button. The page is displayed as it will look when printed.

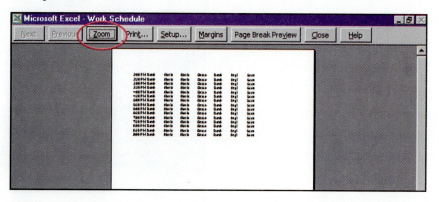

4 Click the <u>Z</u>oom button to switch the magnification. Notice that the column labels in rows 1 and 2 are not shown because they were not part of the print area selected. This problem is addressed in Task 7.

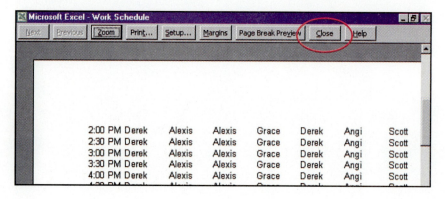

5 Click the Close button on the Print preview toolbar. The worksheet is displayed with a vertical dotted line to indicate how many columns fit on the page.

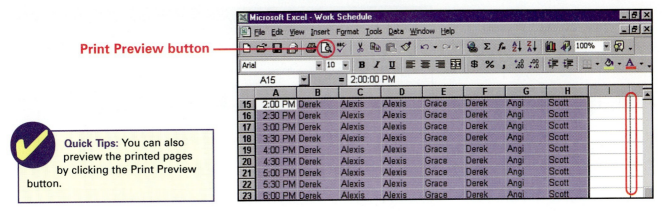

✓ **Quick Tips:** You can also preview the printed pages by clicking the Print Preview button.

TASK 6

Improving the Printed Worksheet

Why would I do this?

There are several options you can use to improve the apperance and readability of your printed worksheet. Sometimes a worksheet has many columns, and the page orientation needs to be changed to accommodate all the information. It is also useful to add information in a header that you want repeated on each page of the printed worksheet. This may include the current date, the name of the file, or your name. Lastly, to give your work a professional appearance, the columns of data can be centered on the page.

In this task, you learn how to change the orientation of the page to handle wider worksheets, center data on the page, and add your name and an automatic date to a header.

1 Choose File, Page Setup. The Page Setup window opens. Click the Page tab, if it is not already selected.

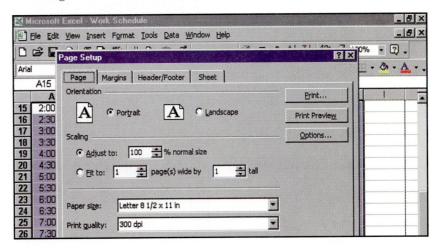

LESSON 4 FILLING, COPYING, AND PRINTING   119

2 Click the Landscape option. This option is useful when printing worksheets that have several columns.

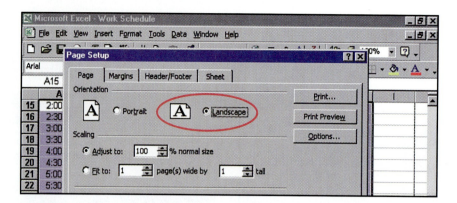

3 Click the Margins tab.

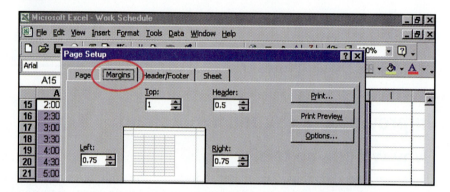

4 Click the Horizontally option under Center on page at the bottom left of the dialog box. The sample layout in the middle of the window shows how the data will be centered on the page.

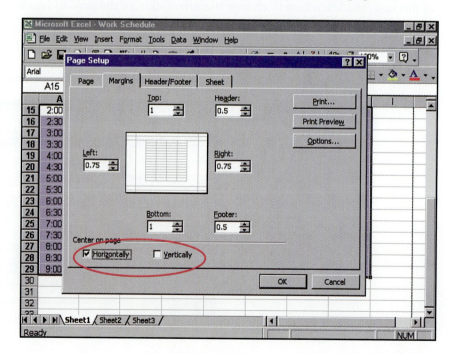

5 Click the **Header/Footer** tab. The Header/Footer window opens. Headers appear at the top and footers appear at the bottom of each page of a printout.

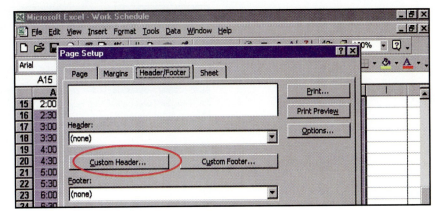

> **Quick Tip:** You may select an existing header or footer design by clicking the down arrow on the **He**a**der** or **F**o**oter** box.

6 Click the **Custom Header** button. The Header window opens. The header is divided into the Left section, the Center section, and the Right section.

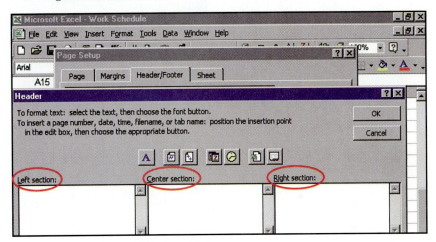

7 Move the pointer to the **Center section** and click. The insertion point appears, centered. Type your name.

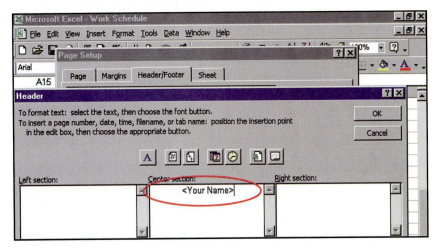

LESSON 4 FILLING, COPYING, AND PRINTING

8 Press Tab to move to the Right section. Click the **Date** button. &[Date] displays. &[Date] is replaced by the current date each time the sheet is printed.

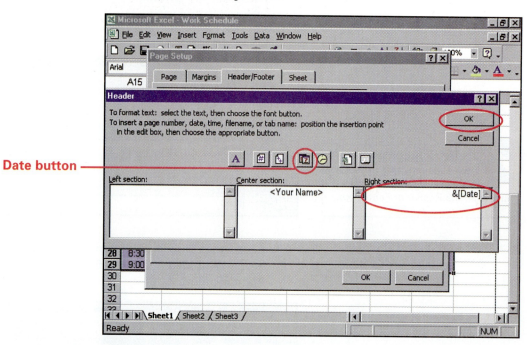

Date button

9 Click the **OK** button in the Header window. The sample displays your name in the center section of the header and the current date in the right section.

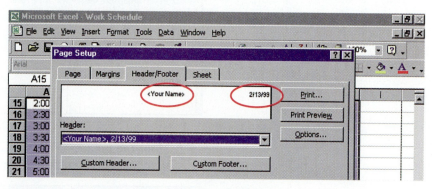

10 Click the **Sheet** tab. The Sheet window opens.

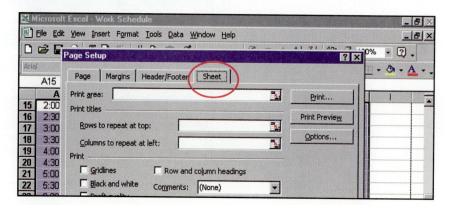

LEARN EXCEL 2000

11 Click the **Gridlines** option to print the *gridlines* that outline the cells and make it easier to follow rows and columns.

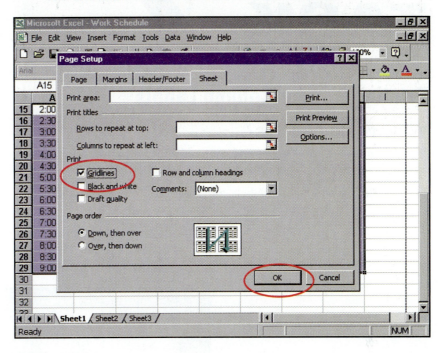

12 Click **OK**. The Page Setup window closes. Scroll to the top of the page. Widen column 0 to display all of the leading.

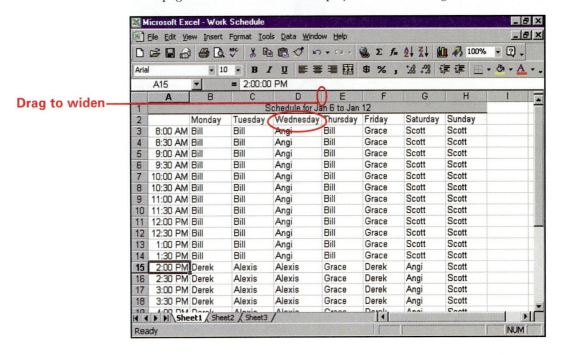

LESSON 4 FILLING, COPYING, AND PRINTING   123

TASK 7

Printing Row or Column Labels

Why would I do this?

If your worksheet prints on several pages, it is useful to have the title of the worksheet and the column headings appear on each page. The information on pages beyond the first page will be properly labeled.

In this task, you add column labels, and then print the worksheet.

1 Select cells **A15** to **H29**. Choose **File**, **Print**, **Selection**, and click **Preview**. The sheet is displayed. Click the **Zoom** button, if necessary, to display the full sheet.

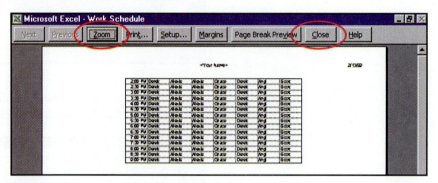

2 Notice that the features you added in the previous task are included. Notice also that the sheet needs column headings. Click the **Close** button.

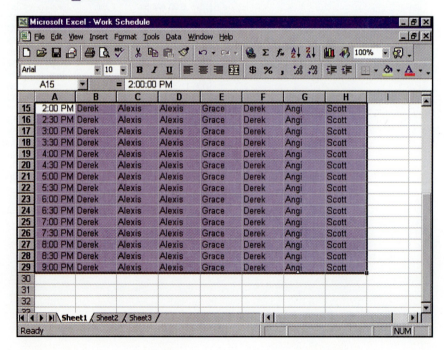

124 LEARN EXCEL 2000

> **Caution:** You may have noticed that there is a Setup button on the Print Preview toolbar. Normally, you could go directly to Setup from within the preview window and set most of the options needed to modify your printout. However, it does not work for the features that are covered in this task.

3 Choose **File**, **Page Setup**, and click the **Sheet** tab if necessary.

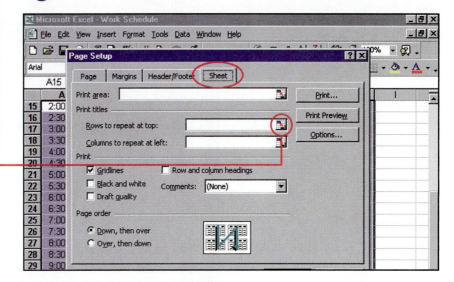

Collapse Dialog Box button

4 Click the **Collapse Dialog Box** button at the right end of the **Rows to repeat at top** box. The dialog box shrinks to a single item so you can see the sheet and select the rows to repeat.

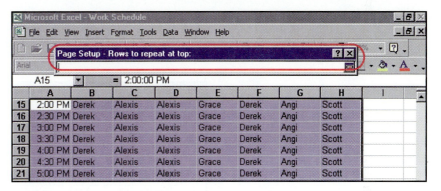

5 Scroll to the top and click and drag to select row headings **1** and **2**. The code for rows 1 and 2 is displayed in the **Rows to repeat at top** box.

Expand dialog box button

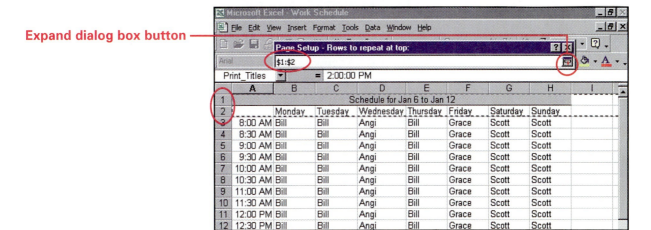

LESSON 4 FILLING, COPYING, AND PRINTING   125

6 Click the **Expand Dialog Box** button to show the entire **Page Setup** window.

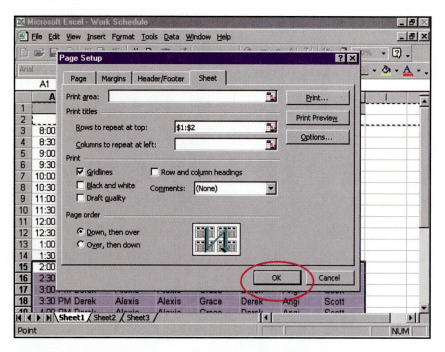

7 Click **OK** to close the dialog box. Choose **File**, **Print**, **Selection**, and click **Preview**. Click the **Zoom** button and scroll the preview to view the table. Notice that the row 1 and 2 headings are now included.

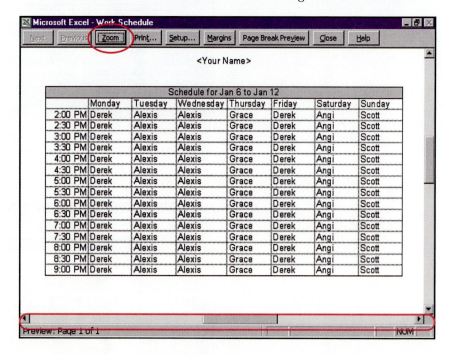

8 Click the Print button to print the selected cells with the column headings from rows 1 and 2.

						<Your Name>							4/23/99

	Monday	Tuesday	Wednesday	Thursday	Friday	Saturday	Sunday
			Schedule for Jan 6 to Jan 12				
2:00 PM	Derek	Alexis	Alexis	Grace	Derek	Angi	Scott
2:30 PM	Derek	Alexis	Alexis	Grace	Derek	Angi	Scott
3:00 PM	Derek	Alexis	Alexis	Grace	Derek	Angi	Scott
3:30 PM	Derek	Alexis	Alexis	Grace	Derek	Angi	Scott
4:00 PM	Derek	Alexis	Alexis	Grace	Derek	Angi	Scott
4:30 PM	Derek	Alexis	Alexis	Grace	Derek	Angi	Scott
5:00 PM	Derek	Alexis	Alexis	Grace	Derek	Angi	Scott
5:30 PM	Derek	Alexis	Alexis	Grace	Derek	Angi	Scott
6:00 PM	Derek	Alexis	Alexis	Grace	Derek	Angi	Scott
6:30 PM	Derek	Alexis	Alexis	Grace	Derek	Angi	Scott
7:00 PM	Derek	Alexis	Alexis	Grace	Derek	Angi	Scott
7:30 PM	Derek	Alexis	Alexis	Grace	Derek	Angi	Scott
8:00 PM	Derek	Alexis	Alexis	Grace	Derek	Angi	Scott
8:30 PM	Derek	Alexis	Alexis	Grace	Derek	Angi	Scott
9:00 PM	Derek	Alexis	Alexis	Grace	Derek	Angi	Scott

9 Save your changes and close the workbook.

Comprehension Exercises

Comprehension exercises are designed to check your memory and understanding of the basic concepts in this lesson. You distinguish between true and false statements, identify new screen elements, and match terms with related statements. If you are uncertain of the correct answer, refer to the task number following each item (for example, T4 refers to Task 4) and review that task until you are confident that you can provide a correct response.

True-False

Circle either T or F.

T F 1. If you select cell B4 and freeze the panes, rows 1 through 3 would be frozen as well as column A. **(T3)**

T F 2. The fill handle is located in the lower-left corner of the selected cell. **(T1)**

T F 3. If you select a cell that contains the word "Jane" and drag the fill handle to an adjacent cell, the adjacent cell would contain the word "Jane." **(T4)**

T F 4. To print a range of cells, select the range and then click the **Print** button on the toolbar. **(T5)**

T F 5. If you select a Zoom percentage of 75%, you can see more cells on the screen. **(T3)**

T F 6. The **Copy** button on the Standard toolbar looks like a small clipboard with a page in front of it. **(T4)**

T F 7. The Preview window has a **Zoom** button but it only toggles back and forth between two sizes. **(T5)**

T F 8. If you had a worksheet that was wider (columns) than it was long (rows), you would use the Portrait page orientation. **(T6)**

T F 9. The **Collapse Dialog Box** button is used to shrink the dialog box to make it easier to make a selection from the worksheet. **(T7)**

T F 10. It is better to print several copies of the worksheet as you create it to make sure the final copy is error-free. **(T5)**

Identifying Parts of the Excel Screen

Refer to the figure and identify the numbered parts of the screen. Write the letter of the correct label in the space next to the number.

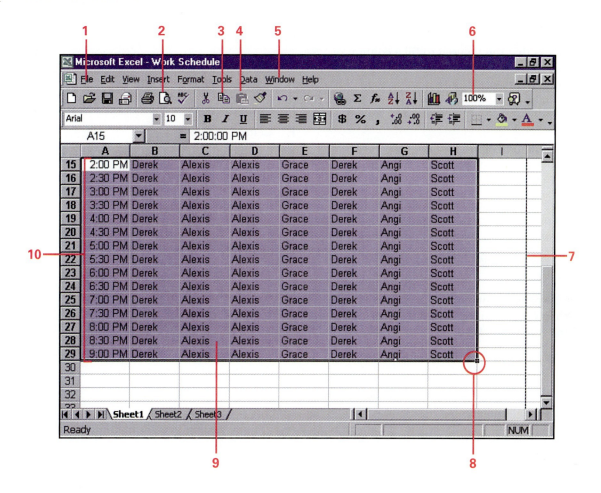

1. _____
2. _____
3. _____
4. _____
5. _____
6. _____
7. _____
8. _____
9. _____
10. _____

A. Fill handle (T1)
B. Copy button (T4)
C. Paste button (T4)
D. Zoom box (T3)
E. Freeze Panes option found here (T3)
F. Indicates the last column that fits on the page (T5)
G. Selected area (T5)
H. Page Setup options found here (T6)
I. Print Preview (T7)
J. Repeating series at half-hour intervals (T2)

Matching

Match the statements below to the word or phrase that is the best match from the list. Write the letter of the matching word or phrase in the space provided next to the number.

1. ___ An example of a first label in a sequence (**T1**)
2. ___ Values that can be used to fill a column or row with times that are separated by fifteen minute increments. (**T2**)
3. ___ Small box at the lower-right corner of a highlighted cell. (**T4**)
4. ___ The method used to fill the cells in two non-adjacent columns with the same word (**T4**)
5. ___ The method used to keep the first row and column visible on the screen even when you scroll (**T3**)
6. ___ To select a range of cells to print, you would do this (**T5**)
7. ___ The page orientation used to print worksheets that are longer (more rows) than they are wide (**T6**)
8. ___ The lines between the cells on a worksheet (**T6**)
9. ___ The option in the Page Setup window that allows you to center the data left-to-right (**T6**)
10. ___ The button that reduces the size of a dialog box to allow you to work with the sheet behind it (**T7**)

A. Portrait
B. Gridlines
C. Freeze Panes
D. Collapse Dialog Box
E. Copy and paste
F. Center Horizontally
G. Select the range and use **File**, **Print**, **Selection**
H. Center Vertically
I. Fill handle
J. January
K. 9:00, 9:15

Reinforcement Exercises

Reinforcement exercises are designed to reinforce the skills you have learned by applying them to a new situation. Detailed instructions are provided along with a figure, where appropriate, to illustrate the final result. The Reinforcement exercises that follow should be completed sequentially. Leave the workbook open at the end of each exercise for use in the next exercise until you are specifically directed to close it.

Open **Less0402** from the **Student\Lesson 04** folder on your CD-ROM disc and save it as **Ex0401** on your floppy disk for use in the following exercises.

R1—Create a Sheet to Track Leases

In this exercise, you create a lease report worksheet for a small office building.

1. Select **Sheet1**. Rename its tab **Leases**.
2. Refer to the figure and fill in the sheet. Check the following steps to make sure that you completed all of the required steps.
3. Fill in the months in column **A**.
4. Select the first two office numbers in cells **B3** and **C3**, then fill in the column labels up to **120** in column **L**.
5. Type **Armstrong** in cell **B4**. Copy the name into the cells as shown for Offices **100**, **102**, and **104**. (Try the Fill method, just to see what happens.)

6. Use Fill and/or Copy to put **Tax** (a tax accounting firm) in Office **104** from **July** to **December** and in offices **108** through **118**. Place **Arch** (an architectural firm) in **106**, and **Admin** (administrative staff) in **120**.

7. Adjust column widths, if necessary, to show all cell data.

8. Center the headers in row **3**.

9. Change the page orientation to **Landscape**.

10. Place your name in the center of the header.

11. Save the workbook.

12. Preview and print the sheet.

R2—Create a Sheet to Track Time

In this exercise, you create a sheet to track time spent on several different accounts during the work week.

1. Select **Sheet2**. Rename the sheet tab at the bottom **Accounts**. Change the **Zoom** to **75%**.

2. Fill in the days of the week (weekdays only) and the dates as shown in the figure. See the steps below for additional information.

3. Select cell **A4**.

4. Click the fill handle with the right mouse button and drag to cell **A23**. Release the mouse button.

5. Select **Fill Weekdays** from the shortcut menu. Make sure that there are no Saturdays or Sundays.

6. Select cell **B4**. Repeat the same process to fill in the dates for the weekdays. Notice how the program displays the year 2000.

7. Add your name to the left side of the footer.

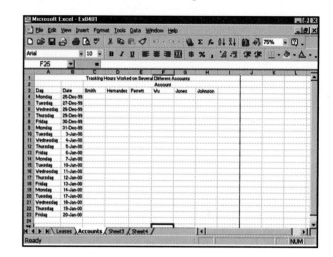

8. Save the workbook. Preview and print the sheet.

R3—Create a Schedule

In this exercise, you create a schedule for a once-a-week activity.

1. Select **Sheet3**.

2. Change the name on the tab from **Sheet3** to **Football**.

3. Fill in the dates to match the figure. Refer to the steps below for additional information.

4. Select the dates in cells **A3** and **A4**. Drag the fill handle down to cell **A14**.

5. Repeat this process for the games in column **C**.

6. Add your name in the left side of the header.

7. Save the workbook. Preview and print the sheet.

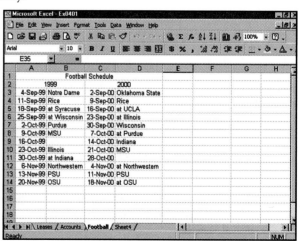

LESSON 4 FILLING, COPYING, AND PRINTING 131

R4—Project Population Growth

In this exercise, you project a population growth of 1 percent per year for the United States for the next twenty years.

1. Select **Sheet4**.

2. Change the name on the tab from **Sheet4** to **Population**.

3. Fill in a sequence of years from **1997** to **2017** in column **A**. Refer to the figure for guidance. All the years do not show in the figure, but it provides a general idea of the layout of the worksheet.

4. Select cell **B3**, which shows the present population of the United States in millions of people.

5. Use the right mouse button to drag the fill handle to cell **B23**. Release the mouse button.

6. When the shortcut menu appears, choose **Series** (not Fill Series).

7. In the Series window, choose **Growth** and set the **Step Value** to **1.01**. This causes the value in each cell to be 1 percent larger than the preceding value. Click **OK**. (The value in the year 2017 will be over 300 million.)

8. Format the population cells to show two decimal places.

9. Add your name in the left side of the header.

10. Save the workbook. Preview and print the sheet.

11. Close the workbook.

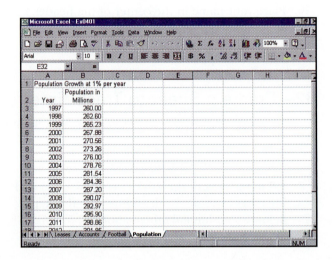

Challenge

Challenge exercises are designed to test your ability to apply your skills to new situations with less detailed instruction. These exercises also challenge you to expand your repertoire of skills by using Excel commands that are similar to those you have already learned. The desired outcome is clearly defined, but you have more freedom to choose the steps needed to achieve the required result.

The following Challenge exercises use the file **Less0403** from the **Student\Lesson 04** folder on your CD-ROM disc. Open this file and save it on your floppy disk as **Ex0402**.

C1—Customize a Fill List

Excel recognizes several common sequences of names. You may want to create your own. For example, if your company works six days a week (closed Sunday) you may want to fill in a sequence of days that does not include Sundays. In this example, three friends decide to buy a car together and take turns paying the car payment. Their names will appear many times, in the same sequence. If you create a custom list, you can fill in a column of names using the fill handle.

Goal: Create a custom list of three names that can be used to fill in the column that shows whose turn it is to pay the loan.

This worksheet contains formulas that you learn about in later chapters. It has also been protected so that you will not accidentally over-write those formulas (see Discovery exercise 3 in Lesson 2).

Use the following guidelines:

1. Select the **Car Payment** sheet.

2. Enter the names **Jack**, **Bill**, and **Mary** in cells **E4**, **E5**, and **E6**, respectively. Select these three cells.

3. Choose **Tools**, **Options**, **Custom Lists**, **Import**. Your list of entries is displayed. Click **OK**.

4. Fill in the rest of the names in column **E**. The three names should repeat so that each person is responsible for a payment every third month.

5. Choose **Tools**, **Options**, **Custom Lists**. Delete the custom list.

6. Save the workbook. Leave the workbook open for use in the next exercise.

C2—Use Header and Footer Options

There are several built-in options for headers and footers. In this exercise, you print the Car Payment sheets using a built-in header and footer.

Goal: Print a two-page worksheet using one of the built-in headers and footers.

Use the following guidelines:

1. Use the workbook **Ex0402** that was created in the previous exercise. If you do not have this file, open **Less0403** from the **Student\Lesson 04** folder on your CD-ROM disc and save it as **Ex0402** on your floppy disk.

2. Choose **File**, **Page Setup**, **Header/Footer**.

3. Click the list arrow at the right end of the **Header** box. Select the built-in header that begins **Prepared by....**

4. Use a similar method to select a built-in footer.

5. Preview the printout. Print the first page.

6. Save the workbook. Leave the workbook open for use in the next exercise.

C3—Include Row and Column Labels for Multiple Sheet Printouts

If a worksheet is too large to print on one sheet, the data prints on additional sheets, but the rows and columns used as labels do not. You can end up with sheets of data that have no labels and are hard to identify. It is possible to specify rows or columns that print on every page in order to provide labels for pages beyond the first page.

Goal: Specify that the first three rows of the Car Payment sheet print on all pages.

1. Use the workbook **Ex0402** that was created in exercise C1. If you do not have this file, open **Less0403** from the **Student\Lesson 04** folder on your CD-ROM disc and save it on your floppy disk as **Ex0402**.

2. Select **File**, **Page Setup**, **Sheet**.

3. Click the **Rows to repeat at top** box.

4. Click the **Collapse Dialog Box** button at the right of the box and drag down the first three rows. Click the **Expand Dialog Box** button. The **Rows to repeat at top** box should indicate the first two rows with the code $1:$3.

5. Preview the second page of the printout to confirm that the first three rows print there as well.

6. Print both pages of the sheet.

7. Save the workbook and close it.

Discovery

Discovery exercises are designed to help you learn how to teach yourself a new skill. In each exercise, you discover something new that is related to the topic taught in this lesson. You may be directed to use built-in wizards or some of the extensive Help features provided in Excel to discover new features and learn new skills with minimum assistance from books or instructors. The required outcome demonstrates your ability to apply the new skill. You determine the choice of topic, worksheet design, and steps of execution.

D1—Use Keyboard Shortcuts

If you have to do a lot of cutting, copying, and pasting, you will find that it is time consuming to take your hand off the keyboard and use a mouse to click a button on a toolbar or select an option from a menu. You may also need to cut, copy, or paste when a dialog box is open and the toolbars and menus are not available. At times like these, you can use Ctrl plus a keyboard letter to perform the task.

Some tasks require that you use menu options, but it would still be faster to use the keyboard to make the selection. In these cases, you can hold down Alt and press the key that is underlined (the hotkey) in the menu option to choose that option.

When you are done specifying your selections in a dialog box or window, you may need to choose a button such as **OK**, **Next**, or **Finish**. If a button has a bold outline, it can be selected by pressing Enter.

Goal: Learn how to use Ctrl with another key to perform functions, Alt to select menu options, Shift with arrow keys to select cells, and Enter to push buttons.

1. Open **Less0404** from the **Student\Lesson 04** folder on your CD-ROM disc and save it on your floppy disk as **Ex0403**. Select the **Keyboard** sheet.

2. Use the Office Assistant to find the quick reference to keyboard shortcuts. Print out the Help page titled **Keys for editing data**.

3. Use the arrow keys to move the selection to cell **A1**. Press Shift and use the down arrow to select cells **A1** through **A12**.

4. Press Ctrl and **C** to copy the contents of the cells.

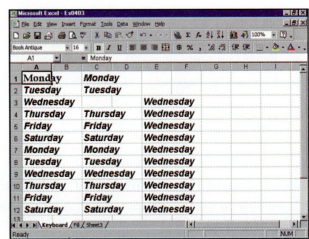

5. Use the arrow key to move the selection to cell **C1**. Press Ctrl and **V** to paste the selection.

6. Cut **Wednesday** out of cell **C3** and paste it into cell **E3** (use Ctrl and **X** to cut).

7. Copy **Wednesday** and paste it into cells **E4** through **E12**.

8. Use Shift and the arrow keys to select cells **A1** through **E12**.

9. Notice that the **Format** menu option has an underlined letter **o** (this is called a hotkey). Hold down Alt and press the **o** key. Use Alt plus the letter **e** in **Cells** to open the Format Cells dialog window.

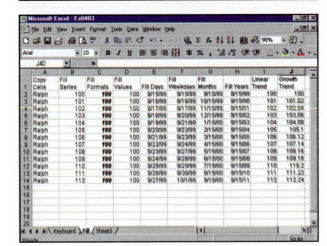

10. Use the arrow keys on the keyboard to select the **Font** tab. Use a combination of arrow keys, Tab, and Alt plus a hotkey to choose **Bold Italic** and **14** points as shown in the figure.

11. Notice that the **OK** button at the bottom of the window has a bold outline. Press ⏎Enter to push the **OK** button.

12. Use these keyboard methods to format cell **A1** as **Book Antiqua, Bold, 16 points** as shown in the figure.

13. Save the workbook. Leave the workbook open for use in the next exercise.

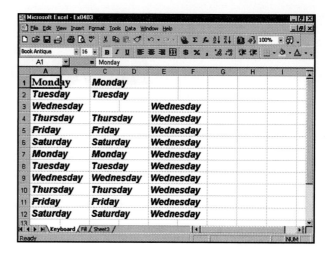

D2—Advanced Fill Options

The right mouse button can be used with the fill handle to provide several useful options.

Goal: Use the fill handle with the right mouse button to fill in the columns as shown in the figure. Use the Series option for the last two and experiment with the step feature to determine how to produce a linear and a growth series.

1. Use **Ex0403** from the previous Discovery exercise. If you did not do that exercise, open **Less0404** from the **Student\Lesson 04** folder on your CD-ROM disc and save it on your floppy disk as **Ex0403**. Select the **Fill** sheet.

2. Fill in the columns as shown. The last column uses a 2 percent growth factor.

3. Save the workbook. Leave it open for use in the next exercise.

D3—Set Print Area and Print Preview

If you click the **Print** button on the toolbar, the entire sheet is printed. You can specify a different default range that will be printed automatically. The range is called the Print Area. If you want to print a small range within a single sheet, use **File**, **Print Area**, **Set Print Area** option. If you want to control the areas printed together in a multipage printout, you want to know how to use the **Page Break Preview** option.

1. Use **Ex0403** from the previous Discovery exercise. If you did not do that exercise, open **Less0404** from the **Student\Lesson 04** folder on your CD-ROM disc and save it as **Ex0403**. Select the **Fill** sheet.

2. Select cells **C1** through **C14**, select the **File**, **Print Area**, **Set Print Area** option to set the print area to cells C1 through C14. Click the **Print** button on the toolbar and print that range automatically.

3. Use Help to learn about setting the print areas with the **Page Break Preview** option. Print the sheet on two pages where the second page has the Linear Growth and Growth Trend columns and the other columns are on the first page.

4. Save the workbook and close it.

Lesson: 5

Making the Computer Do the Math

Task 1 Adding, Subtracting, Multiplying, and Dividing Using Cell References and Numbers

Task 2 Using Formulas with More than One Cell Reference

Task 3 Combining Operations and Filling Cells with Formulas

Task 4 Filling Cells with Relative and Absolute Formulas

Task 5 Applying Basic Formulas to a Loan Repayment

Task 6 Using Built-in Financial Formulas

Task 7 Using Counting and Conditional Formulas

Task 8 Using Excel to Explore Different Possibilities

Introduction

Excel is at your command, whether you need to do basic arithmetic or advanced statistics. Once you set up a spreadsheet, you can change the numbers many times to see how those changes affect the "bottom line." In this lesson, you work on four spreadsheets. The first spreadsheet shows you how to perform basic math calculations using Excel. The next spreadsheet shows you how to use the Fill function with a formula and how to use absolute and relative cell references. In the third spreadsheet, you learn how to use the Paste Function dialog box to calculate a monthly payment on a car or house loan. You also calculate the total amount you will pay for the loan. The last spreadsheet shows you how to use the COUNTIF function to complete an employee's work schedule and to determine total hours worked and wages due.

After you have worked with these four spreadsheets, you make changes to various numbers and see how Excel quickly recalculates the numbers and gives you the results of these changes. The power to recalculate quickly allows you to try out several different options in a short period of time to find the best one.

Visual Summary

When you have completed this lesson, you will have created a reference sheet of math operations, used absolute and relative formulas to calculate sales commissions, and used Excel's library of financial functions to calculate a loan payment.

Sample Numbers:				
8	6			
3	12			

Cell and number:		Two cells		Combinations	
Addition:		Addition:		Grouping - example o.	
	=B3+5		=B2+A3		=(A2+B2)/A3
Subtraction:		Subtraction:		Grouping - example tv	
	=B3-5		=A2-A3		=B3/(A3+B2)
Multiplication:		Multiplication:			Filling:
	=A2*3		=A2*A3	Relative	=A2
					=A3
Division:		Division:			
	=A2/4		=B3/B2	Absolute	=$A$2
					=$A$2

Loan Amount (pv):	$ 10,000
Annual Interest	7.50%
Monthly Interest (rate)	0.625%
Years to Pay Back	4
Number of Payments (nper)	48
Monthly Payment	($241.79)
Total of All Payments	$ (11,605.87)

	A	B	C	D	E	F
		Calculation of Sales Commission				
	Commission rate:		5%			
		Dave	Eric	Sally	Natasha	Siri
	Monday	2,500	2,000	600	800	1,900
	Tuesday	1,500	1,800	3,000	700	2,500
	Wednesday	600	1,400	2,000	550	2,000
	Thursday	1,900	1,500	1,900	3,000	900
	Friday	1,000	1,900	1,400	700	800
	Saturday	1,000	500	900	2,000	2,000
		8,500	9,100	9,800	7,750	10,100
		$ 425.00	$ 455.00	$ 490.00	$ 387.50	$ 505.00

Schedule for Jan 6 to Jan 12							
	Monday	Tuesday	Wednesday	Thursday	Friday	Saturday	Sunday
8:00 AM	Bill	Bill	Angi	Bill	Grace	Scott	Scott
8:30 AM	Bill	Bill	Angi	Bill	Grace	Scott	Scott
9:00 AM	Bill	Bill	Angi	Bill	Grace	Scott	Scott
9:30 AM	Bill	Bill	Angi	Bill	Grace	Scott	Scott
10:00 AM	Bill	Bill	Angi	Bill	Grace	Scott	Scott
10:30 AM	Bill	Bill	Angi	Bill	Grace	Scott	Scott
11:00 AM	Bill	Bill	Angi	Bill	Grace	Scott	Scott
11:30 AM	Bill	Bill	Angi	Bill	Grace	Scott	Scott
12:00 PM	Bill	Scott	Angi	Bill	Grace	Scott	Scott
12:30 PM	Bill	Scott	Angi	Bill	Grace	Scott	Scott
1:00 PM	Bill	Scott	Angi	Bill	Grace	Scott	Scott
1:30 PM	Bill	Scott	Angi	Bill	Grace	Scott	Scott

Employee	Bill	Angi	Grace	Scott
Hourly Wage	$ 6.25	$ 6.50	$ 6.20	$ 6.35
Time Blocks Worked	32	12	12	28
Hours Worked	16	6	6	14
Pay	$ 100.00	$ 39.00	$ 37.20	$ 88.90

TASK 1

Adding, Subtracting, Multiplying, and Dividing Using Cell References and Numbers

Why would I do this?

Spreadsheets have been used in paper form for years as a means of keeping track of financial data. The value of using an electronic spreadsheet program such as Excel is its ability to make mathematical calculations quickly. Before the era of computers, people were employed to calculate rows and columns of numbers for use in navigational charts or other types of computational charts. The job title for the people who performed these calculations was Computer. In today's world, electronic computers keep track of financial data and perform mathematical computations. Computers are faster and more accurate than people for these kinds of tasks.

When you use Excel to perform a mathematical operation, it needs to be done in a way that is similar to ordinary math, but with a few special rules. For example, all formulas must begin with an equal sign (=), and you use cell names in the formulas.

In this lesson, you practice applying the basic formula rules in Excel. The sheet you produce serves as a convenient reference for later use.

1 Open **Less0501** from the **Student\Lesson05** folder on the CD-ROM disc that came with this book. Save it as **Math** on your floppy disk.

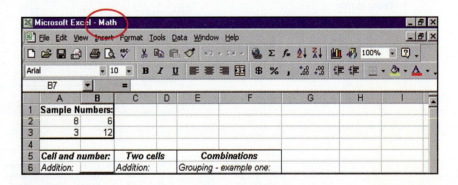

2 Select cell **B7** and type **=B3+5** in the cell. This formula adds the contents of cell B3 and the number 5.

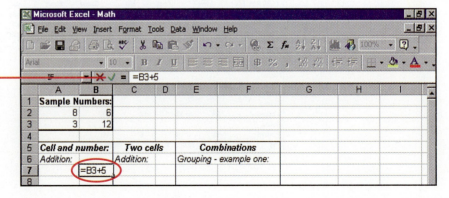

Enter button on the formula bar

3 Click the **Enter** button on the formula bar. Notice that cell B3 contains the number 12, and cell B7 displays the result of adding 5 to the contents of B3.

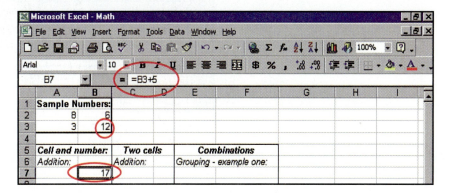

In Depth: You can enter a formula by pressing ⏎Enter or Tab⇄; however, the selection moves to another cell, and you have to move the selection back if you want to see what the formula is in the formula bar. If you click the **Enter** button on the formula bar, the selection does not move to another cell.

4 Select cell **B10**, type **=B3-5**. Determine what you think the answer should be before you proceed. In this case, you subtract 5 from the contents of cell B3. Click the **Enter** button on the formula bar. If you anticipated a different answer, take the time to figure out why.

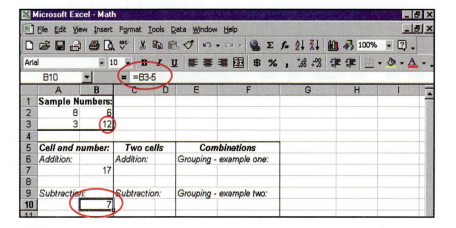

5 Select cell **B13**, type **=A2*3**, determine what you think the answer should be, and click the **Enter** button on the formula bar. Excel uses the asterisk to indicate multiplication.

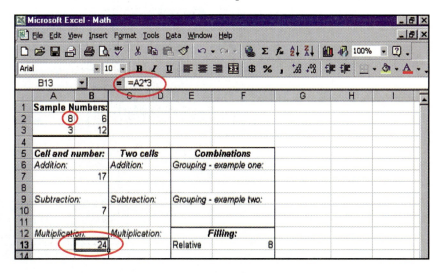

LESSON 5   MAKING THE COMPUTER DO THE MATH   **139**

6 Select cell **B16**, type **=A2/4,** anticipate the answer, and click the **Enter** button on the formula bar. Excel uses the slash to indicate division.

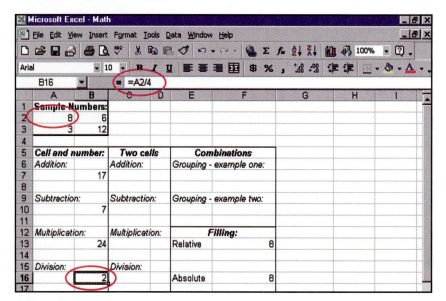

Caution: There are two slash keys. The forward slash (/) is used to indicate division in Excel formulas. If you use the backslash (\) by mistake, Excel displays **#NAME?** to indicate that it does not recognize your entry as a formula, but thinks it is a misspelled cell name.

TASK 2

Using Formulas with More than One Cell Reference

Why would I do this?

When writing a *formula,* an equation used to calculate values in a cell, it is common to refer to numbers entered in more than one cell on your worksheet. For example, if you want to know the profit for your business, you subtract expenses from income. If you want to know the percent increase in sales, you use numbers entered for two different sales periods to make that calculation.

In this task, you learn to use numbers from more than one cell to make calculations.

1 Select cell **D7**, type **=A2+A3**, estimate the answer, and click the **Enter** button on the formula bar. In this case, the formula adds the numbers in cells A2 and A3.

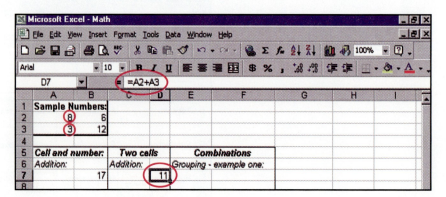

140 LEARN EXCEL 2000

> **2** Select cell **D10**, type **=A2-A3,** estimate the answer, and then click the **Enter** button on the formula bar. This formula tells the program to subtract the number in cell A3 from the number in cell A2.

Quick Tip: After typing an equal sign to begin the formula, you can point to a cell and click to enter its name in the formula. You can then type the math symbol you want to use before you point and click on the next cell you want in the formula. When this method is used, a marquee outlines the cell that has been selected. This method is preferable if you are writing a formula and the cell you want is off the screen where you cannot see the cell reference.

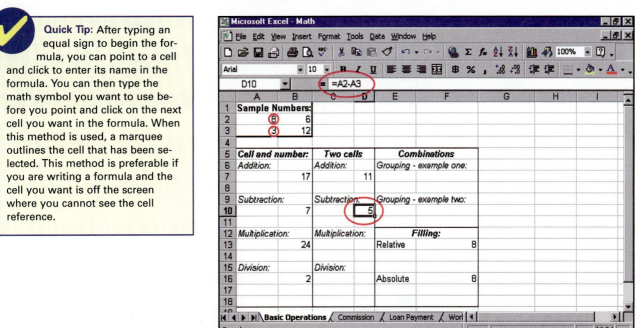

> **3** Select cell **D13**, type **=A2*A3**, determine what the answer should be if the numbers in these cells were multiplied together, and click the **Enter** button on the formula bar. In this case, you told the program to multiply the number in cell A2 by the number in cell A3.

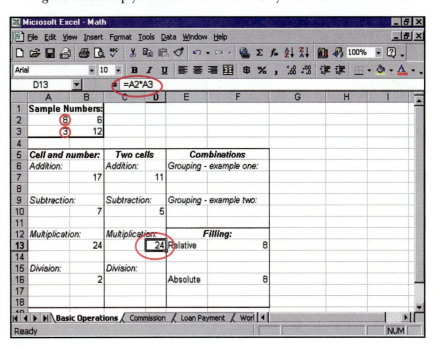

LESSON 5　MAKING THE COMPUTER DO THE MATH

4 Select cell **D16**, type **=B3/B2**, estimate the answer, and click the **Enter** button on the formula bar. In this case, you told the program to take the number in cell B3 and divide by the number in cell B2.

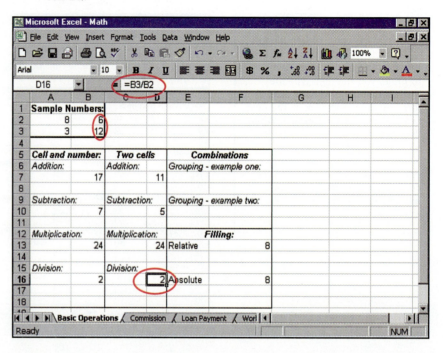

5 Select cell **A2**, then choose **T**ools, A**u**diting, Trace **D**ependants. (You may need to click the double arrow at the bottom of the menu to reveal the A**u**diting option.) Arrows are drawn on the screen to show which cells contain formulas that depend on cell A2.

Quick Tip: If you make a mistake and want to start over, click the Cancel button (X) next to the Enter button on the formula bar.

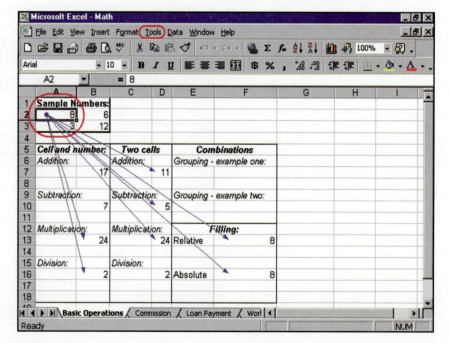

6 Choose **Tools**, **Auditing**, **Remove All Arrows**. The arrows are erased.

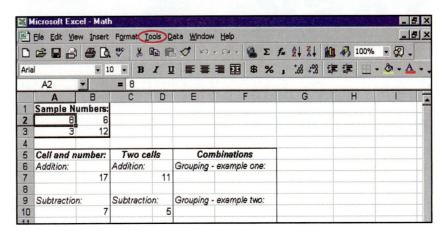

7 Double-click on cell **D7**. The formula is displayed in the cell and in the formula bar. The cell references in the formula and the cells to which they refer change to matching colors. An insertion mark is placed in the formula.

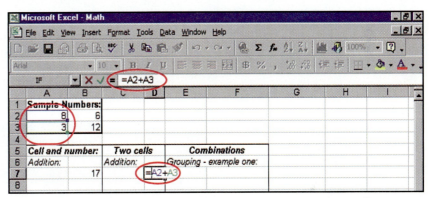

8 Edit the formula the way you would edit ordinary text. Change it to **=B2+A3**. Click the **Enter** button on the formula bar to finish the change.

> ✓ **Quick Tip:** Cell names are not case-sensitive. Excel interprets A2 the same as a2. When entering cell names, it is not necessary to capitalize the column reference letter.

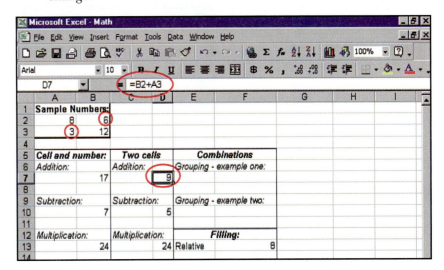

LESSON 5   MAKING THE COMPUTER DO THE MATH   143

TASK 3

Combining Operations and Filling Cells with Formulas

Why would I do this?

You may want to add the contents of several cells together and then divide by the contents of another cell. To do this, use parentheses to group operations together to make sure they are done first.

If the same formula is to be used in several cells, it may be filled into those cells using the fill handle. Sometimes you want cell references to change to adapt to the new position; for example, you may have a formula that totals the cells above it and wish to copy this formula across several cells. In each case, you want the formula to add the column of cells directly above the formula. This is called a relative reference. In other cases, you want the cell reference to always refer to a specific cell. This is called an absolute reference.

In this task, you will learn how to group operations in a formula and how to fill formulas using relative and absolute cell references.

1 Select cell **F7**, type **=(A2+B2)/A3**. Estimate what the result should be if you add the contents of cells A2 and B2 and then divide by the number in cell A3 (it is not a whole number). Click the **Enter** button on the formula bar to confirm your estimate. Notice that the numbers in cells A2 and B2 (8 and 6) are added first and then divided by the number in cell A3 (3).

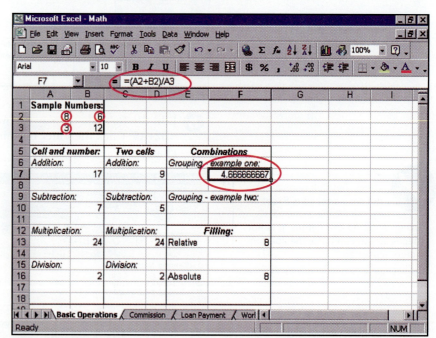

2 Select cell **F10**, type **=B3/(A3+B2)**. Estimate what the answer will be if the number in cell B3 is divided by the sum of the numbers in cells A3 and B2. Click the **Enter** button on the formula bar to confirm your estimate.

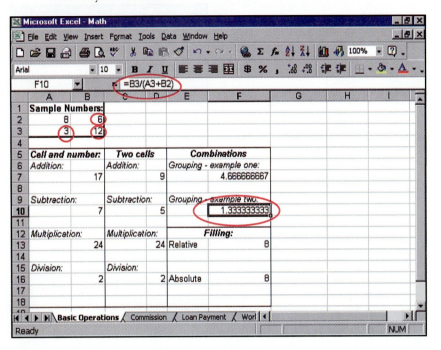

3 Select cell **F13**. Look at the formula in the formula bar. It shows that the formula simply equals the value of cell A2.

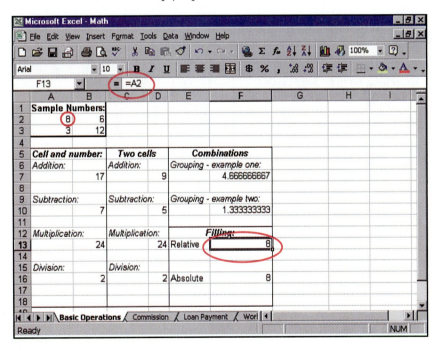

LESSON 5   MAKING THE COMPUTER DO THE MATH   145

4 Click and drag the fill handle down to cell **F14**. Release the mouse button. Notice that cell **F14** displays the number 3, which is the value in cell A3.

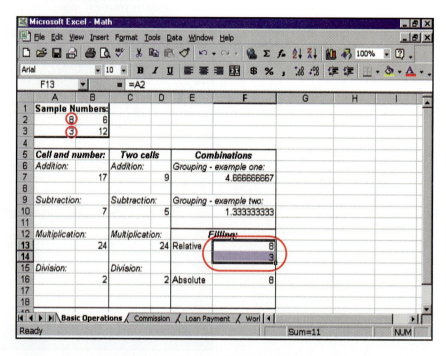

5 Select cell **F14**. Notice that the formula changed and it now equals the value in cell A3. The formulas in cells F13 and F14 both refer to a cell that is eleven rows up and five columns to the left.

In Depth: When you fill a formula from one cell to another, Excel uses a relative cell reference. In this example, Excel used A3 to fill cell F14. Cell F14 is one position below F13, and cell A3 is one position below A2. Excel uses the relative position of the cell that is being referenced to determine the location of the next value to place in the new cell. This is the default method Excel uses to fill a formula from one cell to another.

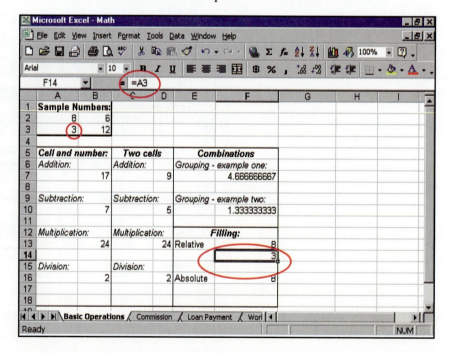

6 Select cell **F16**. Look at the formula in the formula bar. In this case, a dollar sign ($) has been placed to the left of the column and row identifiers to indicate that the cell reference will not change when it is copied.

> **In Depth:** The dollar sign ($) that is used as a code to prevent the reference from changing has nothing to do with currency. It is a symbol that was used in the earliest spreadsheets for this purpose and has been used ever since.

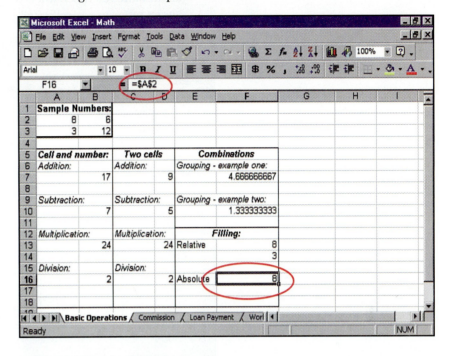

7 Use the fill handle to fill this formula into cell **F17**. Notice that F17 also displays the contents of cell A2.

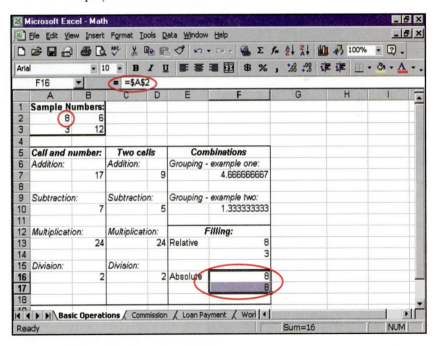

LESSON 5 MAKING THE COMPUTER DO THE MATH **147**

8 Select cell **F17**. Look at the formula in the formula bar. Notice that it did not change when the formula was filled into the cell. This type of cell reference (with the $ sign) is called an *absolute reference*. Use an absolute reference when you want to ensure that the formula always refers to a specific cell.

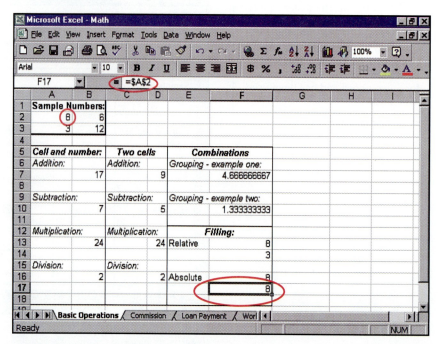

9 Press Ctrl+` (the accent grave mark found on the key to the left of the 1 key.) The formulas for each cell are displayed.

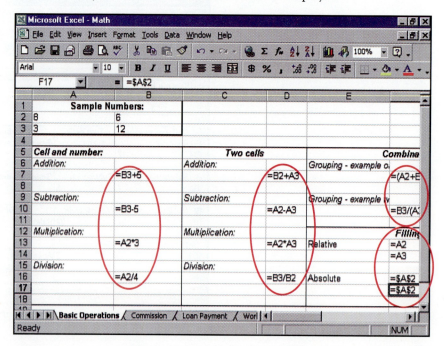

148 LEARN EXCEL 2000

10 Add your name to the header **Center section**, using the **Page Setup** dialog box. Print the worksheet.

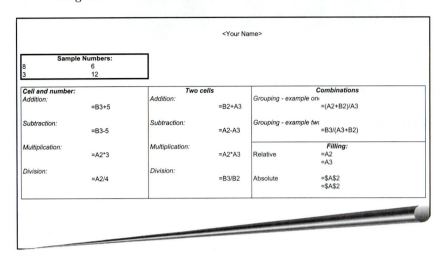

11 Press Ctrl+` to return the worksheet to the Normal view showing numbers. Save your workbook.

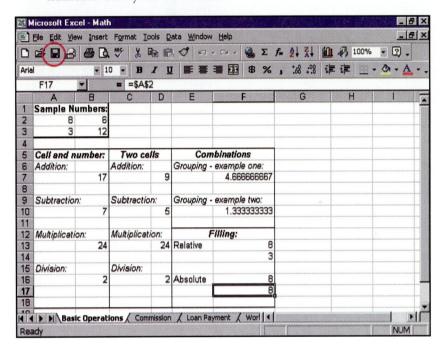

LESSON 5   MAKING THE COMPUTER DO THE MATH

TASK 4

Filling Cells with Relative and Absolute Formulas

Why would I do this?

The capability to fill formulas into adjacent cells greatly increases the speed at which a worksheet can be created.

In this task, you learn how to fill cells using both relative and absolute formulas.

1 Click the **Commission** tab to switch to the **Commission** sheet and select cell **B11 if necessary**. Notice that it contains a formula that adds the contents of cells B5 through B10, which are directly above B11.

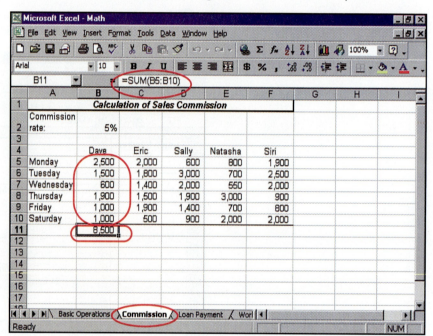

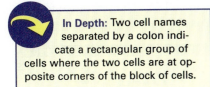

In Depth: Two cell names separated by a colon indicate a rectangular group of cells where the two cells are at opposite corners of the block of cells.

2 Drag the fill handle to the right to cell **F11** and release the mouse. The formula is filled into cells C11 through F11.

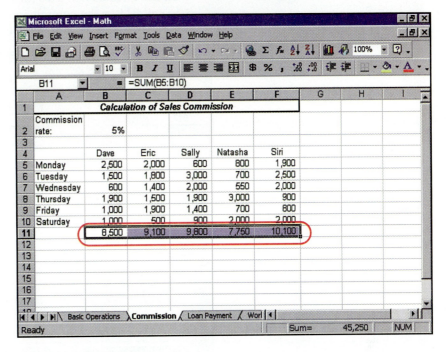

3 Click on cell **D11**, and you see that the formula changed to add the six cells in the column above cell D11. This shows how the use of the fill handle results in a relative reference.

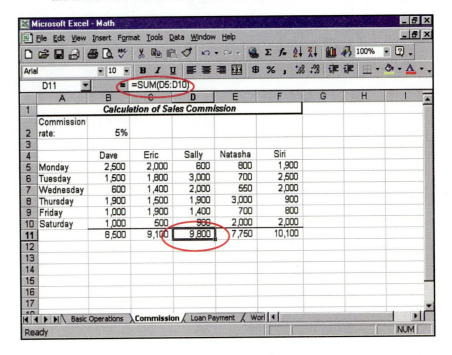

LESSON 5   MAKING THE COMPUTER DO THE MATH

④ Select cell **B12** and type **=B11*$B$2**, then click the **Enter** button on the formula bar. This formula multiplies the sum of Dave's sales in cell B11 by the commission rate in cell B2. The reference to B11 is relative, and the reference to B2 is absolute.

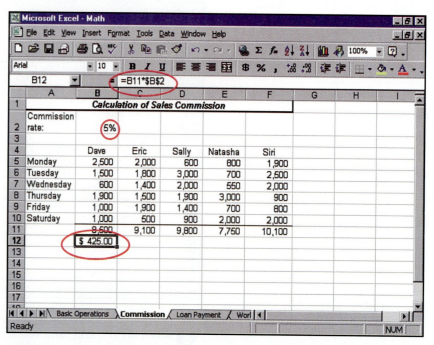

⑤ Drag the fill handle to the right to cell **F12** and release the mouse button. The formula is filled in.

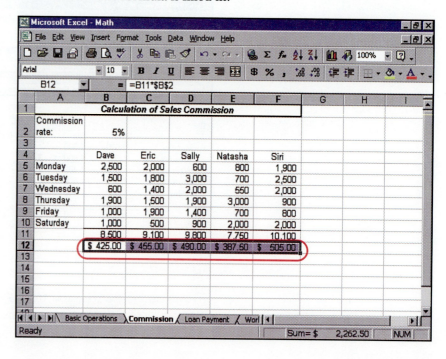

6 Click on cell **D12** and look at the formula bar. The relative reference changed so that it refers to the sum of Sally's sales in cell D11, but the absolute reference to the commission rate in cell B2 did not change.

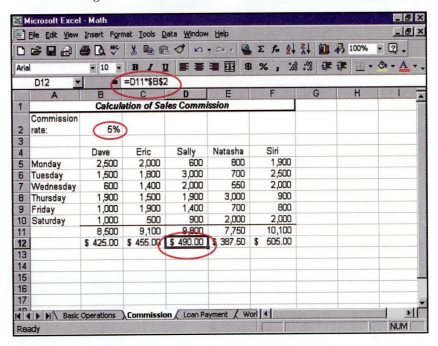

7 Add your name to the sheet header. Save your work and print the worksheet.

LESSON 5   MAKING THE COMPUTER DO THE MATH   153

TASK 5

Applying Basic Formulas to a Loan Repayment

Why would I do this?

When you borrow money for a car or a house, the loan repayment is based on several factors, such as interest rate, time to repay, and the loan amount. With Excel, you can set up a worksheet to calculate your monthly payments based on these factors, and then change the value of the factors to match whatever loan terms you are quoted by a bank or other lender.

In this task, you learn how to set up a worksheet to calculate total monthly payments.

1 Click the **Loan Payment** tab to switch to the **Loan Payment** sheet. Notice that column A is used for labels and column B is used for formulas.

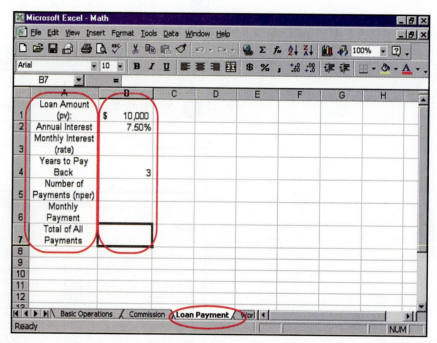

2 Select cell **B3**, type **=B2/12**, and click the **Enter** button on the formula bar. This formula takes the annual interest rate in cell B2 and divides by 12 to calculate the monthly interest rate.

> **In Depth:** To calculate the monthly payment, the formula requires the number of months and the interest rate per month. Most loan interest rates are given as Annual Percentage Rate, or *APR*. If the payment is made every month, the formula needs to use one-twelfth of the annual interest rate to calculate the interest cost per month.

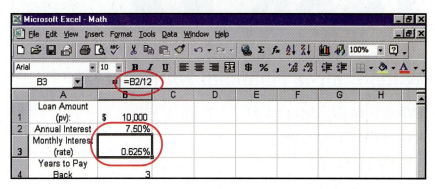

3 Select cell **B5**, type **=B4*12**, and click the **Enter** button on the formula bar. This formula calculates the number of months over which the loan is repaid.

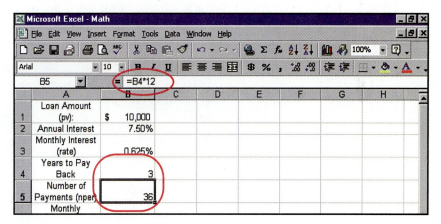

4 Select cell **B7**, type **=B5*B6**, and click the **Enter** button on the formula bar. This formula multiplies the number of payments in cell B5 times the amount of the payment in B6. In this case, no number is displayed in the cell because cell B6 is still empty, and the cell has been formatted to show a dollar sign and a dash when the value is zero.

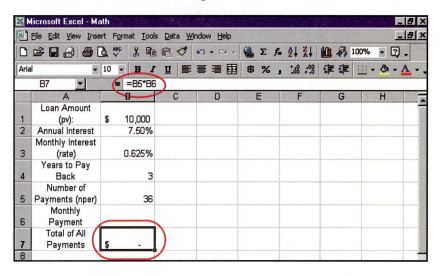

LESSON 5 MAKING THE COMPUTER DO THE MATH

TASK 6

Using Built-in Financial Formulas

Why would I do this?

When you take out a loan, you usually rely on someone else to tell you how much the payment will be. In order to shop around for the best rate or terms, it is helpful to see the effect of different loan terms that may be quoted to you. In the previous task, the factors used to calculate a loan were outlined.

In this task, you learn how to use one of Excel's built-in financial formulas to calculate the monthly payment. Then you change some of the terms of the loan to see what effect they have on the monthly payment and the total amount paid.

1 Select cell **B6.** Click the **Paste Function** button on the Standard toolbar. (If the Office Assistant appears, select **No, don't provide help now.**) The Paste Function dialog box opens.

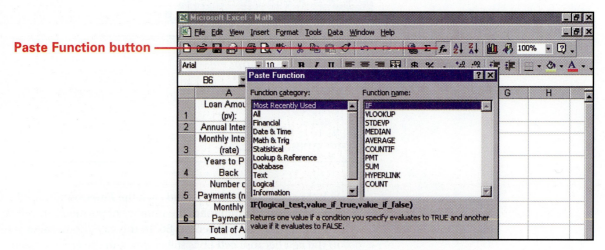

Paste Function button

2 Click the **Financial** option in the **Function category** box. A list of built-in financial formulas appears in the Function name box.

In Depth: The first choice, **Most Recently Used**, displays a list of recently used functions in the box to the right. This list is different for each computer because it is based on personal use.

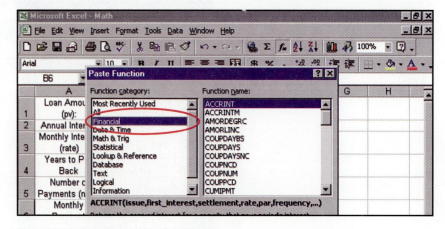

156 LEARN EXCEL 2000

3 If necessary, scroll down and click the **PMT** function. The name of the function and the values it requires are displayed. These values are called *arguments*. This function is used to calculate loan payments.

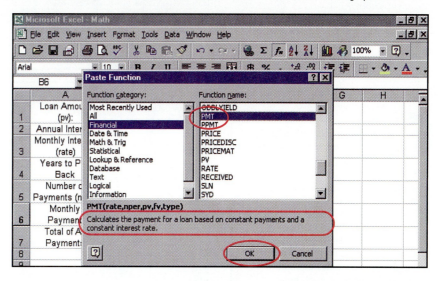

4 Click **OK**. A wizard dialog box opens. You use the wizard to identify the cells that contain values, or arguments, the payment function required. The first three arguments are required, and their names are in boldface type. The last two are optional, and their names are in normal type.

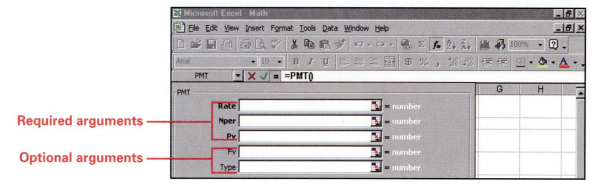

Required arguments

Optional arguments

5 Click the **Collapse Dialog Box** button at the right end of the **Rate** box.

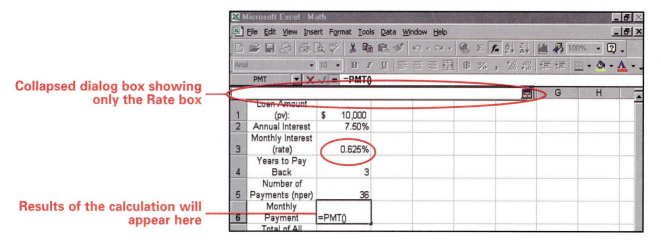

Collapsed dialog box showing only the Rate box

Results of the calculation will appear here

LESSON 5   MAKING THE COMPUTER DO THE MATH   157

6 Click cell **B3**. This cell reference is entered into the formula as the first argument.

Expand Dialog Box button

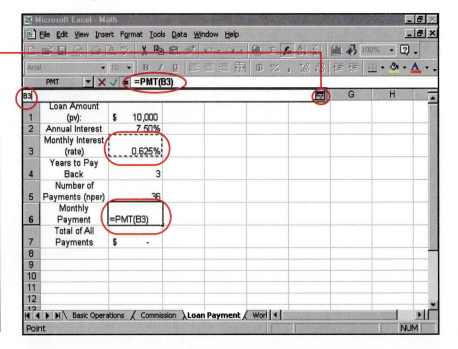

In Depth: Wizards usually consist of a series of questions that guide you through the creation of a formula or a chart. Wizards are used in Excel to help with a number of different processes. These include a Help Wizard known as the Office Assistant, a Chart Wizard used for creating charts, and the wizards in Paste Function that help create complex formulas such as a payment formula.

7 Click the **Expand Dialog Box** button to restore the dialog box. The cell reference is displayed in the Rate box.

In Depth: If the Collapse Dialog Box obscures the range of cells you want to select, expand the dialog box, drag it to another location, then collapse it.

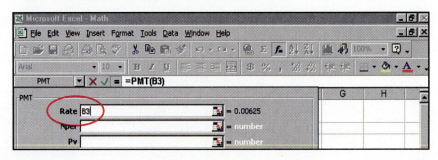

8 Press Tab to move to the **Nper** box. The message at the bottom of the box explains that this is the total number of loan payments.

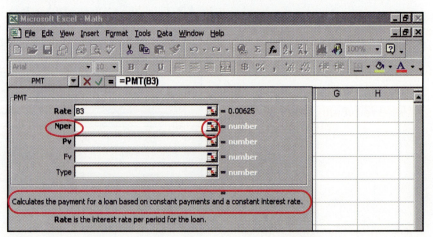

9 Click the **Collapse** Dialog Box button at the right side of the **Nper** box, click on cell **B5**, and click the **Expand Dialog Box** button. The reference to cell B5 is added as the second argument to the formula.

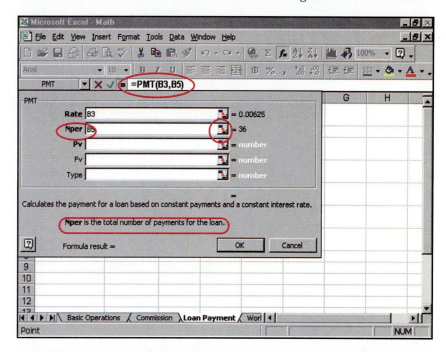

10 Press Tab to move to the **Pv** box. This argument is used to identify the present value of the loan, or the amount you want to borrow.

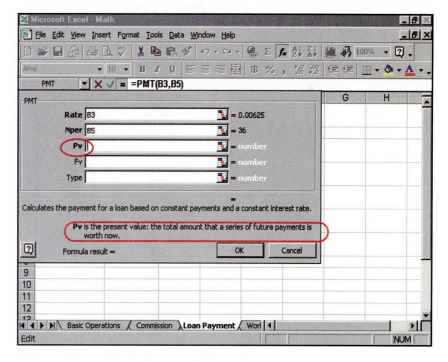

LESSON 5 MAKING THE COMPUTER DO THE MATH

11 Click the **Collapse Dialog Box** button, click on cell **B1**, and click the **Expand Dialog Box** button. The reference to cell B1 is added as the third argument to the formula. The formula now has enough information to calculate the payment. The result is displayed at the bottom of the dialog box.

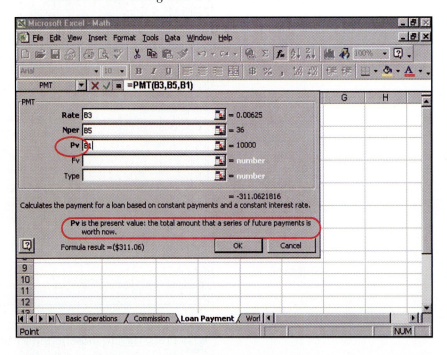

12 Click **OK**. The calculated payment is displayed. The currency format that has been chosen for this cell displays negative numbers in red, enclosed by parentheses. (If the loan amount is entered as a positive number, the payment is negative.) Notice that cell B7 now shows the total amount of all payments.

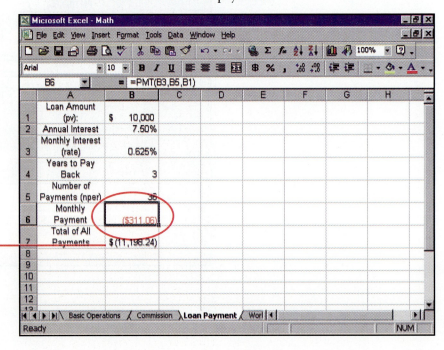

Parentheses indicate negative numbers

13. Add your name to the center of the page header, save your work, preview the printout, then print the sheet.

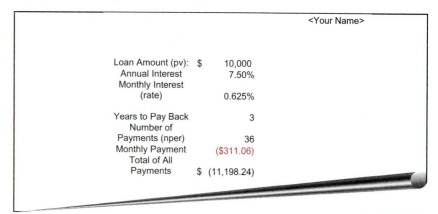

TASK 7

Using Counting and Conditional Formulas

Why would I do this?

The employee time sheet that you filled out in Lesson 4 is useful for posting on a bulletin board to inform workers of when they are scheduled to work. When it comes time to calculate their wages, you may need some help in translating the schedule into dollars earned. Excel has a built-in function, called the *COUNTIF function*, that counts the number of cells in the range you specify that contain words or numbers you specify.

In this task, you learn how to count the number of cells assigned to each worker and calculate the week's wages based on individual salaries and the amount of time worked.

1. Click the **Work Schedule** tab. The Work Schedule sheet is displayed. This is part of the sheet you worked on earlier.

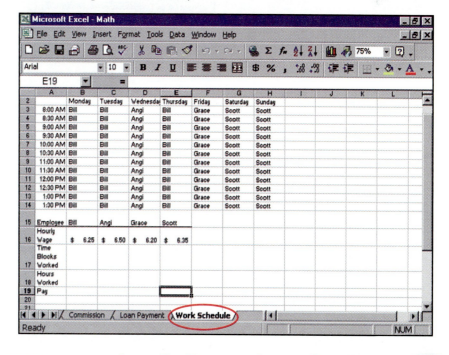

LESSON 5   MAKING THE COMPUTER DO THE MATH   161

2 Select cell **B17** and click the **Paste Function** button. The Paste Function dialog box apprears.

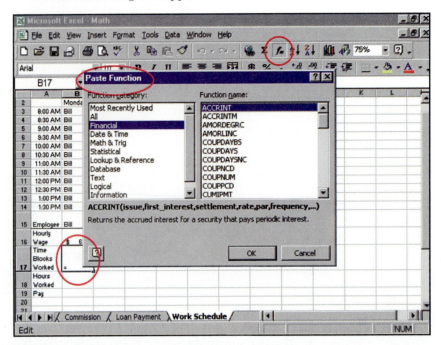

3 Click **Statistical** in the **Function category** box.

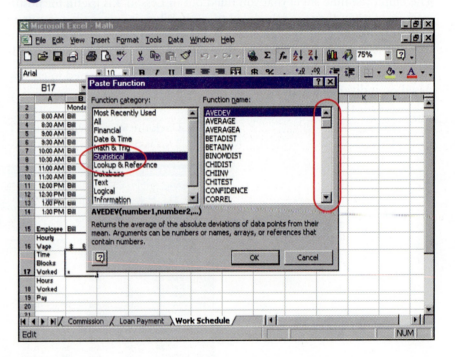

4 Scroll down the list in the **Function name** box and select **COUNTIF**. A message explains that this function counts the number of cells within a specified range that meet a condition.

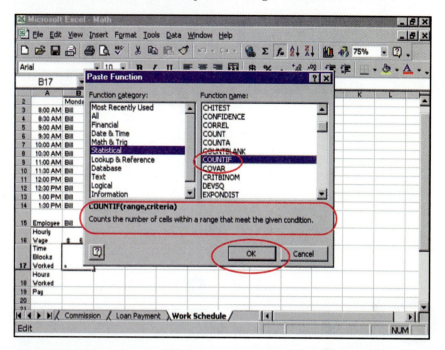

5 Click **OK**. A dialog box appears.

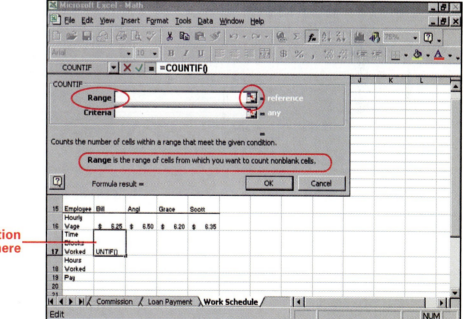

Result of the calculation will appear here

LESSON 5   MAKING THE COMPUTER DO THE MATH

6 Click the **Collapse Dialog Box** button next to the **Range** box.

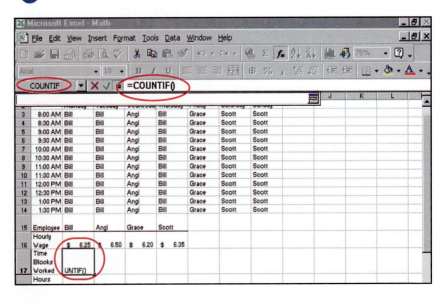

7 Select the range of cells from **B3** to **H14**.

Caution: You may notice that the complete COUNTIF() does not show in the cell. This is only due to a lack of space in the cell. Both the formula bar and the Name Box show the complete name of this function.

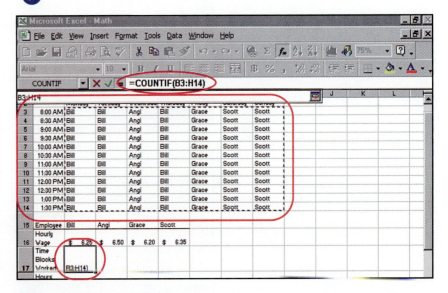

8 Click the **Expand Dialog Box** button. The dialog box reappears with the range filled in.

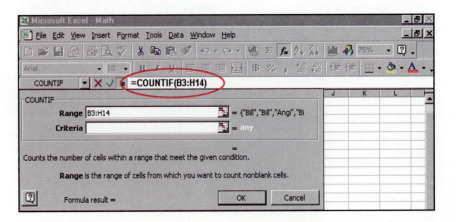

9. Press Tab to move to the **Criteria** box. Type **"Bill"** (include the quotation marks).

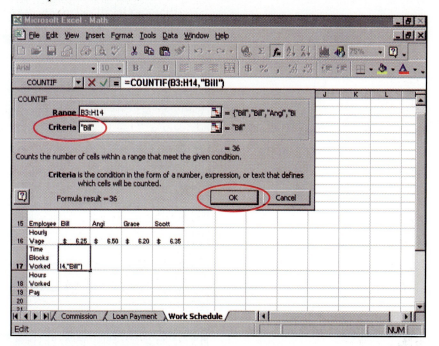

10. Click OK, then select cell **C17**. Use the same method described in the previous steps to count all of the cells that contain Angi's name. Refer to the figure and look at the formula in the formula bar if you have a problem.

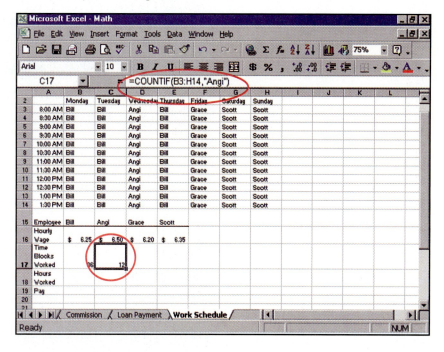

LESSON 5 MAKING THE COMPUTER DO THE MATH

11 Use the same method to place a formula in cell **D17** that counts all of the cells that contain Grace's name and a formula in cell **E17** that counts all occurrences of Scott's name.

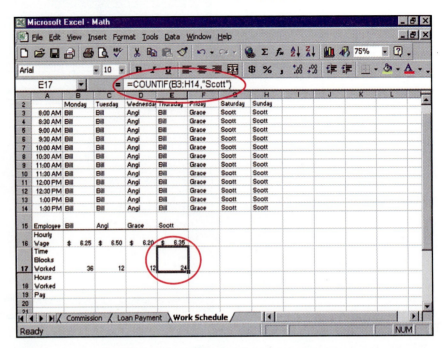

12 Select cell **B18**, type **=B17/2**, and click the **Enter** button on the formula bar. Each cell represents a half hour of work. Therefore, to calculate how many hours the person has worked, you must divide by 2.

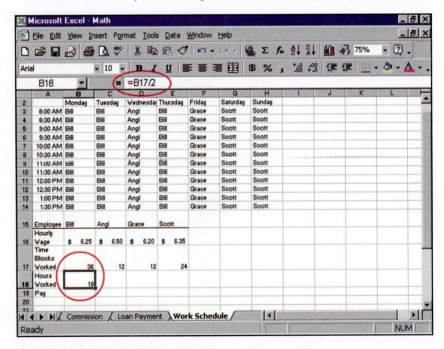

13 Select cell **B19,** type **=B16*B18**, and click the **Enter** button on the formula bar. Notice that the hourly wage in cell B16 was multiplied by the hours worked in cell B18.

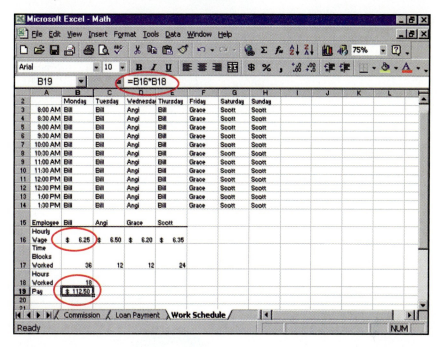

14 Select cells **B18** and **B19**. Drag the fill handle to cell **E19**. Because the formulas in cells B18 and B19 use relative references, Angi's, Grace's, and Scott's pay are automatically calculated the same way Bill's pay was calculated. In each case, the hourly wage was multiplied by the hours worked.

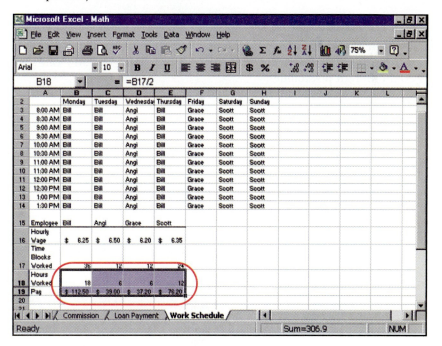

LESSON 5 MAKING THE COMPUTER DO THE MATH   167

15 Add your name to the center of the sheet header as shown in the figure. Turn on the gridlines (use **Sheet** in **Page Setup**), save your work, then preview and print the sheet.

<Your Name>

Gridlines turned on

Schedule for Jan 6 to Jan 12							
	Monday	Tuesday	Wednesday	Thursday	Friday	Saturday	Sunday
8:00 AM	Bill	Bill	Angi	Bill	Grace	Scott	Scott
8:30 AM	Bill	Bill	Angi	Bill	Grace	Scott	Scott
9:00 AM	Bill	Bill	Angi	Bill	Grace	Scott	Scott
9:30 AM	Bill	Bill	Angi	Bill	Grace	Scott	Scott
10:00 AM	Bill	Bill	Angi	Bill	Grace	Scott	Scott
10:30 AM	Bill	Bill	Angi	Bill	Grace	Scott	Scott
11:00 AM	Bill	Bill	Angi	Bill	Grace	Scott	Scott
11:30 AM	Bill	Bill	Angi	Bill	Grace	Scott	Scott
12:00 PM	Bill	Bill	Angi	Bill	Grace	Scott	Scott
12:30 PM	Bill	Bill	Angi	Bill	Grace	Scott	Scott
1:00 PM	Bill	Bill	Angi	Bill	Grace	Scott	Scott
1:30 PM	Bill	Bill	Angi	Bill	Grace	Scott	Scott
Employee	Bill		Angi		Grace	Scott	
Hourly Wage	$ 6.25		$ 6.50		$ 6.20	$ 6.35	
Time Blocks Worked	36		12		12	24	
Hours Worked	18		6		6	12	
Pay	$ 112.50		$ 39.00		$ 37.20	$ 76.20	

TASK 8

Using Excel to Explore Different Possibilities

Why would I do this?

One of the rewards of designing a spreadsheet using formulas is that the computer does all of the recalculations any time you change any of the data. This means you can easily see the effects of your changes and rapidly try out different possibilities.

In this task, you learn more about how Excel recalculates formulas.

1 If necessary, click the left tab-scrolling button to scroll the sheet tabs to the left. Click the **Basic Operations** tab to return to that sheet.

168 LEARN EXCEL 2000

2 Select cell **B2**. Choose **Tools, Auditing, Trace Dependants**. The arrows quickly identify which cells contain formulas that depend upon the value in this cell.

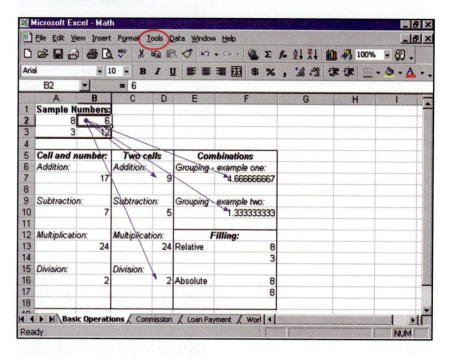

3 Type **200** and click the **Enter** button on the formula bar. All of the cells that depend on cell B2 are recalculated with the new number.

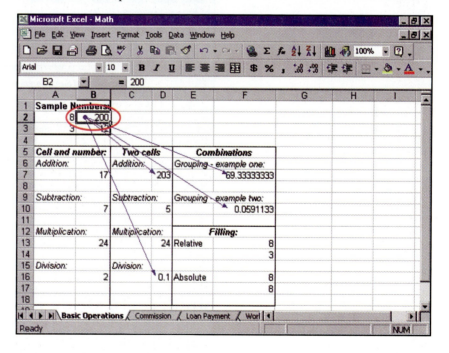

LESSON 5   MAKING THE COMPUTER DO THE MATH

4 Click the **Commission** tab to switch to that sheet and select cell **B2**.

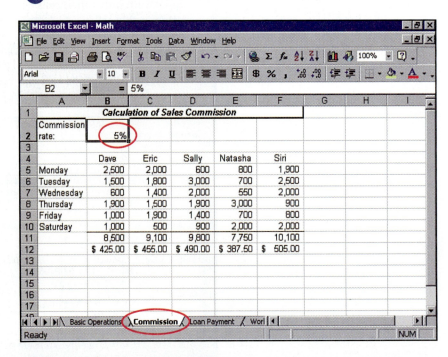

5 Type **7** and click the **Enter** button on the formula bar. Notice that all of the commissions have been recalculated.

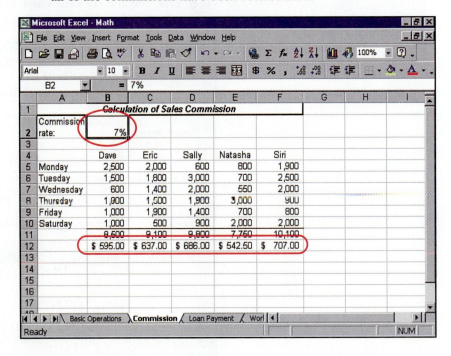

6 Click the **Loan Payment** tab to switch to that sheet.

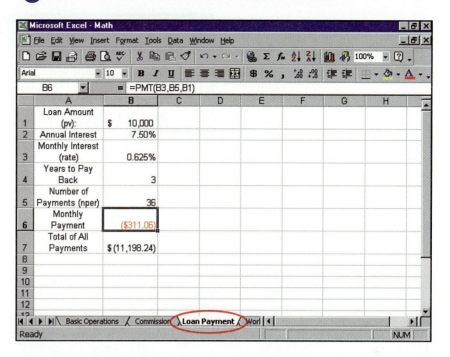

7 Select cell **B4**, type **4**, and click the **Enter** button on the formula bar. Notice that the new payment ($241.79) is less, but the total paid for the loan is more.

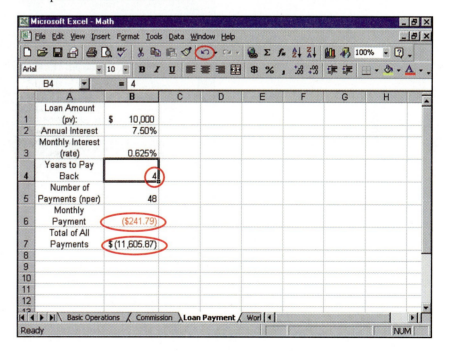

LESSON 5   MAKING THE COMPUTER DO THE MATH

8 Click the **Undo** button to see the previous values.

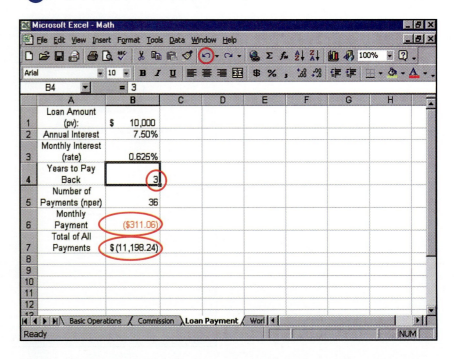

9 Click the **Redo** button to go back to the four-year payment plan.

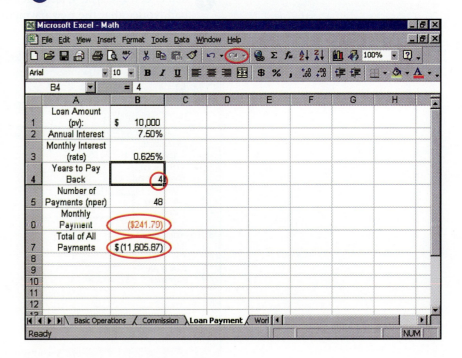

10 Click the **Work Schedule** tab.

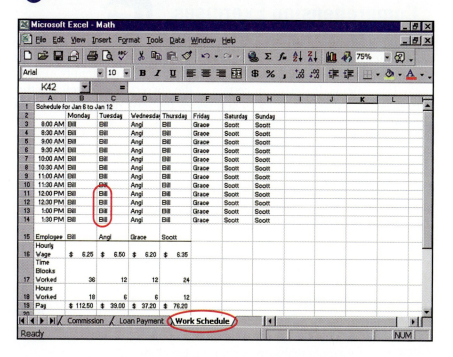

11 Assume that Bill asked Scott to take his Tuesday lunch shift from 12 to 2. Enter Scott's name in cells **C11** through **C14**. Notice that the hours worked and pay are automatically recalculated for both employees.

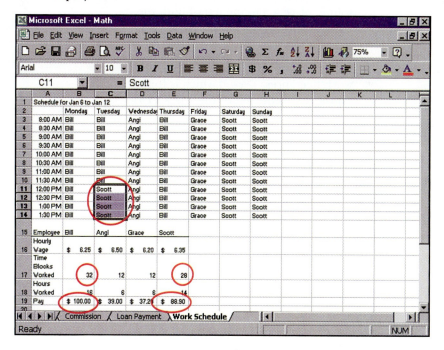

12 Save the changes and close the workbook.

LESSON 5 MAKING THE COMPUTER DO THE MATH

Comprehension Exercises

Comprehension exercises are designed to check your memory and understanding of the basic concepts in this lesson. You distinguish between true and false statements, identify new screen elements, and match terms with related statements. If you are uncertain of the correct answer, refer to the task number following each item (for example, T4 refers to Task 4) and review that task until you are confident that you can provide a correct response.

True-False

Circle either T or F.

T F **1.** You can only use one cell reference in a formula. **(T2)**

T F **2.** Math operations that are grouped inside parentheses are calculated first in a formula. **(T3)**

T F **3.** When you use the fill handle to copy a formula that sums a column, Excel assumes an absolute reference to the numbers in the original column. **(T3)**

T F **4.** To designate a cell reference as absolute, place a **$** to the left of both the column and row identifiers. **(T4)**

T F **5.** To view the formulas used in an Excel worksheet, press Ctrl+` which is found on the key to the left of the 1 key. **(T3)**

T F **6.** The loan payment formula uses an annual interest rate and the number of years of the loan to calculate the monthly payment amount. **(T6)**

T F **7.** The Paste Function button on the Standard toolbar opens a wizard that can be used to enter formulas for making a variety of financial calculations. **(T6)**

T F **8.** Relative reference is a cell reference that will change when the formula is copied, moved, or filled. **(T4)**

T F **9.** The COUNTIF function in Excel can be used to count the number of cells that contain a selected word or number. **(T7)**

T F **10.** When you change a number in a cell, it automatically changes the results of every formula that uses that cell. **(T8)**

Identifying Parts of the Excel Screen

Refer to the figure and identify the numbered parts of the screen. Write the letter of the correct label in the space next to the number.

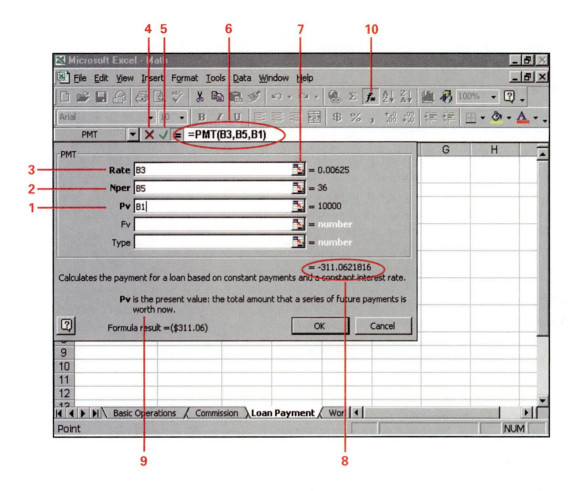

1. _____
2. _____
3. _____
4. _____
5. _____
6. _____
7. _____
8. _____
9. _____
10. _____

A. Paste Function button **(T6)**
B. Enter button **(T1)**
C. Projected payment amount **(T6)**
D. Interest rate per loan period **(T6)**
E. Amount of money that is borrowed **(T6)**
F. Number of payments in a loan **(T6)**
G. Collapse Dialog Box button **(T6)**
H. Formula with arguments **(T6)**
I. Description of the selected argument **(T6)**
J. Cancel button **(T2)**

LESSON 5 MAKING THE COMPUTER DO THE MATH

Matching

Match the statements below to the word or phrase that is the best match from the list. Write the letter of the matching word or phrase in the space provided next to the number.

1. ___ Symbol used to represent division **(T1)**
2. ___ The term used for numbers or words that are used by a function to perform a calculation or operation **(T6)**
3. ___ Symbol used to represent multiplication **(T1)**
4. ___ Enter button on the formula bar **(T1)**
5. ___ An example of a relative cell reference **(T3)**
6. ___ Used to begin every formula **(T1)**
7. ___ Used to count the number of occurrences of a word or a number in a range of cells **(T7)**
8. ___ An example of an absolute cell reference **(T4)**
9. ___ A cell reference that will change when copied or filled **(T4)**
10. ___ Used to group math operations **(T3)**

A. $B$3
B. ( )
C. B3
D. =
E. COUNTIF function
F. ✓
G. Relative reference
H. Arguments
I. APR
J. /
K. *

Reinforcement Exercises

Reinforcement exercises are designed to reinforce the skills you have learned by applying them to a new situation. Detailed instructions are provided along with a figure, where appropriate, to illustrate the final result. The Reinforcement exercises that follow should be completed sequentially. Leave the workbook open at the end of each exercise for use in the next exercise until you are specifically directed to close it.

Open **Less0502** from the **Student\Lesson05** folder on the CD-ROM disc that came with your book and save it as **Ex0501** on your floppy disk for use in the following exercises.

R1—Using Basic Excel Formulas

1. Select **Sheet1** and change the sheet tab name to **Patio Division**.

2. Modify the **Patio Furniture Division** worksheet to match the figure. See the following steps for more detail. (The sheet Zoom is set at 80% to provide a full view of the worksheet.)

3. To calculate the total cost of each item, select cell **D3** and enter **=B3*C3**. Adjust the column width as necessary.

4. Use the fill handle to copy the formula in **D3** to cells **D4** through **D9**. Format the values in this column to be currency with no decimals. Adjust the column width as shown in the figure.

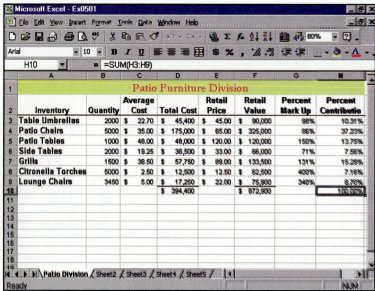

5. To calculate the retail value, select cell **F3** and enter **=B3*E3**.

6. Use the fill handle to copy the formula in **F3** to cells **F4** through **F9**. Format the values in this column as currency with no decimals.

7. Place a bottom border in cells **D9** and **F9**. Use the **AutoSum** button to place a sum function in cells **D10** and **F10** to add the numbers in the column above.

8. To calculate the percent markup, select cell **G3** and enter **=(E3-C3)/C3**. Fill the formula to the other cells in the column. Format the values in this column as percentages with no decimals. (Use the % button on the Formatting toolbar).

9. To calculate the percent contribution, select cell **H3** and type **=F3/$F$10**. Fill the formula to the other cells in the column. Format the values in this column as percentages with two decimals.

10. Place a bottom border in cell **H9** and sum the column in cell **H10**.

11. Add your name to the sheet header and choose **Landscape** orientation.

12. Preview and print the sheet.

13. Change the worksheet to show the formulas. Adjust the columns and wrap the column headings so the worksheet will print on one page. Print the sheet showing the formulas.

14. Change the worksheet back to show the values rather than the formulas and use the **Undo** button to restore the previous column widths.

R2—Using Absolute and Relative Reference

1. Select **Sheet2** and change the sheet tab name to **Tech Support**.

2. Modify the **Computer Technical Support Inc.** worksheet to match the figure. See the following steps for more detail.

3. Select cell **B5** and enter **=B3*$B$15**. Use the fill handle to copy the formula to the right to cell **G5**. With the cells still selected, use the **Comma Style** button to format the cells, if needed, then decrease the decimals to show no decimals.

4. Select cell **B6** and type **=B3*.20**. Use the fill handle to copy the formula to the right to cell **G6**. Format row **6** the same as row **5**.

5. Select cell **B7** and type **=B3*$B$16**. Use the fill handle to copy the formula to the right to cell **G7**. Format row **7** the same as rows **5** and **6**.

6. Select cell **B8**. Write a formula that will multiply the salaries by an absolute reference to the Medicare Tax percent (refer to the Fixed Percentages table in the figure). Use the same format for these cells. Use the fill handle to copy the formula to the right of cell G6.

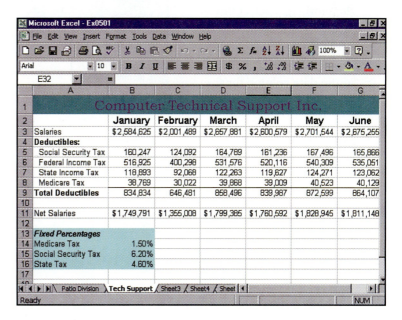

7. Add a bottom border to the figures in row **8** and sum the deductibles in each column in row **9**. Notice that the empty cell in row 4 prevents the AutoSum function from accidentally selecting the salaries in row 3.

8. Calculate the net salary figures by writing a formula in cell **B11** that takes the salaries for the month and subtracts the deductibles for the month. Copy the formula to cell **G11**.

9. Check the results of your formulas against the figure to be sure they are working properly. Change the state tax to **6%**. The workshet is recalculated.

10. Add your name to the sheet header. Change the orientation to **Landscape** and print a copy of the worksheet. Save your work.

R3—Calculate a House Payment Schedule

In this exercise, you use the Payment (PMT) function to calculate a house payment. Then you use Excel's ability to copy relative and absolute cell references to calculate a list of payments and balances for each month. You also learn how to use this table of payments to determine how much you would need to refinance if you select a common form of loan known as a 5-year balloon mortgage.

1. Select **Sheet3** and change the sheet tab name to **Mortgage**.

2. Modify the **Mortgage** worksheet to match the figure. See the steps that follow for more detail.

3. Select cell **B5** and write a formula to determine the monthly interest rate. Format it as a percent showing three decimal places.

4. Select cell **B7** and write a formula to determine the number of monthly payments over the term of the loan.

5. Select cell **B8** and use the **Paste Function** button to insert the payment formula for the mortgage. Select the appropriate arguments for the formula.

6. Select cells **D5** and **D6** and fill in the date column for five years. The last date should be **1/1/03** in row **64**.

7. Select cells **E6** through **G6**. Drag these three cells to the bottom of the date column to complete the amortization schedule. Look in cell **G64**. If you need to refinance the home loan in five years, you will need to borrow $118,688.88 (and pay closing costs again).

9. Change the Annual Percentage Rate (APR) to **8%**.

10. Add your name to the sheet header, set the first four rows to repeat on the second page (see Lesson 4, Task 7), and print a copy of the worksheet (two pages).

11. Save the workbook.

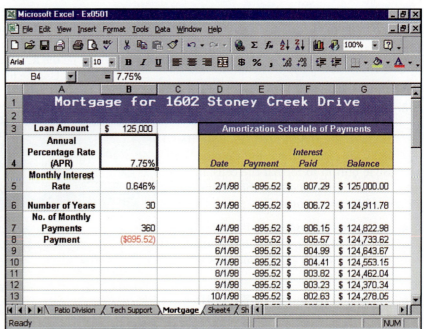

R4—Use the COUNTIF Function to Calculate Wages

1. Select **Sheet4** and change the sheet tab name to **Metro Hospital**.
2. Modify the **Metro Hospital** worksheet to match the figure. See the steps below for more detail.
3. Select cell **C16** and use the COUNTIF function to calculate the number of shifts that were worked by Bertha.
4. Each shift is 12 hours. Select cell **D16** and write a formula that will multiply the number of shifts by 12 to arrive at the number of hours worked.
5. Select cell **E16** and write a formula to multiply the hourly wage times the hours worked for Bertha.
6. Select cell **C16** and change the COUNTIF formula so the cell references will not change and the name to count is found in the adjacent cell, =COUNTIF($B$6:$H$13,A16).
7. Copy the formula in **C16** into cells **C17** through **C30**.
8. Select **D16** and **E16**. The fill handle appears at the corner of the pair of selected cells. Click and drag the fill handle down to cell **E30** to copy both formulas at the same time into their respective cells in columns **D** and **E**. This completes the table of hours and wages.
9. Use the AutoSum function to sum the **Wages Earned** column. If your work is correct, the sum of wages is $9,550.20. Fix any problems.
10. Change the head nurse, second shift assignment from **Martha** to **Robert** on Sunday, July 6. The worksheet is recalculated.
11. Add your name to the sheet header and print a copy of the worksheet. Save the workbook and close it.

Challenge

Challenge exercises are designed to test your ability to apply your skills to new situations with less detailed instruction. These exercises also challenge you to expand your repertoire of skills by using Excel commands that are similar to those you have already learned. The desired outcome is clearly defined, but you have more freedom to choose the steps needed to achieve the required result.

The following Challenge exercises use the file **Ex0503**. Open **Less0503** from the **Student Lesson 05** folder on the CD-ROM disc that came with your book and save it as **Ex0502** on your floppy disk.

C1—Using Goal Seek

Sometimes you know what the answer needs to be, but you do not know how to get there. If you have a spreadsheet set up to calculate an answer based on one or more cells, you can use an Excel tool named Goal Seek that will try different numbers in the cell you select until the answer in another cell matches the value you set.

Goal: Use the Goal Seek tool to determine the value in one cell that will produce the desired result in another cell.

Use the following guidelines:

1. Select the **Goal Seek** sheet tab.
2. Select **Tools**, **Goal Seek** from the menu.
3. Use the **Goal Seek** dialog box to set cell **B6** to **600** by changing the annual interest rate in cell **B2**. The resulting Annual Interest Rate is 7.02%.
4. Use this method to determine how big a loan you can afford (Loan Amount) on a five-year car loan at an Annual Interest Rate of 8.5% if the most you can afford for a monthly car payment is $350. See the steps below for more detail.
5. Change cell **B2** to **8.5%**. Change cell **B4** to **5**. Use Goal Seek to find out what loan amount will yield a payment of $350. (The sheet is protected so that you do not accidentally overwrite the formulas.)
6. Save the workbook. Leave the workbook open for use in the next Challenge exercise.

C2—Percentage Increases or Decreases

Prices are often determined by marking up a wholesale price by a certain percentage. When those items go on sale, the price is reduced by a certain percentage.

In this exercise, you will see how formulas are used to increase or decrease a price by a given percentage. In general, if you want to increase a value by 40 percent, you multiply the value by (1+40%). If you want to decrease the price by 20 percent, you multiply by (1-20%). An example is provided to show how a merchant starts with a wholesale price for a pair of boots, increases the price by 40 percent to get the retail price, decreases the retail price by 20 percent for a sale, and then determines the gross profit and percent profit.

Goal: Learn how to calculate percentage increases and decreases.

1. Select the **Percent** sheet.
2. Look at the formula in cell **C2**. Notice how the retail price for the boots was calculated by multiplying the wholesale price in cell B2 by (1+40%).
3. Enter a similar formula in cell **C3** that calculates a retail price for gloves at a 50 percent increase over the wholesale price.
4. Observe the formula in cell **D2** to see how the sale price for boots was determined by multiplying the retail price by (1-20%).
5. Enter a similar formula in cell **D3** to calculate the sale price for gloves if their price is reduced by 30 percent.
6. Fill the formulas in cells **E2** and **F2** into cells **E3** and **F3**, respectively. The percent profit on the gloves will be 5% if you have written the formulas correctly.
7. Enter two similar formulas for the hats. Use an increase of 120 percent to determine the retail price, then determine the sale price for a 50-percent-off sale. Fill the **Gross Profit** and **Percent Profit** formulas into cells **E4** and **F4**.
8. Save the workbook. Leave the workbook open for use in the next Challenge exercise.

C3—Statistics: Average, Median, and Standard Deviation

When we describe a set of numbers, such as the income of a certain group, we often use terms such as average or median. We can use Excel to compute these numbers and see how they describe a set of numbers. Average and median are two ways of describing where the "center" of a set of numbers is. They do not describe whether the numbers are all close to that central number or if they vary greatly. The statistic that describes this type of variation is the standard deviation.

In this exercise, you look at the monthly rainfall in Buffalo and Seattle.

Goal: Use Excel's statistical functions to compare the average, median, and standard deviation of rainfall.

1. Select the **Stats** sheet. Notice that both cities have almost the same total annual rainfall. Look at the rainfall for each month of the year—it is apparent that the rainfall in Seattle varies much more from month to month.

2. Paste the Average function in cell **B16** (it is one of the Statistics functions). Use cells **B3:B14**; do not include the total in cell B15. Use the same method to find the average rainfall in Seattle.

3. The median of a set of numbers is the value that has as many values above it as below it. Find the median rainfall for both cities and place them in the table.

4. To see how much the numbers vary from the average, find the standard deviation of the rainfall for both cities. Use the STDEVP function. About 2/3 of the values will be within this range of the average. A small standard deviation means that the numbers are closely grouped around the average. Does the city with the smaller standard deviation have about the same amount of rain each month? If so, you have done the assignment correctly.

5. Save the workbook and close it.

Discovery

Discovery exercises are designed to help you learn how to teach yourself a new skill. In each exercise, you discover something new that is related to the topic taught in this lesson. You may be directed to use built-in wizards or some of the extensive Help features provided in Excel to discover new features and learn new skills with minimum assistance from books or instructors. The required outcome demonstrates your ability to apply the new skill. You determine the choice of topic, worksheet design, and steps of execution.

The following Discovery exercises use the file **Less0504**. Open **Less0504** from the **Student Lesson 05** folder on the CD-ROM disc that came with your book and save it on your floppy disk as **Ex0503**.

D1—Using the Vlookup Function

If you are providing a quotation for a job, the price often depends on the cost of parts and labor. These costs vary depending on the item and the quantity purchased. It can be very time-consuming to look up information in tables to include in your calculations. Excel has two functions that are designed to look up values in a table, column, or array. These are called Vlookup and Hlookup. Vlookup is used to look up values in a vertical column, and Hlookup is used to look up values in a horizontal row. In this exercise, you will learn how to use the Vlookup function.

To use the Vlookup function to find the correct value in a table and use it in a calculation, follow these steps.

1. Select the **Lookup** sheet, if necessary.

2. Use Help to find the description of the VLOOKUP function. Read the description and examine the example in cell **C4**. There are three arguments included in this formula. The first defines the value that is looked up in a table. The second argument defines the table or range of cells that should be examined. The third is the column that should be used to locate the matching value. Each column in the defined table is identified with a number, **1**, **2**, **3**, etc. (Note: The values in the first column of a table that is used with this function must be sorted in increasing order.)

3. Test the function by changing values in cells **A4** and **B4**. Use one of the codes from column **1** of the **Quantity Charge** table for cell **A4**, and either a **2** or **3** for cell **B4**. The number in cell B4 indicates whether column 2 or 3 of the Quantity Charge table should be used to look up the value that matches the code in cell A4.

4. Find the **Multi-Color Charge** table. Paste the VLOOKUP function into cell **C18** and select the arguments so that it will find the correct charge for additional shirt colors and display it in cell **C18**.

5. Test the function by trying different numbers in cells **A18** and **B18**.

6. Save the workbook and leave it open for use in the next Discovery exercise.

D2—Determine Frequency Distribution Using the Histogram Tool

This exercise requires the Analysis ToolPak Add-in. Look under the **Tools** menu to determine if you have the Data Analysis option. If not, select **Tools**, **Add-Ins**, **Analysis ToolPak**. If you plan to do the Solver exercise, D3, select the **Solver Add-in**. You may need your Office 2000 CD-ROM disc, or ask your lab administrator to install these features.

If you are trying to determine how many of each kind of number you have in a group, you want to know the frequency distribution. For example, 25 people have answered a question that has five possible answers numbered 1 through 5, and you would like to know how many people chose each answer.

Excel provides two options for determining the frequency distribution. There is a Frequency Distribution function, which can be found by using the Paste Function button. The other option is part of the Histogram tool in the Analysis ToolPak. The Histogram tool is much easier to use and can also produce a chart, which will be used in the next lesson.

Goal: Learn how to use the Histogram tool to determine the number of people answering each option for a question.

1. Select the **Frequency** sheet.
2. Search for Help on the Histogram analysis tool.
3. Look at the example analysis that was done on the first question.
4. Use the Histogram analysis tool to produce a similar analysis of the second question. Select cell **Y14** as the output cell that will be used as the upper-left corner of the output range.
5. Save the workbook and leave it open for use in the next Discovery exercise.

D3—Using the Solver Tool

Solver is similar to Goal Seek, but it has more options. It can change more than one input cell and you can specify constraints on several cells. You can have it determine the inputs to produce a match, a maximum, or a minimum value.

A classic physics problem is to determine how high a projectile will go if it is shot straight up at a given initial speed. The formula is $H = -16T^2 + ST$. This formula can be written in Excel as =-16*(time cell reference)^2+(speed cell reference)*(time cell reference). In the example sheet used for this exercise, the formula is =-16*B3^2+B4*B3. There are two ways to solve this problem. You could use differential calculus to find the derivative, set it equal to zero, solve for T, and then plug the value of T into the original formula. A second way would be to try increasing values of time in the formula until the value of the height stopped increasing and started decreasing. In order to solve for the time down to the nearest tenth of a second, you would have to do the formula many times.

The Solver works by trying different values in the formula, subject to the constraints you have imposed, until the target cell matches the value you have chosen or is a maximum or minimum if you have selected either of those options.

Goal: Use the Solver tool to find the maximum height to which a projectile will rise given an initial speed.

1. Select the **Solver** sheet.
2. Search for Help on guidelines for using the Solver.
3. Use the Solver to determine the maximum value for the formula in cell **B5** by changing the time values in cell **B3**.
4. Keep the Solver solution.
5. Save the workbook and close it.

Lesson: 6

Understanding the Numbers Using a Chart

Task 1   Creating a Chart to Show a Trend

Task 2   Creating a Chart to Show Contributions to a Whole

Task 3   Creating a Chart to Make Comparisons

Task 4   Editing the Elements of a Chart

Task 5   Changing Chart Types

Task 6   Printing a Chart

Introduction

People process information in several different ways. Most of us recognize trends more readily if a line or a series of columns of differing height represents them. We also recognize how one member of a group compares to the others if all members are represented by slices of a pie chart.

This lesson is designed to provide you with the basic skills you need to create a variety of *charts* to represent your numerical data graphically. Excel's *Chart Wizard* guides you through the necessary steps.

Visual Summary

When you have completed this lesson, you will have created three charts to represent the sales performance of a company.

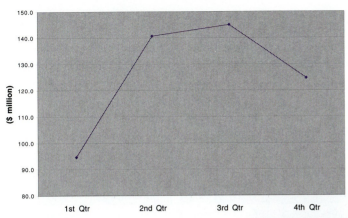

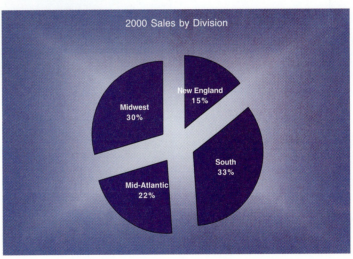

<Your Name>

TASK 1

Creating a Chart to Show a Trend

Why would I do this?

It is sometimes easier to analyze numbers when looking at a visual representation. A picture or *chart* helps, and some types are better than others for specific purposes. For instance, when you want to show a trend (change over time), a *line chart* is usually most effective.

In this task, you learn how to create a line chart to show the trend in sales for a real estate firm.

1 Launch **Excel**. Open **Less0601** from the **Student\Lesson 06** folder on the CD-ROM disc that came with this book, and save the file on your floppy disk as **Sales**. The new title appears in the title bar.

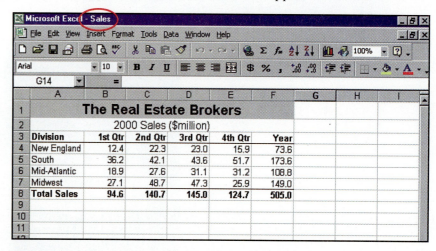

2 Move the pointer to cell **A3**. Click and drag to select cells **A3** through **E3**, then release the mouse button. Hold down Ctrl and select cells **A8** through **E8**.

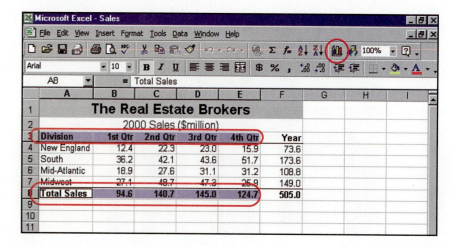

186 LEARN EXCEL 2000

3 Click the **Chart Wizard** button. The first Chart Wizard dialog box is displayed. (If the Office Assistant opens, click the **Close** button to close it.) Click **Line** in the **Chart type** area, and observe that the default *Chart sub-type* is a line with data markers. Each chart type has several variations that you can use to display the data.

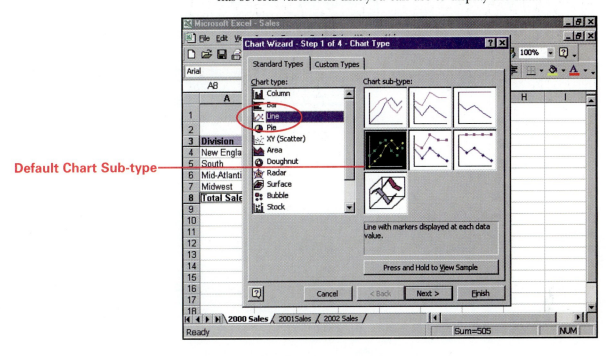

Default Chart Sub-type

4 Click **Next**. The second Chart Wizard dialog box is displayed. Make sure **Rows** is selected from the **Series in** area.

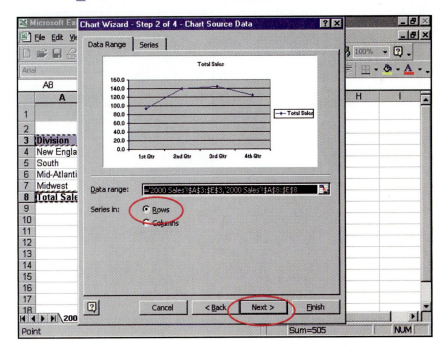

LESSON 6   UNDERSTANDING THE NUMBERS USING A CHART

5 Click **Next**. The third Chart Wizard dialog box is displayed. Click the **Titles** tab if necessary. Type **2000 Real Estate Sales** in the **Chart title** box. Type **($ million)** in the **Value (Y) axis** box.

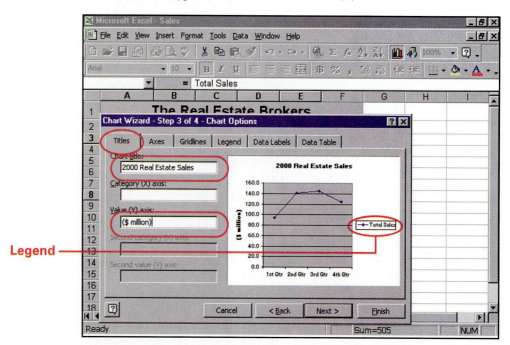

6 Click the **Legend** tab. A *legend* is a list that identifies a pattern or color used in an Excel chart. Click the **Show legend** box to turn off the legend.

> **In Depth:** The first three Chart Wizard dialog boxes contain multiple tabs. These tabs let you control such things as the chart scale, whether to show vertical or horizontal gridlines, and how to label the data points.

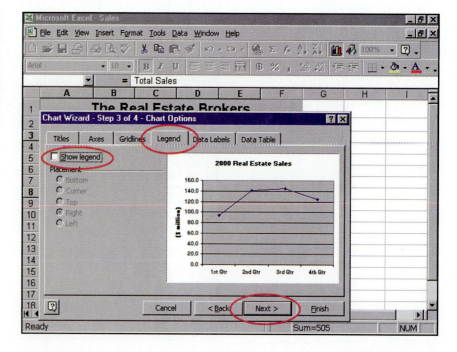

188 LEARN EXCEL 2000

7 Click **Next**. The fourth Chart Wizard dialog box is displayed. Click **As new sheet** to select it and type **2000 Sales Chart** in the adjacent box.

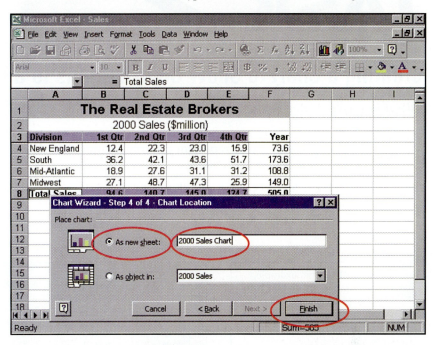

8 Click **Finish**. The chart is shown full-size on its own sheet. Click the **Save** button to save your work. If the Chart toolbar appears, close it.

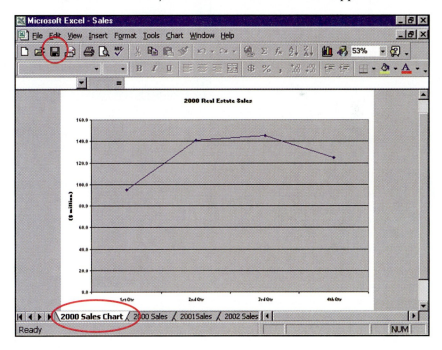

TASK 2

Creating a Chart to Show Contributions to a Whole

Why would I do this?

In the previous task, you took a set of data and created a line chart to show a trend over time. You may find that it is often beneficial to graphically represent the contribution of various elements to the whole. The best way to illustrate parts of a whole is to use a *pie chart*.

In this task, you learn how to create a pie chart that shows the contribution each region made to the total sales amount for the year.

1 Click the **2000 Sales** sheet tab. Select cells **A3** through **A7**. Hold down Ctrl and select cells **F3** through **F7**.

> **In Depth:** In this example, the company is divided into four operating divisions that are based on geographic regions. The terms, division, and region are used interchangeably.

2 Click the **Chart Wizard** button. The first Chart Wizard dialog box is displayed. Click **Pie** in the **Chart type** area, and select **Pie** in the **Chart sub-type** area.

> **Caution:** When you create a pie chart, you want to show the contribution each part makes to the whole. A common mistake when building a chart from a worksheet that contains totals is to include the totals with the data. Doing this would defeat the purpose of a pie chart, since the total figure would appear to be a piece of the pie rather than the sum of the parts.

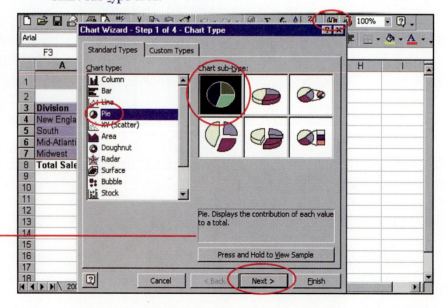

Description of Sub-type

190 LEARN EXCEL 2000

3 Click **Next**. The second Chart Wizard dialog box is displayed. Make sure **Columns** is selected from the **Series in** area, because the data you are charting is in a column.

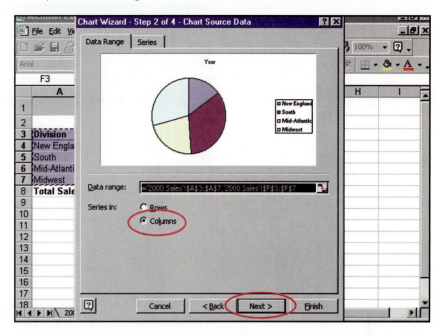

4 Click **Next**. The third Chart Wizard dialog box is displayed. Click the **Titles** tab, if it is not already selected. Type **2000 Sales by Region** in the **Chart title** box.

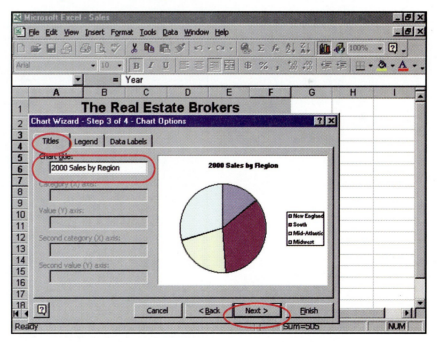

LESSON 6 UNDERSTANDING THE NUMBERS USING A CHART   191

5 Click **Next**. The fourth Chart Wizard dialog box is displayed. Select **As new sheet** and type **2000 Sales by Division** in the adjacent box.

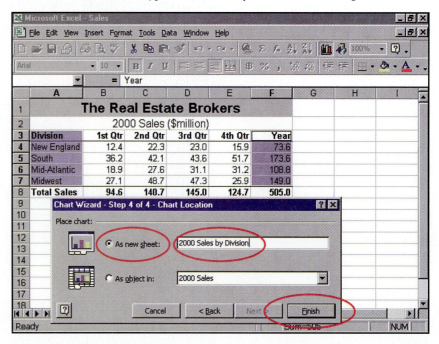

6 Click **Finish**. The chart is placed on its own sheet. (You learn how to change the size of the title and legend in a later task.) Save your work.

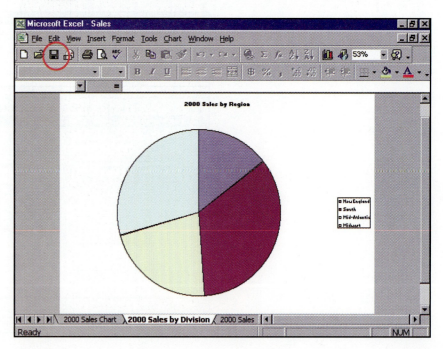

TASK 3

Creating a Chart to Make Comparisons

Why would I do this?

Perhaps the most common use for a chart is to make comparisons. For example, you might want to compare oil production by country over a series of years. To illustrate this type of comparison, a *column chart* (with vertical bars) or *bar chart* (with horizontal bars) is most often used.

In this task, you learn how to create a column chart that compares a company's regional sales for each quarter in 2000.

1 Click the **2000 Sales** sheet tab. Select cells **A3** through **E7**.

> **In Depth:** It is important that you do not include the total rows or columns when doing a comparison chart. If you included these figures, it would distort the chart, since the totals would be compared to regional and quarterly sales amounts.

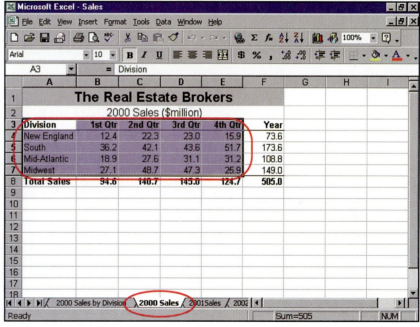

LESSON 6　UNDERSTANDING THE NUMBERS USING A CHART　193

2 Click the **Chart Wizard** button. The first Chart Wizard dialog box is displayed. Click **Column** in the **Chart type** area, and accept the **Clustered Column** option in the **Chart sub-type** area.

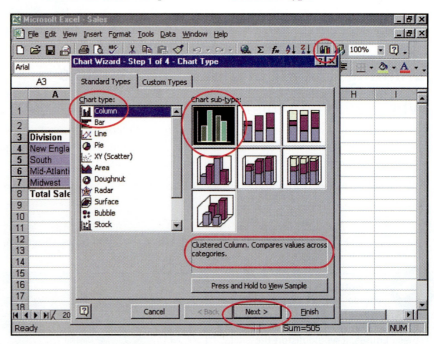

3 Click **Next**. The second Chart Wizard dialog box is displayed. Make sure **Rows** is selected from the **Series in** area. This keeps all of the sales figures from each quarter together.

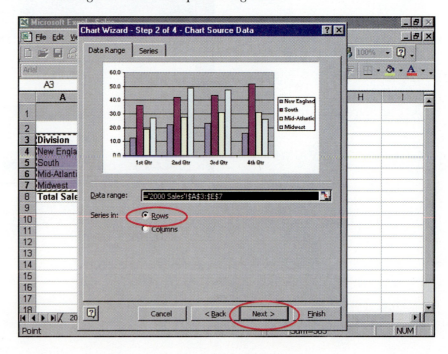

4 Click **Next**. The third Chart Wizard dialog box is displayed. Click the **Titles** tab, if necessary, and type **2000 Regions** in the **Chart title** box. Type **($ millions)** in the **Value (Y) axis** box.

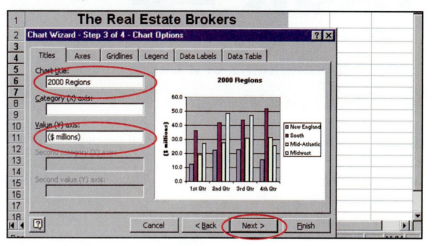

5 Click **Next**. Select **As new sheet** and type **2000 Regions** in the adjacent box.

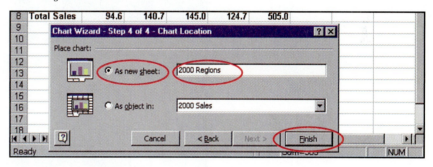

6 Click **Finish**. The chart is on its own sheet. Save your work.

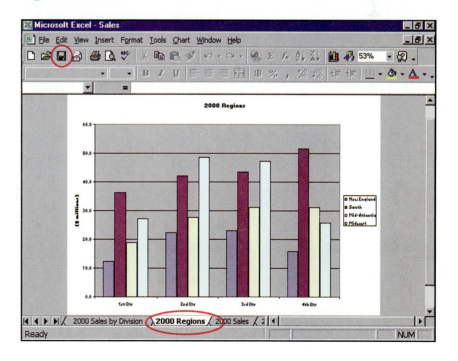

LESSON 6   UNDERSTANDING THE NUMBERS USING A CHART   195

TASK 4

Editing the Elements of a Chart

Why would I do this?

When you create a chart in Excel, the proportions of the various elements often need to be adjusted. For example, the text on the axes, titles, and legends on the charts might be too small. There are many options for customizing your charts in Excel, and they are easy to use.

In this task, you make changes to the 2000 Sales Chart to make it easier to read and to emphasize the variation from one quarter to the next.

1 Click the **2000 Sales Chart** sheet tab. Right-click on the title, **2000 Real Estate Sales**. A shortcut menu appears.

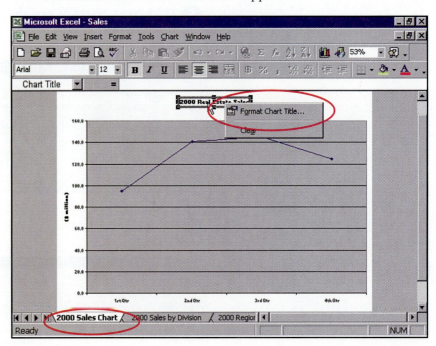

196 LEARN EXCEL 2000

2 Select **Format Chart Title** from the shortcut menu and click the **Font** tab in the **Format Chart Title** dialog box. Scroll down the list of available font sizes and select **18**.

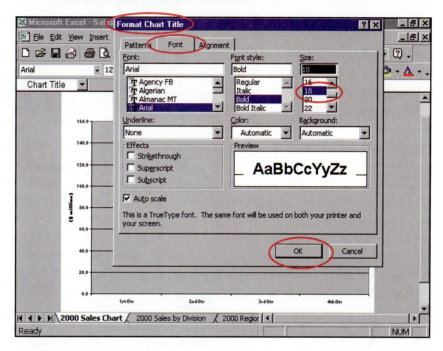

3 Click **OK**. The title is now much easier to read.

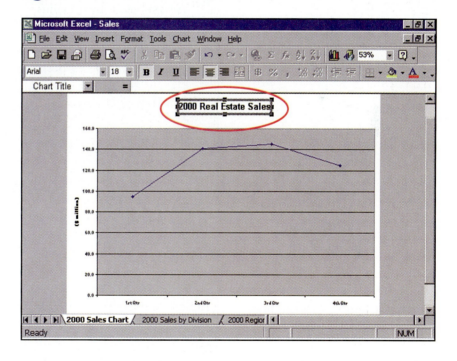

LESSON 6   UNDERSTANDING THE NUMBERS USING A CHART

4 Right-click on the value (y) axis label, **($ million)**, and choose **Format Axis Title** from the shortcut menu. Change the size of the font to **14** points.

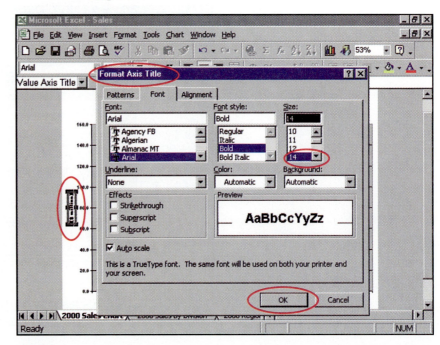

5 Click **OK**. Use this procedure to change the size of the category (x) axis labels to **14** points.

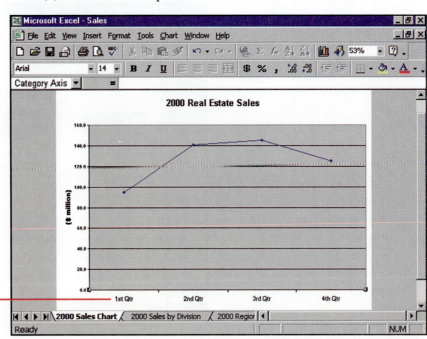

Category (x) Axis Labels displayed with 14 pt. font

6 Move the pointer onto the numbers on the value (y) axis. The ScreenTip Value Axis is displayed.

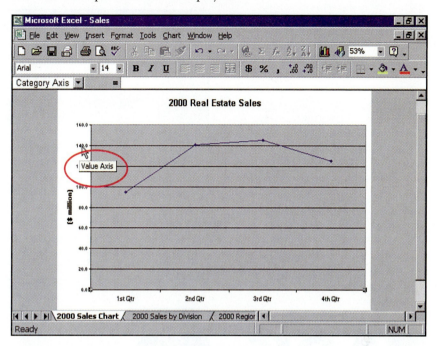

7 Right-click and select **Format Axis** from the shortcut menu. Click the **Scale** tab. Change the **Minimum** value to **80**.

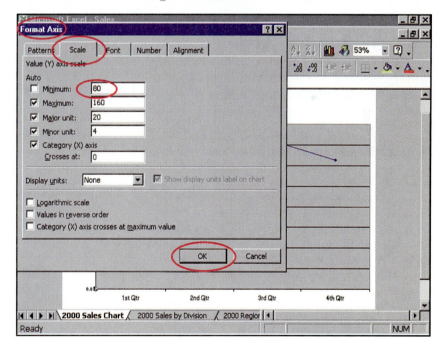

LESSON 6 UNDERSTANDING THE NUMBERS USING A CHART

8 Click **OK**. Notice the new scale exaggerates the difference in the values. Save the changes you have made.

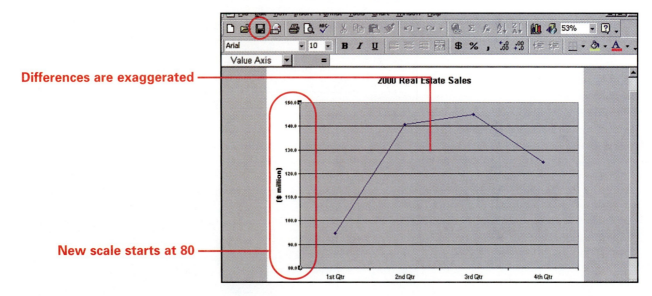

Differences are exaggerated

New scale starts at 80

TASK 5

Changing Chart Types

Why would I do this?

Sometimes it is difficult to imagine how data will look using a different type of chart. Fortunately, it is easy to preview chart types, or to change chart types until you find the one that is most effective for the data you want to display. There are several ways you can change the chart type or chart sub-type.

In this task, you learn to change the chart sub-types for a more effective display of data.

1 Click the **2000 Sales by Division** sheet tab. Right-click on an empty area of the chart. A shortcut menu is displayed.

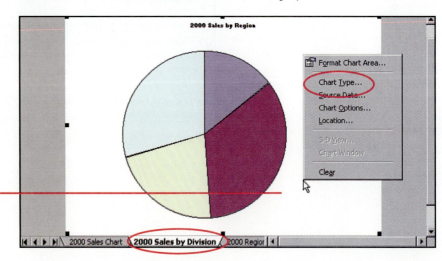

Right-click empty area of chart

200 LEARN EXCEL 2000

2 Click **Chart Type** to display the **Chart Type** dialog box. Confirm that the **Chart type** is **Pie** and click the **Pie with a 3-D visual effect** sub-type.

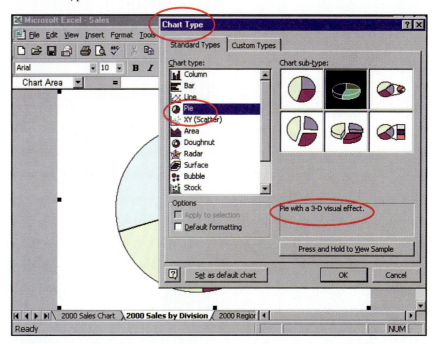

3 Move the pointer to the **Press and Hold to View Sample** button. Click and hold the left mouse button. An example of how the chart would look is displayed.

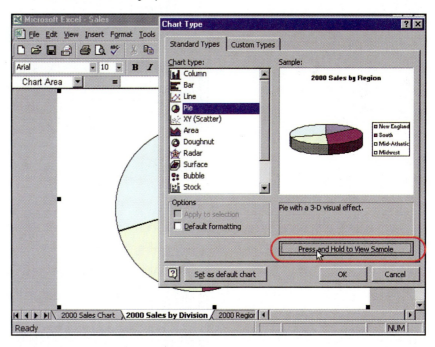

LESSON 6 UNDERSTANDING THE NUMBERS USING A CHART

4 Release the mouse button. Select the **Exploded pie with 3-D visual effect** sub-type. Click and hold the **Press and Hold to View Sample** button.

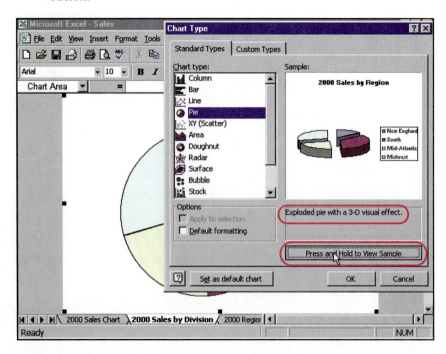

5 Release the mouse button. Click the **Custom Types** tab and select the **Blue Pie** option. This is an example of one of the many custom designs.

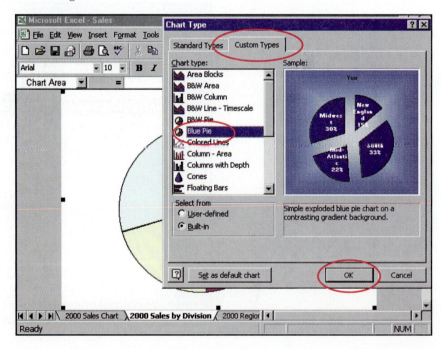

6 Click **OK**. Notice that the wording of the title needs to be changed; it should be larger, and it would be easier to read if it were white instead of black. Also, the labels should be larger.

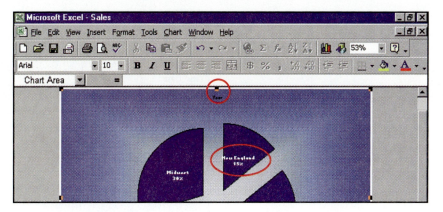

7 Right-click the title and select **Format Chart Title** from the shortcut menu. Select the **Font** tab if necessary. Change the font size to **18** and click the down arrow next to the **Color** box to display a list of available colors.

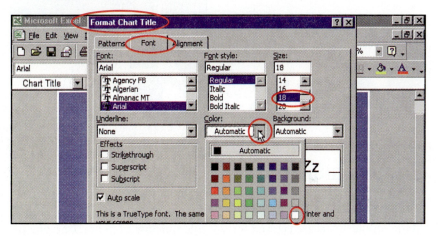

8 Click the **white** box, then click **OK**. Notice that the title is still selected. Type **2000 Sales by Division**. Notice the new title appears in the formula bar.

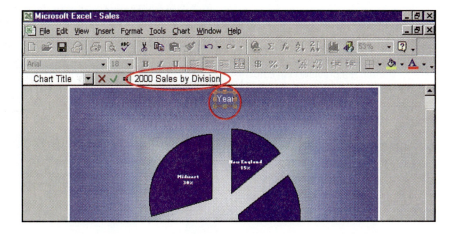

LESSON 6 UNDERSTANDING THE NUMBERS USING A CHART   203

⑨ Press **Enter**. Right-click on one of the four labels and select **Format Data Labels** from the shortcut menu. Change the size of the font to **14** points. Click **OK**. Save your changes.

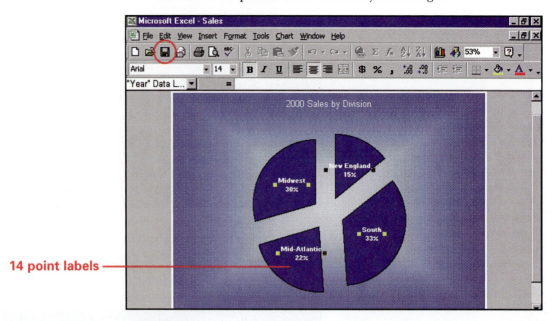

14 point labels

TASK 6

Printing a Chart

Why would I do this?

Many spreadsheets are created for the sole purpose of generating one or more charts. These charts might be printed on paper to be included in a report or on overhead transparencies to be used as part of a presentation.

In this task, you learn how to print a chart.

① Click the **2000 Regions** sheet tab. Click the **Print Preview** button.

In Depth: If your computer is connected to a color printer, the preview is in color and the chart will print in color.

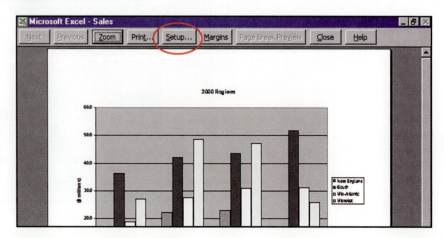

204 LEARN EXCEL 2000

2 Click **Setup**. Click the **Header/Footer** tab if necessary. Click **Custom Header** and type your name in the **Left section** of the header.

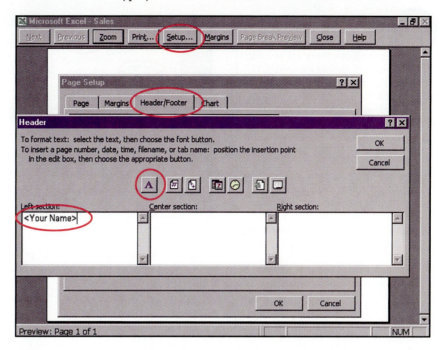

3 Click the **Font** button and change the size of the font to **14** points and the **Font style** to **Bold Italic**.

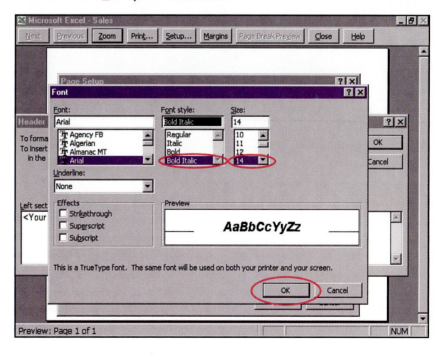

LESSON 6   UNDERSTANDING THE NUMBERS USING A CHART

Caution: If you plan to create transparencies from your charts, there are several problems you should know about. If you plan to print the transparency directly from your printer, you must use a transparency that is designed for your type of printer. Colors seldom look as dark or saturated as onscreen or on paper. If your office has transparencies that work with your copier, you would be wise to print the charts on regular paper and then use the copier to transfer them to transparencies. Transparency material is expensive, and you usually have to buy an entire box. Preview your work and print samples on paper to avoid costly reprints. Transparencies often jam when you try to feed several through the printer or copier.

4 Click **OK** to return to the **Header** dialog box. Click **OK** to return to the **Page Setup** dialog box. Click **OK** to return to the **Print Preview**.

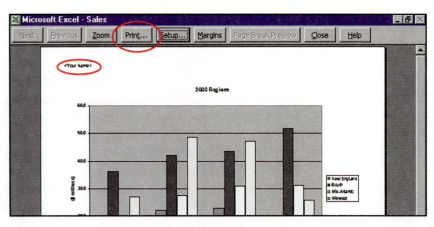

5 Click the **Print** button to print the chart. Click **OK** in the **Print** dialog box. Close the workbook and save the changes.

Comprehension Exercises

Comprehension exercises are designed to check your memory and understanding of the basic concepts in this lesson. You distinguish between true and false statements, identify new screen elements, and match terms with related statements. If you are uncertain of the correct answer, refer to the task number following each item (for example, T4 refers to Task 4) and review that task until you are confident that you can provide a correct response.

True-False

Circle either T or F.

T F **1.** The Chart Wizard walks you through the creation of a chart. **(T1)**

T F **2.** Pie charts are used to show trends. **(T1)**

T F **3.** A 3-D Pie chart requires at least three columns (or rows) of selected data. **(T5)**

T F **4.** When selecting data to chart, always include the row and column totals. **(T2)**

T F **5.** When you right-click on a chart title, it automatically sizes the font to produce a title that spans 3/4 of the printed page. **(T4)**

T F **6.** Column charts and bar charts are both used to illustrate data that shows comparisons. **(T3)**

T F **7.** When you increase the font size of the y-axis, the size of the plot area remains the same. **(T4)**

T F **8.** One of the choices you can make in the Chart Wizard is whether you want your chart to be on the same worksheet as the data or on its own sheet. **(T1)**

T F **9.** Once a line chart is created, the y-axis scale must always start at zero. **(T4)**

T F **10.** Right-clicking on a chart element will call up a shortcut menu that allows you to make changes. **(T4)**

Identifying Parts of the Excel Screen

Refer to the figure and identify the numbered parts of the screen. Write the letter of the correct label in the space next to the number.

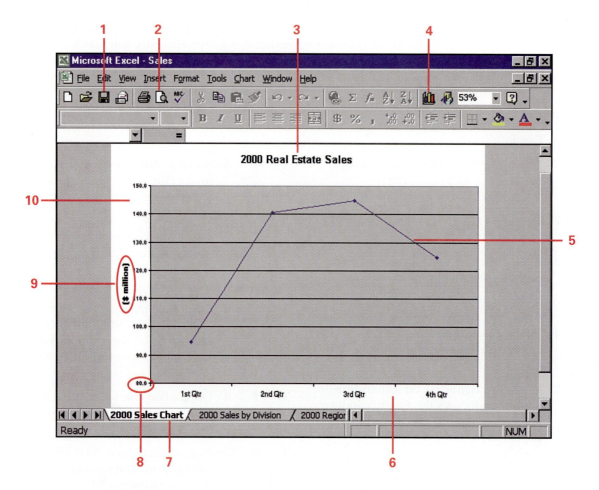

1. _____
2. _____
3. _____
4. _____
5. _____
6. _____
7. _____
8. _____
9. _____
10. _____

A. Save button (T1)
B. Category (x) axis (T4)
C. Print Preview button (T6)
D. Value (y) axis (T4)
E. Value (y) axis title (T4)
F. Chart Wizard button (T1)
G. Sheet tab (T2)
H. Chart title (T1)
I. Minimum scale value (T4)
J. Line connecting data points (T1)

Matching

Match the statements below to the word or phrase that is the best match from the list. Write the letter of the matching word or phrase in the space provided next to the number.

1. ___ A chart type used to make comparisons (T3)
2. ___ Displays chart as it will look when printed (T6)
3. ___ Where you can add a header to the printout (T6)
4. ___ A chart type used to show trends over time (T1)
5. ___ A way to quickly change the chart type (T5)
6. ___ A variation of a chart type (T5)
7. ___ Contains several special chart designs (T5)
8. ___ A list that identifies a pattern or color used in an Excel worksheet chart (T1)
9. ___ A chart type used to show contributions to a whole (T2)
10. ___ A way to choose chart elements (T4)

A. Legend
B. Right-click
C. Column chart
D. Right-click empty area of chart and use shortcut options
E. chart
F. Page Setup dialog box
G. Print Preview button
H. Line chart
I. Custom tab
J. Sub-type
K. Pie chart

Reinforcement Exercises

Reinforcement exercises are designed to reinforce the skills you have learned by applying them to a new situation. Detailed instructions are provided along with a figure, where appropriate, to illustrate the final result. The Reinforcement exercises that follow should be completed sequentially. Leave the workbook open at the end of each exercise for use in the next exercise until you are specifically directed to close it.

Open **Less0602** from the CD-ROM disc and save it as **Ex0601** on your floppy disk for use in the following exercises.

R1—Create and Print a Pie Chart

1. Change the **Sheet1** tab name to **Casualties**.
2. Create a 3-D pie chart showing how tornadoes in each decade have contributed to the total number of casualties. See the following steps for more details.
3. Select cells **A2** through **A6** and cells **E2** through **E6**.
4. In the first dialog box, click the **Chart Wizard** button. Choose the **Pie** chart type, then choose the **Pie with 3-D visual effect** chart sub-type (the middle choice on the top row). In the second Dialog box, choose columns, if necessary.

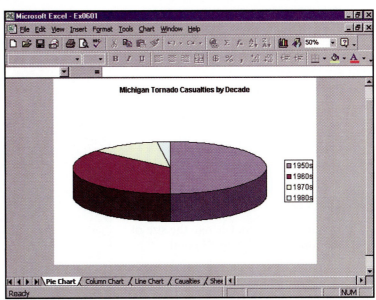

5. In the third dialog box, change the title to **Michigan Tornado Casualties by Decade**.

6. In the fourth dialog box, choose to save the chart as a new sheet named **Pie Chart**. Save your work.

7. Change size of the font in the title and the legend to **18** point.

8. Add your name to the header using **Bold**, **Italic**, **12** point font. Preview and print the chart.

R2—Create and Print a Column Chart

1. Select the **Casualties** sheet.

2. Create a Column chart to compare the number of tornadoes in each decade. See the following steps for more detail.

3. Select cells **A2** through **B6**.

4. Click the **Chart Wizard** button. Choose the **Column** chart type, then choose the **Clustered column with a 3-D visual effect** chart sub-type (the first choice in the second row).

5. View a sample of the chart and compare it to the figure.

6. Change the title to **Michigan Tornadoes by Decade**.

7. In the fourth dialog box, place the chart on a new sheet named **Column Chart**.

8. Change the size of the title font to **18** points. Select and delete the legend. Change the size of the x and y axis labels to **12** points.

9. Add your name to the footer in the lower-left. Print the chart.

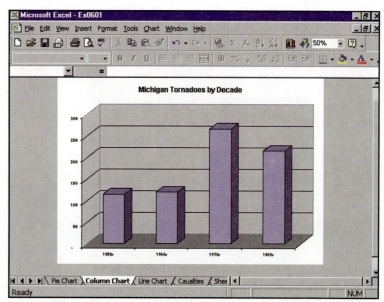

R3—Show a Trend with a Line Chart

1. Select the **Casualties** tab.

2. Create a chart to show the trend in Total Casualties. See the steps below for more detail.

3. Select cells **A2** through **A6** and cells **E2** through **E6**.

4. Click the **Chart Wizard** button and select the **Line** chart type and **3-D Line** as the sub-type.

5. Change the title to **Tornado Casualties in Michigan**.

6. Save as a new sheet with the name **Line Chart**.

7. Delete the legend. Change the size of the font in the title to **18** point.

8. Add your name to the header in the upper-left. Preview and print the chart.

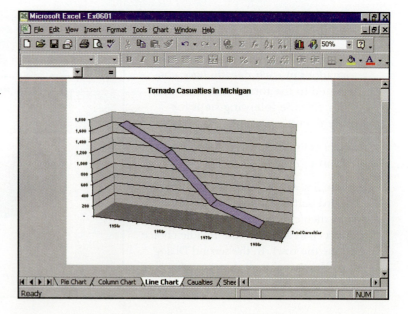

210   LEARN EXCEL 2000

R4—Change the Chart Type

1. Select the **Column Chart** worksheet.

2. Change the column chart into a bar chart as shown in the figure. See the steps below for more detail.

3. Right-click on an empty (white) part of the chart and select **Chart Type** from the shortcut menu.

4. If necessary, selected the Standard types tab. Select the **Bar** chart type and the **Clustered bar with 3-D visual effect** sub-type.

5. Preview the printout and confirm that your name will appear in the lower left corner.

6. Print the chart.

7. Change the sheet tab name to **Column-Bar Chart**. Save the changes you have made. Close the workbook.

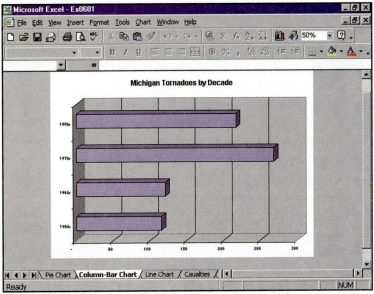

Challenge

Challenge exercises are designed to test your ability to apply your skills to new situations with less detailed instruction. These exercises also challenge you to expand your repertoire of skills by using Excel commands that are similar to those you have already learned. The desired outcome is clearly defined, but you have more freedom to choose the steps needed to achieve the required result.

In these Challenge exercises, you work with data concerning the consumption of energy compared to gross national product (GNP) for sixteen countries around the world. You will use Excel's charting capability to determine if the amount of energy that a person uses is proportional to the amount of goods they produce. In other words, if a person in an affluent country consumes ten times as much energy as a person in a poor country, do they produce ten times as much? If the amount of goods produced is directly proportional to the energy consumed, a line chart of the data should be a fairly straight line.

In these exercises, you examine this data to see if such a relationship exists, using some of the advanced Excel charting tools. First, you create a simple chart that displays the energy used per person for each country and save it as an object in the worksheet. Then you create a line chart of the energy consumption and GNP as a first attempt to show data with unequal category (x) axis intervals. Last, you create a chart of the data to show the relationship between energy consumption and GNP using an x-y scatter chart.

Open **Less0603** and save it as **Ex0602**. This file is used for both Challenge and Discovery exercises.

C1—Place a Chart on the Same Sheet as the Data

If a chart is small, it may be placed on the same sheet as the rest of the data. In this example, you will chart the energy used per person by country and then save it onto the same sheet as the data.

Goal: Create a column chart that displays the country and the energy used per capita and place it on Sheet1 with the data. Adjust the font size of the category labels so that they all display.

Use the following guidelines:

1. If necessary, open **Ex0602** and select **Sheet1**.
2. Select the data (and headings) in the **Country** and **Energy** columns.
3. Create a column chart and save it as an object in **Sheet1**.
4. Notice that all the country names do not fit on the x axis. Double-click on one of the country names on the chart and change the font size to **8** point.
5. Deselect the chart and change the **Zoom** to **50%**.
6. Change the **Page Setup** to **Landscape** orientation.
7. Move the chart to a place below the data and drag one of its handles to stretch the chart to display all the names. Work with the **Print Preview** option to make sure the chart will fit on one page and that all the country names will print.
8. Add your name to the header. Print the page with the chart. Change the Zoom back to 100%.
9. Save the workbook. Leave the workbook open for use in the next exercise.

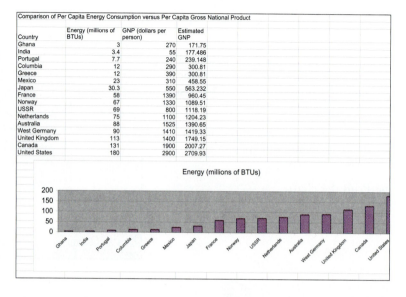

C2—Chart Data with Unequally Spaced Category Values Using a Line Chart

If the value on the value (y) axis is supposed to depend on its corresponding value on the category (x) axis, it is important that the numeric intervals between the values on the category (x) axis are equal. If you use a line chart, the data in the left-most column is automatically placed along the category (x) axis, spaced at even intervals, even if the values between the data points are not equal. The result is a chart where it is not easy to determine if a proportional or "straight line" relationship exists. In this exercise, you chart the energy used per capita compared to the GNP per capita using a line chart so you can see what the problem looks like. In the next exercise, you will use an x-y chart so you can compare the two types of graphs.

Use **Ex0602** that was opened in the previous exercise.

Goal: Chart related data using a line chart.

1. Select the data and column heading for GNP (cells **C3** through **C19**).
2. Create a line chart like the one in the figure. See the steps below for more detailed instruction.
3. In the second dialog box of the Chart Wizard, select the **Series** tab.
4. Click the **Collapse dialog box** button on the **Category (X) axis labels** box and select the data in the **Country** and **Energy** columns (**A4** through **B19**; do not include the column labels).
5. Create the chart on its own sheet named **Line Chart**.
6. Add your name to the page header. Print the chart. Save the workbook.

7. Examine the chart. The values along the category (x) axis are evenly spaced even though they do not represent equal intervals. For example, Columbia and Greece both use 12 BTUs per person, but these two points are displayed at different locations along the horizontal or category (x) axis. Obviously, a graph with two data points of the same value in two different locations creates a misleading picture. It is not a good idea to represent data where the value shown on the value (y) axis depends on the number shown on the category (x) axis using a line chart unless the intervals between the values on the category (x) axis are already equally spaced. Do the next exercise to see how this example data should be charted.

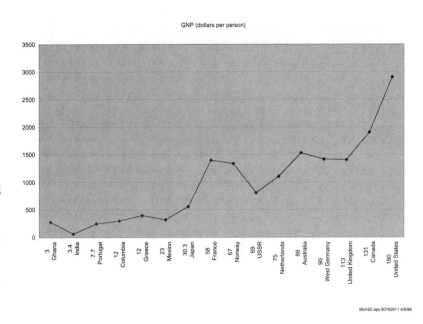

C3—Chart Related Data Using the X-Y Chart

If you are charting two columns of numbers where the second column is dependant on (or related to) the first column, you should use an x-y chart, sometimes called a scatter chart. The data points are scattered on the chart to indicate each intersection of the x and y coordinates, and the intervals on the category (x) axis are forced to be equal.

When plotting real-life data, you seldom get an exact relationship. You look to see if the points represent a general trend such as a straight line or a curve. In our example, the energy used per person is displayed on the category (x) axis and the GNP per person is displayed on the value (y) axis.

Use the file **Ex0602** that was created in a previous exercise.

Goal: Represent the per capita gross national product as it relates to the amount of energy used per person.

1. Open **Sheet1**. Select the **Energy** and **GNP** columns (cells **B3** through **C19**). Chart the energy and GNP data using an x-y scatter chart as shown.

2. Use a chart title of **GNP per Energy Used**, **Millions of BTUs** for the x axis title, and **Dollars** for the y axis title.

3. Do not show the legend.

4. Save the chart on its own sheet named **X-Y chart**.

5. Add your name to the header and print the chart.

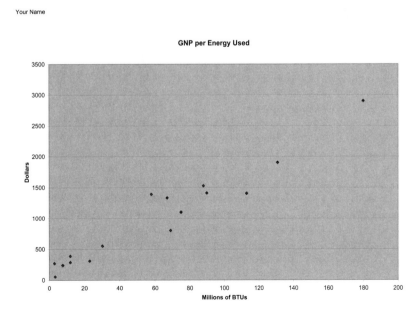

LESSON 6   UNDERSTANDING THE NUMBERS USING A CHART   213

6. Notice that the values on the category (x) axis have evenly spaced intervals and the relationship between the two factors appears to be more linear. The two data points with 12 BTUs are at the same location on the category (x) axis and vary slightly on the value (y) axis because of a difference in GNP.

Leave the workbook open for use in the Discovery exercises.

Discovery

Discovery exercises are designed to help you learn how to teach yourself a new skill. In each exercise, you discover something new that is related to the topic taught in this lesson. You may be directed to use built-in wizards or some of the extensive Help features provided in Excel to discover new features and learn new skills with minimum assistance from books or instructors. The required outcome demonstrates your ability to apply the new skill. You determine the choice of topic, worksheet design, and steps of execution.

These exercises continue the exploration of using advanced Excel charting concepts and statistical analysis. The the x-y chart that was created in Challenge exercise 3 is used, and the exercises should be completed in order as presented.

D1—Add Data Labels to an X-Y Chart

You can add information to a chart using the shortcut menu that displays when you right-click on a data point on the chart.

Goal: Use the shortcut menu to display the y-axis value next to each data point on an x-y chart.

1. Select the x-y chart sheet that you created in Challenge exercise 3 and right-click on one of the chart's data points.

2. Format the **Data Series** so that the data labels show.

3. Leave the workbook open for use in the next Discovery exercise.

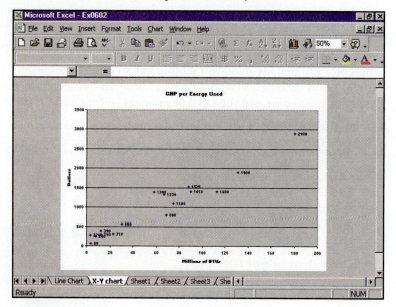

D2—Add Trend Line to an X-Y Chart

If there is a linear relationship between the values displayed on the category (x) axis and those on the y-axis of an x-y chart, the data points will be close to a straight line. Excel can calculate the straight line that is the best fit to the data points and add it to the chart.

The method of determining the formula for the best-fitting straight line is called a linear regression analysis. The degree of fit is represented by the R^2 value. A perfect fit would have an R^2 value equal to 1.

Goal: Add the trend line to the x-y chart that is the best fit to the data. Use the R2 value to determine if the best fit is a straight line or one of the other shapes.

1. Select the **X-Y chart** sheet.

2. Right-click on one of the data points and add a trend line.

3. Choose one of the six types of trend lines. Click the **Options** tab and choose to display the R-squared value.

4. Look at the trend line and its R-squared value, then delete the trend line.

5. Try each of the trend lines and decide which one is the best fit (has the highest value of R-squared).

6. Once you determine which trend line is the best fit, add it to the data and display the R-squared value on the chart.

7. Save the workbook and leave it open for use in the next exercise.

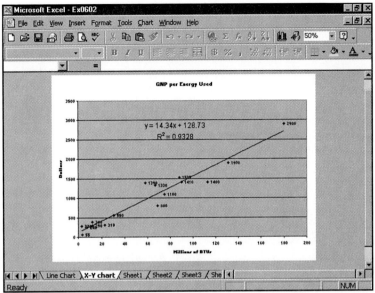

D3—Use the Trend Line Formula to Estimate Values

Excel displays the formula for the line that you select. You can use this formula to estimate new values or determine how much a given point differs from the trend line. For this example, we will use the straight trend line to keep the formula as simple as possible.

Goal: Determine the formula for the straight trend line and use it to generate a new column of estimated GNP values.

1. Select the **X-Y chart** sheet. Use the shortcut menu to add a straight trend line to the data points. Set the option to display the formula of the line.

2. Right-click on the formula and change its font size to **18** points. Drag the formula to a clear space on the chart.

3. Select **Sheet1**. Rewrite this formula so that you can use it in cell **D4** to estimate the GNP based on the value in cell **B4**. Use a cell reference in place of X in the formula. (The estimated value for Ghana will be 171.75. Ghana's GNP per energy used, 270, is much higher than the estimate.)

4. Fill this formula into the cells below to create a new column of estimated GNP for each country.

5. Print **Sheet1**.

6. Save the workbook and close it.

LESSON 6 UNDERSTANDING THE NUMBERS USING A CHART

Lesson: 7

Sorting, Grouping, and Filtering Data

Task 1 Sorting Rows by Department

Task 2 Grouping and Subtotaling by Department

Task 3 Displaying Totals and Subtotals Without the Details

Task 4 Filtering Information to Show Specified Rows

Task 5 Identifying Overdue Orders Using the Logical IF Function

Task 6 Removing Filters, Totals, and Outlines

Introduction

Worksheets are normally used to keep track of financial information such as expenditures and receipts. To manage such information effectively, you need to produce periodic reports showing expenditures by category or department. To do this, the information needs to be sorted, grouped, or filtered much like you would in a database file. In this lesson, you learn how to *sort* and group rows of data in the same way a *database management* system does.

Visual Summary

When you have completed this lesson, you will have a worksheet that looks like this:

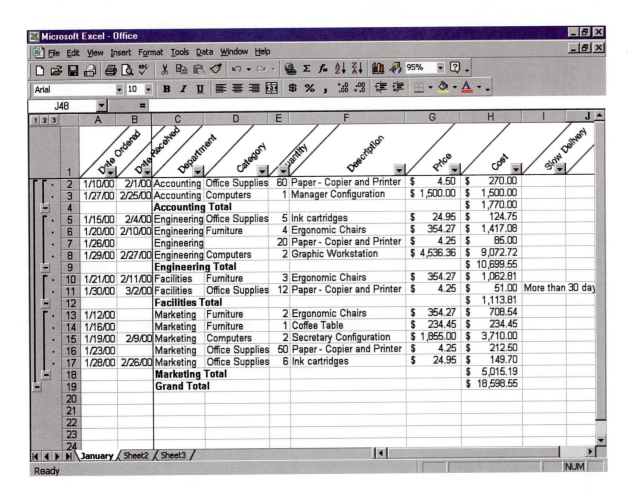

TASK 1

Sorting Rows by Department

Why would I do this?

Sometimes information in a worksheet is not organized in the order you need for a report. To organize information to meet your needs, you must sort it. For example, in the worksheet you are about to open, the orders for office supplies, computers, and furniture were recorded as they occurred. As a result, the orders are in date sequence.

In this task, you learn how to prepare a report showing the orders by department, rather than by date, which means you have to sort the data.

1 Open **Less0701** from the **Student\Lesson 07** folder on the CD-ROM disc and save the file on your floppy disk as **Office**. The new title appears in the title bar.

2 Select cells **A1** through **H14**.

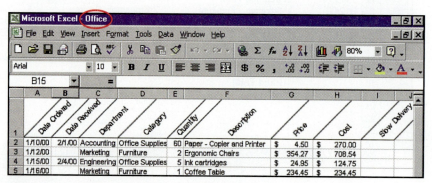

In Depth: If you set up your own worksheet for use as a database, you need to arrange the data in rows and columns. The columns should each have a label in row 1. These labels are called *field names*. Each field name identifies a category of information. The other rows are used to store data. Each row is used to store data about one transaction, person, or event. These rows are called *records*. In this example, Department is a field name and the information about the coffee table that Marketing ordered on January 16 is a record. If you set your worksheet up using these guidelines, it is easy to sort, group, and subtotal. It is also easy to export or embed your worksheet into a table in Word or Access.

218 LEARN EXCEL 2000

> **Caution:** With the slanted headings in this worksheet, it may appear to you as though Cost is the title for column I. This is really column H and should be included in the selection of the cells.

❸ Choose **Data**, **Sort**. The Sort dialog box opens.

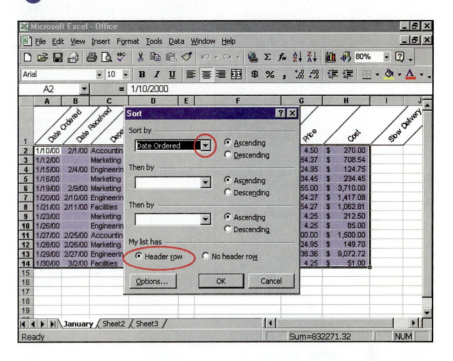

❹ Make sure that the **Header row** option is selected. Click the down arrow at the right side of the **Sort by** box. A list of the column labels is displayed.

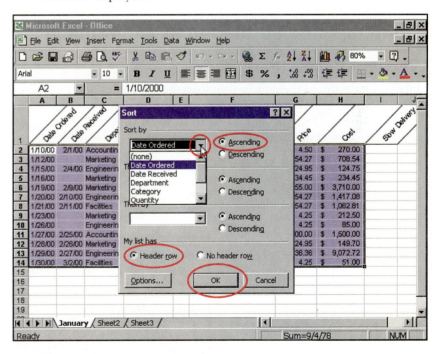

LESSON 7 SORTING, GROUPING, AND FILTERING DATA

5 Click **Department**. Make sure that the **Ascending** option is selected and click **OK**. The rows are reordered so that they are sorted alphabetically by department.

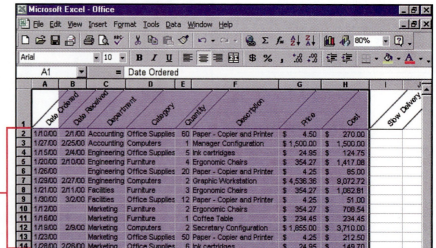

Rows sorted by department

TASK 2

Grouping and Subtotaling by Department

Why would I do this?

Once you have sorted the data in your worksheet, you may want to show subtotals, as well as a grand total. You could do this by applying the AutoSum function for each department, but Excel provides an easier way to make such calculations. Once the data has been sorted by the desired category or field name, Excel can automatically insert subtotals and grand totals.

In this task, you learn how to insert departmental order subtotals, as well as a grand total.

1 Confirm that cells A1 through H14 are still selected, then choose **Data**, **Su_b_totals**. The Subtotal dialog box opens.

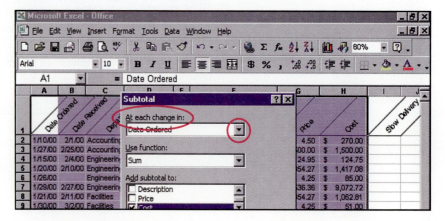

220 LEARN EXCEL 2000

2 Click the down arrow next to the <u>A</u>t each change in box. A list of the column labels (field names) drops down.

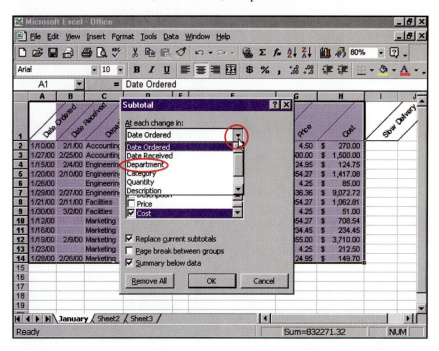

3 Click **Department**. Make sure that **Sum** is the choice in the **<u>U</u>se function** box and that **Cost** is the only field that has been selected in the **A<u>d</u>d subtotal to** box for subtotaling.

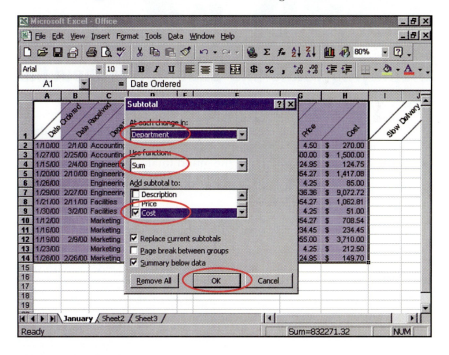

LESSON 7   SORTING, GROUPING, AND FILTERING DATA   221

④ Click **OK**. Totals are added for each department, and a grand total is included in row 19. A *collapsible outline* is also provided at the left of the screen.

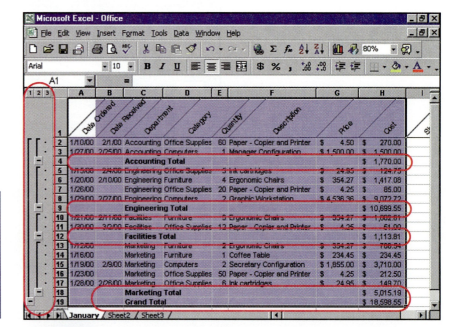

In Depth: Adding subtotals automatically produces an outline framework at the left side of your worksheet that can be collapsed or expanded to hide or reveal the details of each change in category. This outline is used in the next task.

TASK 3

Displaying Totals and Subtotals Without the Details

Why would I do this?

When you use the subtotals feature, Excel displays an outline of the data with the data, subtotals, and grand total on different levels of the outline. You can choose to hide the details and just show the subtotals and grand total, or hide everything but the grand total.

In this task, you learn how to display only the subtotals and the grand total of the report.

① Move the pointer to the level **2** symbol for the Accounting department. Notice that it has a ⊡ sign in the box to indicate that it can be collapsed.

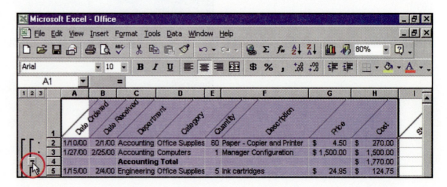

222 LEARN EXCEL 2000

2 Click the ⊖ button. The detail records of the Accounting department's expenses (rows 2 and 3) are hidden, and only the subtotal for the department is displayed. The outline button now has a ⊕ on it to indicate that it can be expanded.

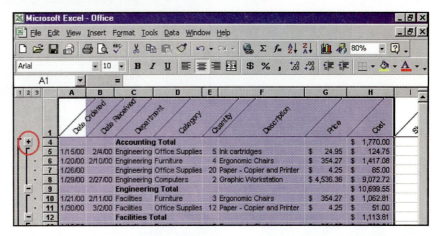

3 Click the level **2** outline button to collapse all of the detail rows. Only the departmental subtotals and the grand total are displayed.

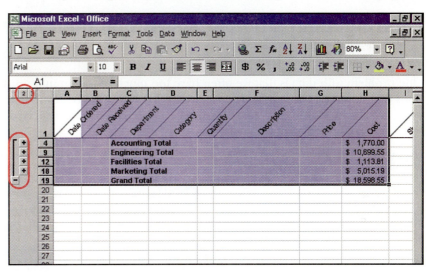

4 Use the options found under **File, Page Setup** to change the orientation to landscape and add your name to the left side of the page header. Preview the sheet.

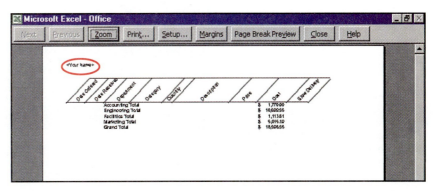

LESSON 7   SORTING, GROUPING, AND FILTERING DATA

5. Print the sheet. Click the level 3 outline button to fully expand the outline.

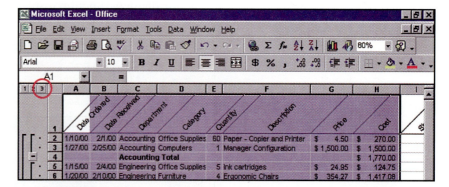

TASK 4

Filtering Information to Show Specified Rows

Why would I do this?

One problem with data is that we often have too much of it. You may want to see the rows that show transactions that occurred between two dates or were for amounts greater than a certain minimum. Excel allows you to set criteria in any column that determines which rows will be displayed. You learn how to *filter* the rows to show only those that meet your criteria.

In this task, you learn how to display the purchases that have not yet been received.

1. Select a cell anywhere in the table of data. Choose **Data**, **Filter**, **AutoFilter**. An *AutoFilter* arrow button appears at the top of each column of data.

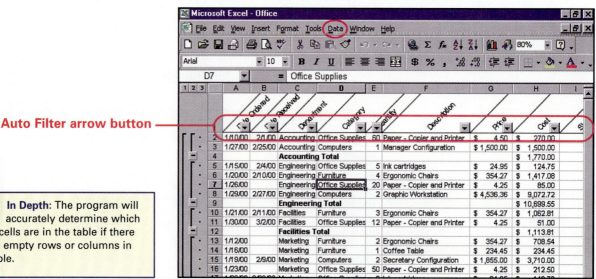

Auto Filter arrow button

In Depth: The program will accurately determine which cells are in the table if there are no empty rows or columns in the table.

LEARN EXCEL 2000

2 Click the AutoFilter arrow in column **B** (Date Received) and choose **Blanks**. The rows with no entry in column B are displayed. All of the purchases that do not have an entry in the Date Received column are displayed.

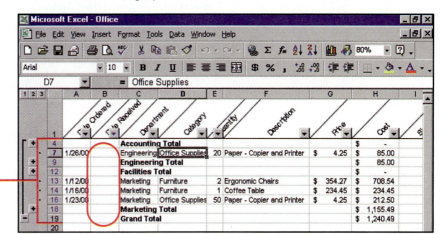

Rows with a blank in Date Received

3 Click the AutoFilter arrow in column **A** (Date Ordered) and choose **NonBlanks**. Notice that all of the subtotal rows are filtered out, but not the grand total. It is now easy to see that there are $1,240.49 worth of supplies that have been ordered but not received.

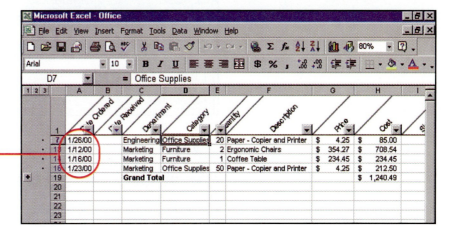

Filter does not apply to Grand Total row

4 Select the AutoFilter arrow in column **A** and choose **All**. Repeat this process for column **B**. All of the rows are now displayed.

In Depth: When you add a filter to data that already has been subtotaled, Excel re-calculates the subtotal to reflect the impact of the filter. Notice that the total amounts in the cost column have changed to reflect the total by department for only the rows that are displayed. Excel recalculated the subtotals to fit the filter that you just placed on the data.

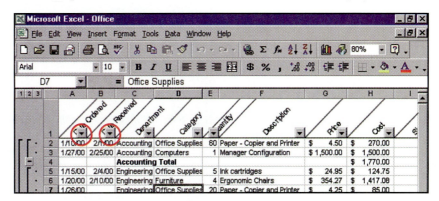

LESSON 7 SORTING, GROUPING, AND FILTERING DATA

5 Assume that this company considers any piece of equipment that costs more than $1,000 to be capital equipment that must have an ID tag. To display and total those records, click the AutoFilter arrow at the top of the **Price** column and choose **Custom**. The Custom AutoFilter dialog box opens.

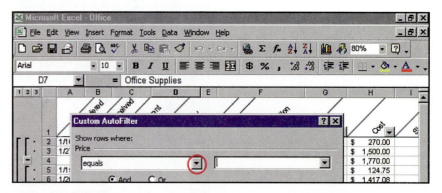

6 Click the down arrow next to the first condition box and choose **is greater than**.

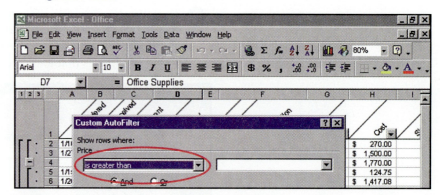

7 Press Tab to move to the next condition box and type **1000**.

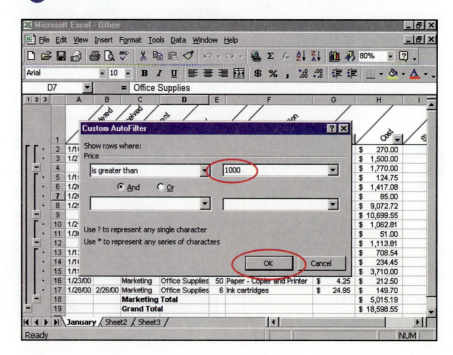

8 Click **OK**. The purchases over $1,000 are displayed.

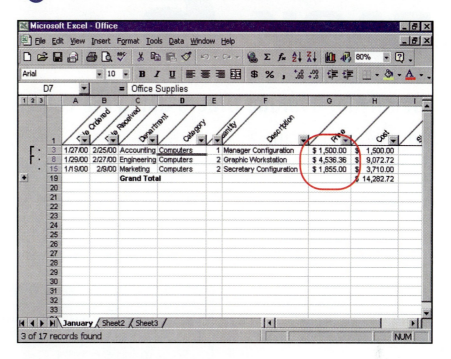

9 Click the AutoFilter arrow at the top of the **Price** column and choose **All**. The entire list is displayed.

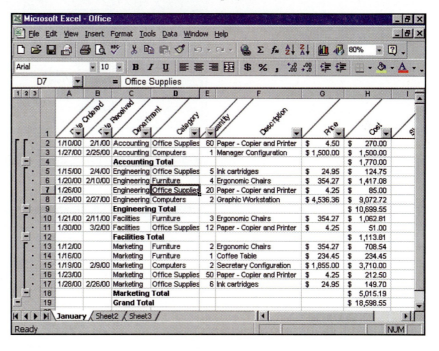

TASK 5

Identifying Overdue Orders Using the Logical IF Function

Why would I do this?

The filters that were used in the previous task are very effective for limiting the display if the condition is limited to the values in one column. If you need to compare two columns, you need a different tool.

In this task, you learn how to use the IF function to compare the difference between the Date Ordered and the Date Received and then to print a message if any of the orders took more than thirty days to fill.

1 Select cell **C2**. Choose **Window, Freeze Panes**.

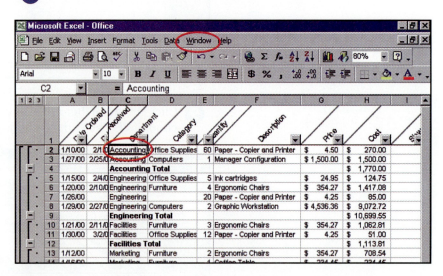

2 Scroll to the right, if necessary, so that column **I, Slow Delivery**, is on the screen.

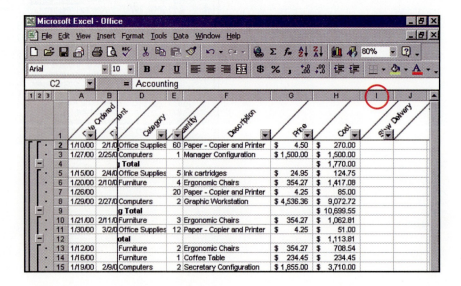

228 LEARN EXCEL 2000

3 Select cell **I2** and click the **Paste Function** button. The Paste Function dialog box opens. Select **Logical** in the **Function category** on the left.

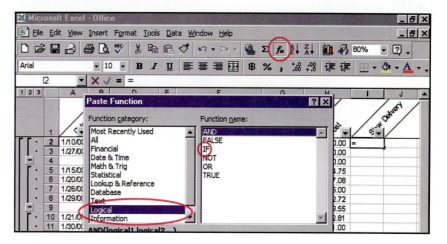

4 Select **IF** from the **Function name** list on the right.

A description of the function

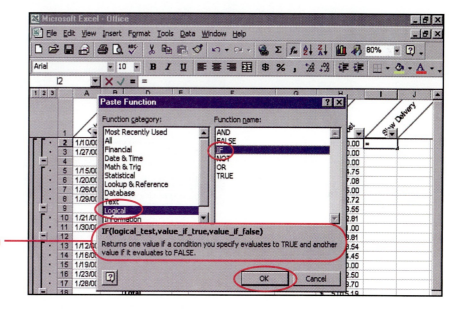

5 Click **OK**. The IF dialog box opens with the insertion point in the Logical_test box.

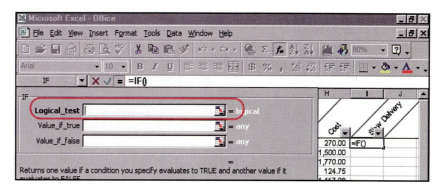

LESSON 7 SORTING, GROUPING, AND FILTERING DATA   229

6 Type **(B2-A2)>30** in the **Logical_test** box.

> **In Depth:** The computer thinks of dates as sequential numbers that are formatted to represent dates. Later dates are larger numbers than earlier dates. To find the difference between two dates, you subtract the earlier date (Date Ordered in cell A2) from the later date (Date Received in cell B2).

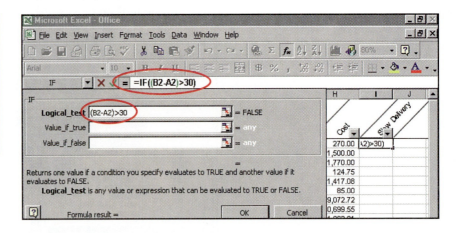

7 Press Tab to move to the **Value_if_true** box. This box contains the formula or statement to use if the condition is true. In this case, we want to print a statement. Words are enclosed in quotation marks. Type **"More than 30 days."**

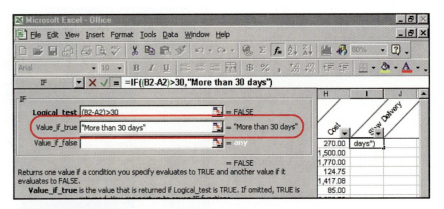

8 Press Tab to move to the **Value_if_false** box. This box contains the formula or statement to use if the condition is false. In this case, we do not want to print anything. To print nothing, we use two quotation marks with nothing between them. Type **""**.

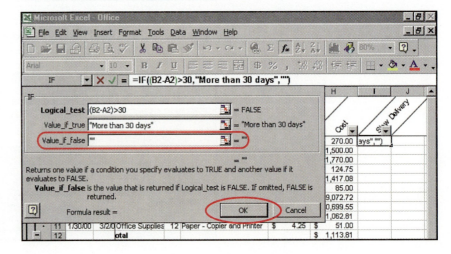

230 LEARN EXCEL 2000

9 Click **OK**. The function appears in the formula bar and nothing prints in cell I2 because these two dates are less than 30 days apart.

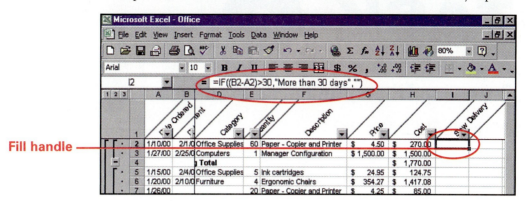

Fill handle

10 Drag the fill handle down to cell **I17** to fill this function into the other cells in this column. Notice that one of the orders took longer than 30 days to deliver.

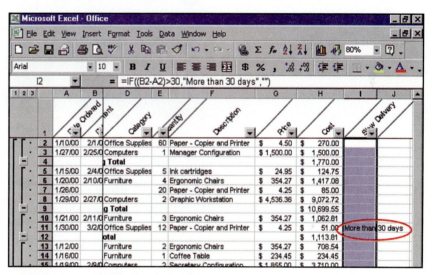

11 Print this sheet and save it.

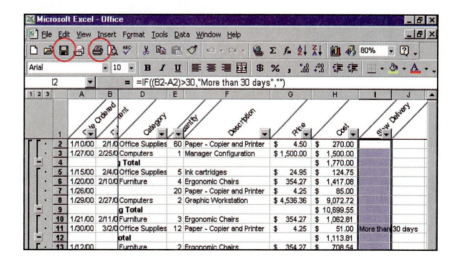

LESSON 7 SORTING, GROUPING, AND FILTERING DATA

TASK 6

Removing Filters, Totals, and Outlines

Why would I do this?

After you have applied filters and totals, you may need to apply different filters to your data based on other criteria, or you may need to subtotal the data based on a different category. Before you can change filters or totals, you must first remove the ones you have created. Then you can apply new filters or total the data based on different categories.

In this task, you learn how to remove filters, totals, and the outline.

1 Choose **Window, Unfreeze Panes.**

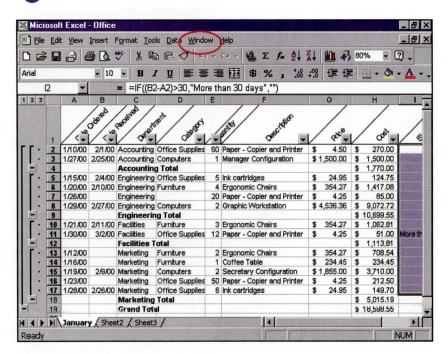

232 LEARN EXCEL 2000

2 Choose **Data**, **Filter**. Notice the AutoFilter option is shown next to a button with a check mark and that the button appears to be pressed. This indicates a *toggle* type button. The filter may be removed by clicking the button again.

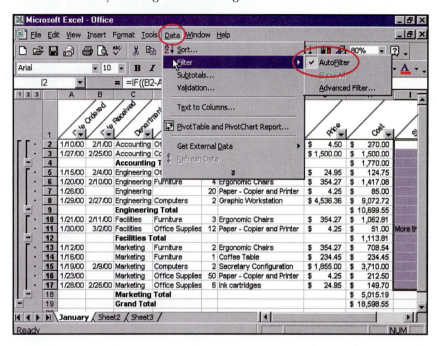

3 Click the **AutoFilter** button. The AutoFilter arrows are removed from each column.

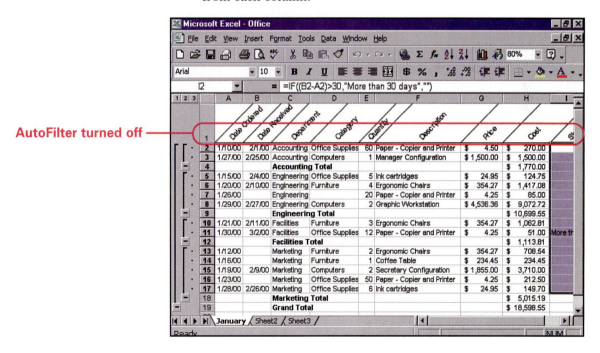

AutoFilter turned off

LESSON 7   SORTING, GROUPING, AND FILTERING DATA   233

4 Click on any cell in the table. Choose **Data**, **Subtotals** from the menu. The Subtotal dialog box appears.

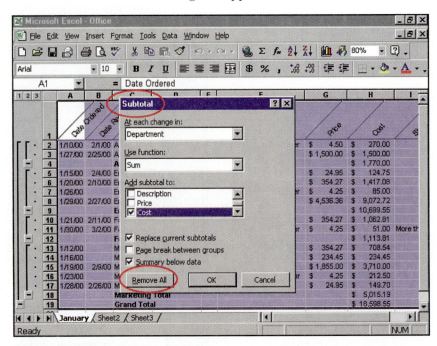

5 Click the **Remove All** button. The totals and outline are removed.

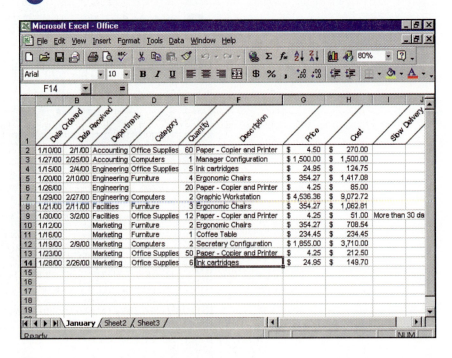

6 Click the **Close Window** button to close the workbook. A window with a caution message appears. (You may see the Office Assistant.)

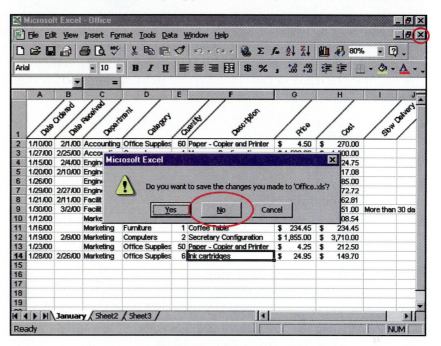

7 Click **No**. Do not save the changes this time. The file on your disk has the filters and outlines that you saved at the end of the last task.

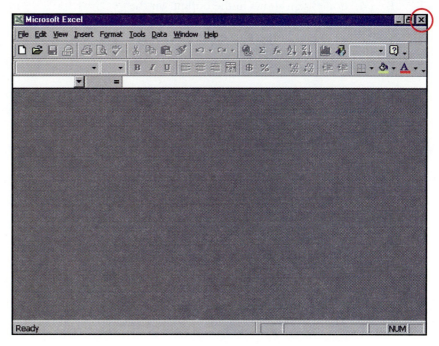

Comprehension Exercises

Comprehension exercises are designed to check your memory and understanding of the basic concepts in this lesson. You distinguish between true and false statements, identify new screen elements, and match terms with related statements. If you are uncertain of the correct answer, refer to the task number following each item (for example, T4 refers to Task 4) and review that task until you are confident that you can provide a correct response.

True-False

Circle either T or F.

T F 1. To use an Excel worksheet for grouping and sorting data, the information needs to be organized with labels or field names in the first column (A). **(T1)**

T F 2. A record is a row of information about one transaction, person, or event. **(T1)**

T F 3. Excel can insert a subtotal after each identifiable group, such as departments. **(T2)**

T F 4. If a ⊞ sign shows in the outline on the left side of a worksheet, it indicates that all details of the worksheet are currently visible. **(T3)**

T F 5. To filter data in a worksheet, you must first select all the cells to which the filter applies. **(T4)**

T F 6. To limit the data displayed, you can use the Custom AutoFilter and set conditions on several columns. **(T4)**

T F 7. To compare data in two columns, you use the If-Then function. **(T5)**

T F 8. To remove a filter from a worksheet, click the **Remove-Filter** button on the Standard toolbar. **(T6)**

T F 9. In a logical test, you type two quotation marks with nothing between them to indicate a value is false. **(T5)**

T F 10. To compare dates, you subtract the oldest date from the newest date if you want the difference to be a positive number. **(T5)**

Identifying Parts of the Excel Screen

Refer to the figure and identify the numbered parts of the screen. Write the letter of the correct label in the space next to the number.

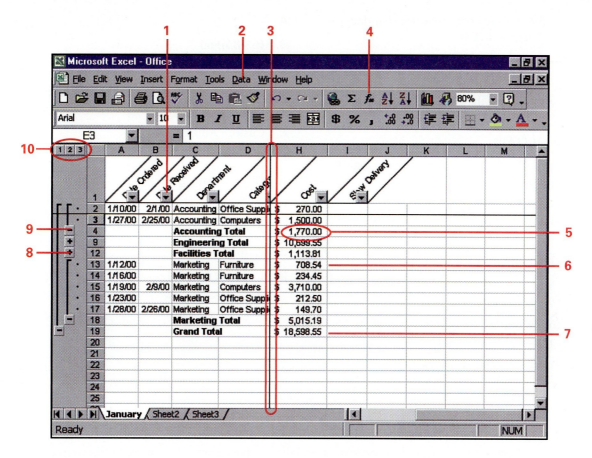

1. _____
2. _____
3. _____
4. _____
5. _____
6. _____
7. _____
8. _____
9. _____
10. _____

A. Collapse button (T3)

B. Expand button (T3)

C. Subtotal (T3)

D. Grand total (T3)

E. Collapse (or expand) all second outline level details (T3)

F. A detail row (T3)

G. Paste Function (T5)

H. Columns to the left of this line are frozen (T5)

J. AutoFilter arrow (T4)

K. Menu item used to sort, filter, and subtotal (T1)

LESSON 7 SORTING, GROUPING, AND FILTERING DATA   237

Matching

Match the statements below to the word or phrase that is the best match from the list. Write the letter of the matching word or phrase in the space provided next to the number.

1. ___ In the outline area, indicates that data can be expanded (T3)
2. ___ Information about one person, event, or transaction (T1)
3. ___ Used to limit the data that is shown (T4)
4. ___ Used to add or remove filters from a worksheet (T4)
5. ___ Example of a comparison using a logical operator (T5)
6. ___ Column headings in a worksheet used to identify categories of information so the data can be sorted like a database (T1)
7. ___ To add a subtotal to sorted records (T2)
8. ___ Used to set special criteria on a particular column (T4)
9. ___ In the outline area, indicates that all data for that group is visible (T3)
10. ___ To sort data in a worksheet (T1)

A. -
B. (B3-B5)>60
C. Field names
D. Highlight a column and click the **Sort Ascending** button
E. Custom AutoFilter
F. +
G. Choose **Data, Sort**
H. Filter
I. Record
J. AutoFilter button
K. Choose **Data, Subtotals**

Reinforcement Exercises

Reinforcement exercises are designed to reinforce the skills you have learned by applying them to a new situation. Detailed instructions are provided along with a figure, where appropriate, to illustrate the final result. The Reinforcement exercises that follow should be completed sequentially. Leave the workbook open at the end of each exercise for use in the next exercise until you are specifically directed to close it.

Open **Less0702** from the **Student\Lesson 07** folder on your CD-ROM disc and save it as **Ex0701** on your floppy disk for use in the following exercises.

R1—Sort by Product

In this exercise, you take a list of sales that is sequential by date and sort it by product.

1. Select **Sheet1** and change the name to **Sales**.
2. Sort the rows by the **Product or Service** column as shown in the figure. See the steps below for more detail.
3. Click anywhere in the table of data (except the title), then choose **Data, Sort**.

238 LEARN EXCEL 2000

4. Confirm that this table has a header row and that the appropriate item is checked. Sort the records by the **Product or Service** field in ascending order.

5. Save your work.

R2—Group and Subtotal by Product

1. In the **Sales** sheet, make sure a cell within the table of data is selected.

2. Insert subtotals and a grand total into the table to display the total amount for each type of product or service as shown in the figure. See the following steps for further instruction.

3. Choose **D**ata, S**u**btotals. Add a subtotal to the **Deposit/Loan Amount** field at each change in **Product or Service**. Deselect the Points Awarded check box.

4. Collapse all the details so that the sheet displays only the subtotals and grand total.

5. Add your name to the sheet header and print the worksheet.

6. Expand the outline to display all the level 3 detail rows. Save the workbook.

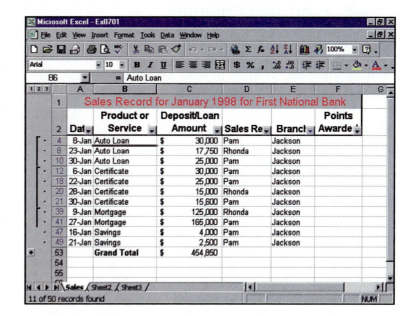

R3—Filter by Branch

1. Make sure that a cell in the table is selected.

2. Filter the records so that the only records showing are those for the **Jackson** branch, as shown in the figure. For further instructions, see the steps below.

3. Choose **D**ata, **F**ilter, Auto**F**ilter.

4. Click the filter arrow in the **Branch** column and select **Jackson** from the list.

5. Print the sheet.

6. Save the changes to the workbook.

LESSON 7 SORTING, GROUPING, AND FILTERING DATA

R4—Remove Subtotals and Filters

1. Remove the filters, subtotals, and outline from the **Sales** worksheet to match the figure. See the steps below for more details.

2. Choose **Data**, **Filters**, and click the **AutoFilter** button to deselect it.

3. Choose **Data, Subtotals, Remove All**.

4. Print the sheet.

5. Close the workbook, but do not save the changes.

Challenge

Challenge exercises are designed to test your ability to apply your skills to new situations with less detailed instruction. These exercises also challenge you to expand your repertoire of skills by using Excel commands that are similar to those you have already learned. The desired outcome is clearly defined, but you have more freedom to choose the steps needed to achieve the required result.

Open **Less0703** from the **Student\Lesson 07** folder on your CD-ROM disc and save it on your floppy disk as **Ex0702**.

C1—Sort on Two Columns

If you sort a table of data by the values in one column, you may want to sub-sort by the values in a second column.

Goal: Sort the sales record by product and then sub-sort by branch. Add a subtotal to the Deposit/Loan column for each change in product.

Use the following guidelines:

1. Select the **Sort on Two Columns** tab.

2. Open the **Sort** dialog window and sort on **Product or Service**, then use the second dialog box in that window to sort by **Branch**. Sort both in ascending order and make sure that the **Header row** option is selected.

3. Use the **Subtotals** option to subtotal the **Deposit/Loan Amount** for each change in **Product or Service**. Deselect the Points Awarded check box, if necessary.

4. Save the workbook. Leave the workbook open for use in the next exercise.

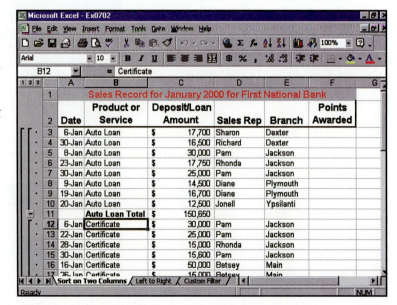

240 LEARN EXCEL 2000

C2—Sort Left to Right

Some worksheets are organized with the data in rows rather than columns. You can sort the data left to right as well as with the top to bottom default option.

The left to right option does not recognize row headers in the first column, so it is necessary to select the range of cells before you start to sort.

Goal: Sort the table from left to right based on the Product or Service row.

1. Click the **Left to Right** sheet tab.
2. Select cells **B2** through **AS5**.
3. Begin the sorting process. When the **Sort** window opens, select **Options** and choose **Sort left to right**.
4. Sort on the **Product or Service** by selecting the number of that row. Sort in **Ascending** order.
5. Save the workbook. Leave the workbook open for use in the next exercise.

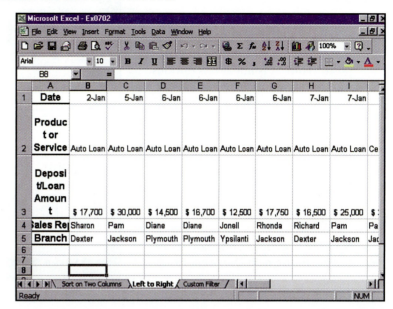

C3—Custom Filters

You can use Excel's filters and subtotals to answer fairly complex questions such as "How many Auto Loans did we process that were larger than $15,000?" To answer a question like this, you need to use filters on more than one column and use the Custom Filter feature.

Goal: Learn how to use the Custom Filter feature and use filters on two columns at the same time.

1. Select the **Custom Filter** sheet.
2. Turn on the **AutoFilter** feature and select **Auto Loan** in the **Product or Service** column.
3. Use the **Custom Filter** option in the **Deposit/Loan Amount** column to show the amounts that are greater than or equal to $15,000.
4. Save the workbook and close it.

Discovery

Discovery exercises are designed to help you learn how to teach yourself a new skill. In each exercise, you discover something new that is related to the topic taught in this lesson. You may be directed to use built-in wizards or some of the extensive Help features provided in Excel to discover new features and learn new skills with minimum assistance from books or instructors. The required outcome demonstrates your ability to apply the new skill. You determine the choice of topic, worksheet design, and steps of execution.

Open the file **Less0704** from the **Student\Lesson 07** folder on your CD-ROM disc and save it as **Ex0703** on your floppy disk for use in the following Discovery exercises.

D1—Compound Filters Using Logical AND and OR

There are times when more than one condition should be used in a filter. If both conditions must apply to display the row, you use the AND option. If meeting either condition is sufficient, use the OR option.

Goal: Filter the data to display auto loans and certificates of deposit that are from $15,000 to $30,000 (including $15,000 and $30,000).

1. Select the **And and Or** sheet.

2. Use a custom filter on the **Product or Service** column to display all the auto loans and all the certificates of deposit. (Hint: It is not always obvious whether to use the AND or the OR option. If you get no rows showing after you apply the filter, it means that none of the rows met your condition.)

3. Apply a custom filter to the **Deposit/Loan Amount** column. Be sure to include the limiting numbers in the conditions.

4. Save the workbook and leave it open for use in the next Discovery exercise.

D2—Nesting Formulas Inside Logical IF Functions

It is possible to place a formula in an IF statement as one of the true or false options. In the example problem, points are awarded to each employee for signing up new customers based on the amount of the deposit or loan. Three points are awarded per thousand dollars if the amount is less than $10,000, and two points are awarded for amounts that are greater than or equal to $10,000.

Goal: Use formulas nested inside a logical IF function to determine the amount of bonus points awarded for each transaction.

1. Open **Ex0704**, if necessary, and select the **IF** sheet.

2. Paste a **Logical IF** function in cell **F3**.

3. Enter a condition that determines if the amount in **C3** is less than $10,000.

4. Enter a formula (without an equal sign) in the **Value_if_true** box that takes the amount in **C3**, divides by 1,000, and multiplies by the appropriate number of points.

5. Determine the appropriate formula (without equal sign) to put in the **Value_if_false** box.

6. Fill this formula into the rest of the cells in column **F**.

7. Save the workbook and leave it open for use in the next exercise.

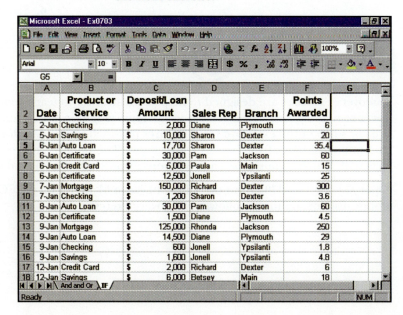

242   LEARN EXCEL 2000

D3—Pivot Tables

You can create tables of summary data that can be easily analyzed using the Pivot Table option. Unfortunately, the name of the option does not describe what it does and may cause some confusion. You may think of this option as a way to produce a summary table that has built-in filters to allow for easy analysis.

Goal: Learn how to use a pivot table to summarize the amount of loans and deposits by branch bank and by the product. Provide totals by branch and by product.

1. Search for Help on the subject **Pivot Table.**

2. Read the section on **When to use a Pivot table and Pivot Chart Wizard - Layout dialog box**.

3. Open **Ex0703** and select the **IF** sheet.

4. Select a cell in the table.

5. Choose **Data**, **Pivot Table and Pivot Chart Report**. Create the table on a new sheet.

6. Use the **Product or Service** field for row fields, **Branch** for column fields, and **Deposit/Loan Amount** for data items. Drag the names of these fields onto the layout boxes provided by the wizard.

7. Rename the sheet **Dollars**.

8. If you have done the preceding exercise, D2, return to the **IF** sheet and create a second pivot table that uses **Sales rep** (rows), **Branch** (columns), and displays the points (data items). Name the sheet **Points**.

9. Save the workbook and close it.

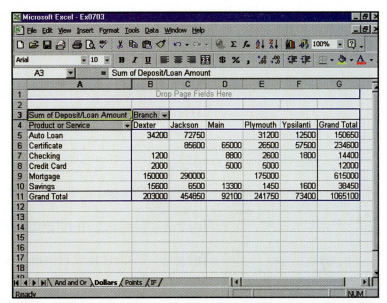

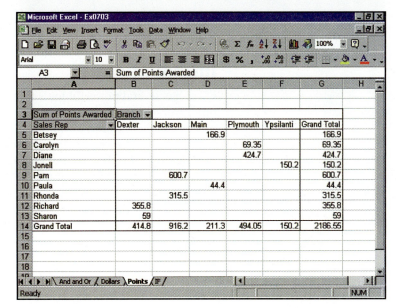

LESSON 7 SORTING, GROUPING, AND FILTERING DATA

Creating Connections to Build Summaries, Improve Teamwork, and Work on the Web

Task 1 Inserting and Moving a New Sheet

Task 2 Designing a Summary Sheet for Convenient Charting

Task 3 Linking the Results of Several Sheets to a Summary Sheet

Task 4 Inserting a Hyperlink to Another Workbook

Task 5 Saving a Worksheet as a Web Page

Task 6 Using a Worksheet on the Web

Introduction

Excel has several powerful tools that you can use to connect your worksheet to other worksheets or documents that are on your computer or on other computers anywhere in the world over the *Internet*. The Internet is a worldwide communications network of computer connections that allows people to have access to thousands of online resources. You can also use this connectivity to share files with co-workers or to get help.

Visual Summary

In this lesson, you create summary sheets and publish worksheets as Web pages.

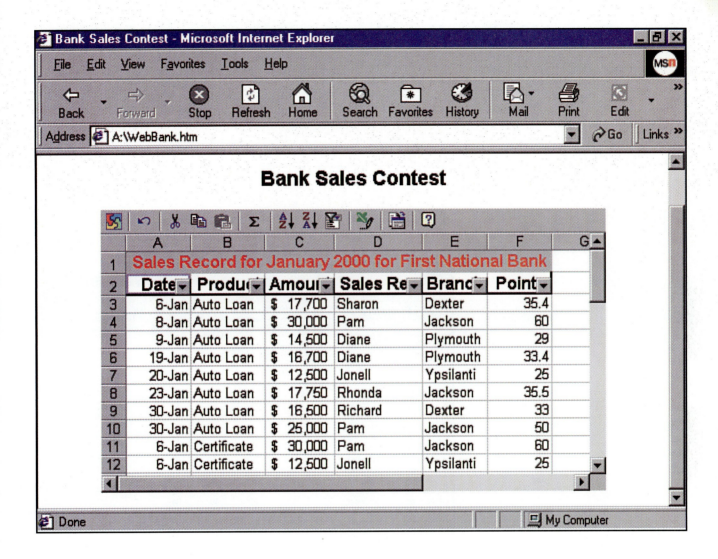

TASK 1

Inserting and Moving a New Sheet

Why would I do this?

It may make sense to divide your data into several separate sheets. This makes the data easier to manage and to chart. However, you often need to bring the results of these sheets together in one place so that they can be compared and summarized. When you are ready to summarize your work, you may need to add a worksheet and place it into your workbook in a particular location.

In this task, you add a new sheet to use as a year-end summary sheet and change the order of the sheet in the workbook.

1 Open **Less0801** from the **Student\Lesson08** folder on your CD-ROM disc and save the file on your floppy disk as **Summary**. The new title appears in the title bar.

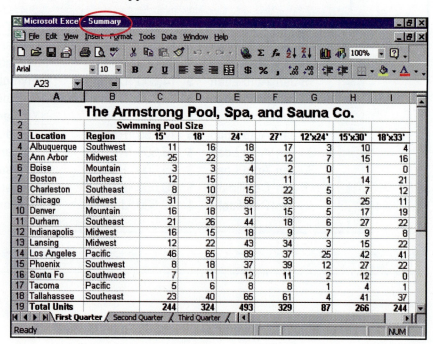

246 LEARN EXCEL 2000

2 Choose **Insert, Worksheet.** A blank worksheet is added. It is called **Sheet1**.

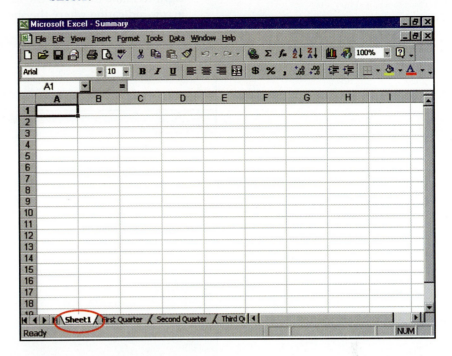

3 Double-click the **Sheet1** tab to select it and type **Year-End Summary**. Press ⏎Enter.

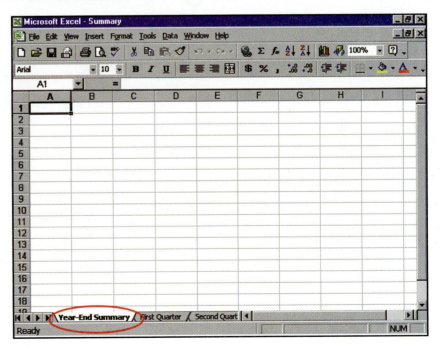

LESSON 8 CREATING CONNECTIONS 247

4 Move the pointer onto the new tab. Click and drag the tab to the right to make this sheet the last one. Notice that there is a small arrow indicating where the sheet will be placed.

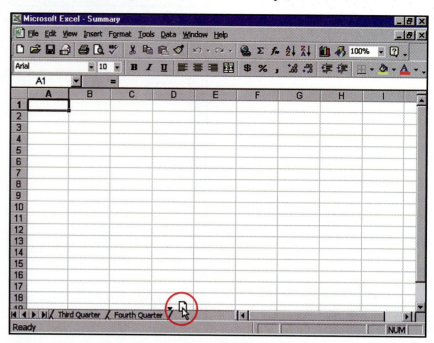

5 Release the mouse button. The sheet is placed last.

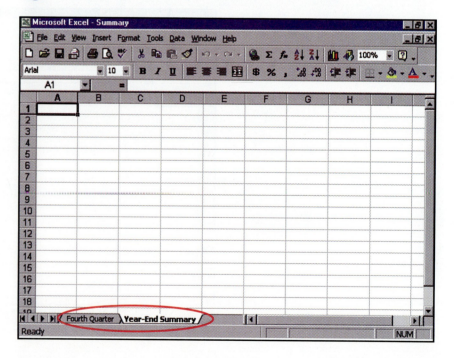

TASK 2

Designing a Summary Sheet for Convenient Charting

Why would I do this?

The summary sheet consolidates the data from several other sheets. Because this is summary information that may be communicated to others, you want to organize it so that it is easy to chart. To create charts, the data must be arranged into adjacent cells in rows or columns. Therefore, it is important that the design of the worksheet allows for easy comparison charting.

In this task, you design labels for a sheet that summarizes the sales from each of the quarters represented by the other four sheets.

1 Select the **Year-End Summary** sheet, if necessary. Select cell **A1**, if it is not already selected. Type **The Armstrong Pool, Spa, and Sauna Company**. Press **Enter**.

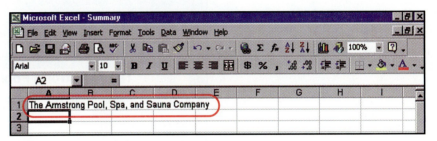

2 Select cells **A1** through **I1**. Click the **Merge and Center** button.

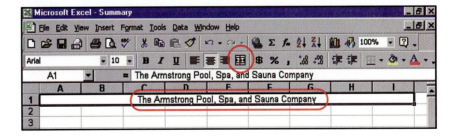

3 Select cell **B2**. Type **Swimming Pool Size**. Press **Enter**.

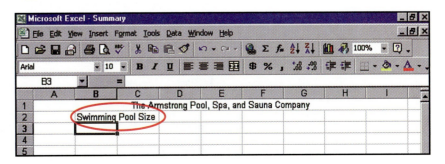

LESSON 8 CREATING CONNECTIONS 249

4 Select cells **B2** through **H2**. Click the **Merge and Center** button.

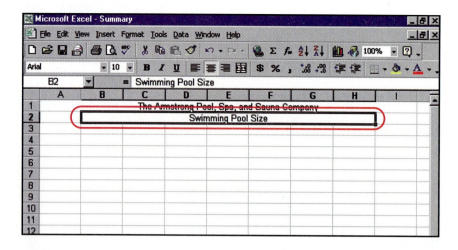

5 Click the **Fourth Quarter** sheet tab and select cells **C3** through **I3**.

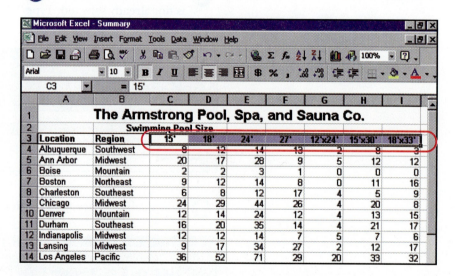

6 Click the **Copy** button. Cells **C3** through **I3** have a marquee around them to show that they have been copied.

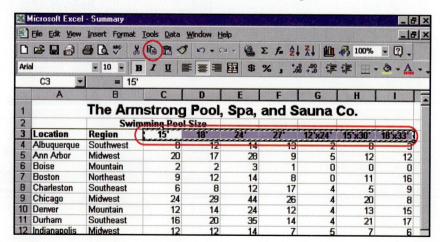

7 Click the **Year-End Summary** sheet tab and select cell **B3**.

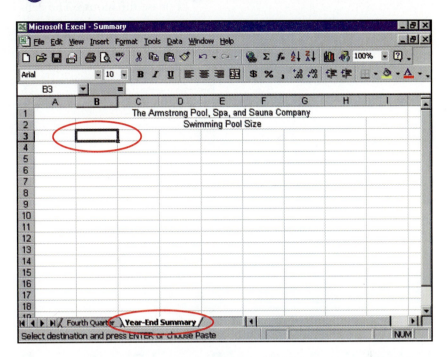

8 Click the **Paste** button. The column headings from the Fourth Quarter sheet are pasted into these cells.

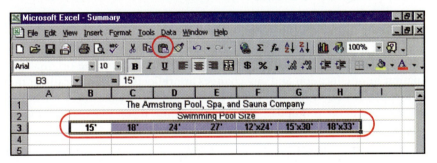

9 Select cell **A4**, type **Q1**, and press ⏎Enter. (Note: When labeling columns or rows that will be charted at a later time, use brief labels that will not take up too much space on the chart, such as the Q1 label.)

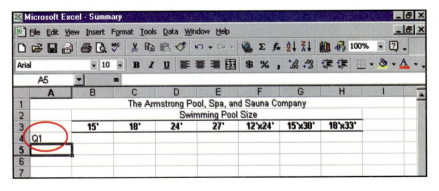

LESSON 8 CREATING CONNECTIONS **251**

10 Select cell **A4**. Drag the fill handle down from cell **A4** to **A7** and release the mouse. The cells fill with a series from Q1 through Q4.

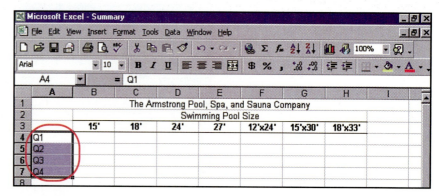

TASK 3

Linking the Results of Several Sheets to a Summary Sheet

Why would I do this?

When you copy information from one sheet to another, there is no link established between the data in the two worksheets. To be able to change data in one sheet and have that change reflected in a summary worksheet, you need to create a link between the worksheets. You do this by using a relative reference technique that points directly to a key cell in the worksheet that contains the original data. Then you only have to enter information in one location and any changes are reflected automatically in the summary worksheet. For example, if you copy the data from the First to Fourth Quarter sheets into your Year-End Summary sheet, the values do not change whenever you update the data. However, if you place a formula in a cell in the Year-End Summary sheet, you can make it refer to specific cells in the quarterly worksheet.

In this task, you place formulas in the summary sheet that refer to the totals by category in each of the quarterly sales sheets.

1 Make sure that the **Year-End Summary** sheet is selected and select cell **B4**.

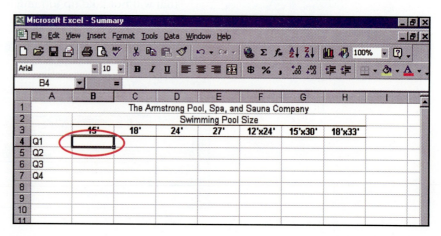

LEARN EXCEL 2000

In Depth: After the = , you could type the complete formula in cell B4 if you knew the cell references you wanted to select. In this case, as you will see, it is easier to use your mouse to locate the cell references, because the cells to which you refer are on another sheet.

2 Type = to indicate that the following entry is a formula.

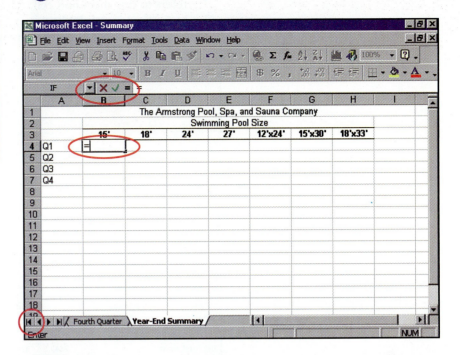

3 Click the left-most **Tab Scrolling** button to find the **First Quarter** sheet tab. Click the **First Quarter** tab. Notice that the name of the sheet is written in the formula bar between single quotation marks, followed by an exclamation mark.

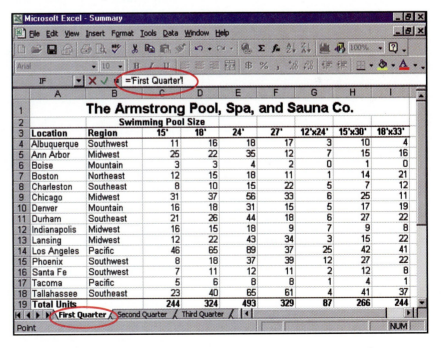

LESSON 8   CREATING CONNECTIONS   253

④ Click cell **C19**. Notice that the formula in the formula bar now refers to this sheet and cell. (Note: This is the formula you would have typed in cell B4 in step 2, if you knew the cell reference was C19 and how to state the formula.)

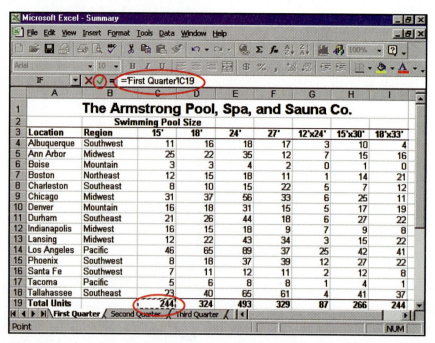

⑤ Click the **Enter** button on the formula bar. The screen automatically returns to the **Year-End Summary** sheet, and the value from cell C19 on the **First Quarter** sheet is displayed in cell B4 where you placed the formula.

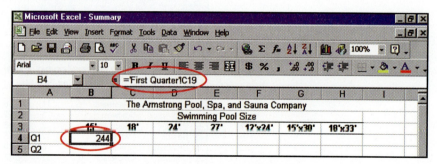

⑥ Drag the fill handle from cell **B4** to **H4** and release the mouse. The cells from C4 through H4 are filled with relative formulas that refer to cells D19 through I19 on the **First Quarter** sheet.

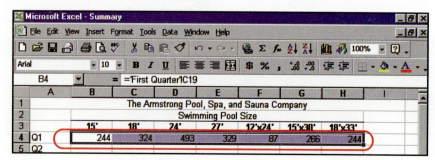

254   LEARN EXCEL 2000

7 Select cell **B5** and type =. Switch to the **Second Quarter** sheet, select cell **C19**, and click the **Enter** button on the formula bar.

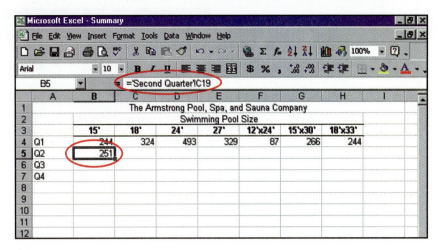

8 Drag the fill handle from cell **B5** to **H5** and release the mouse button. The values from the second quarter are filled in.

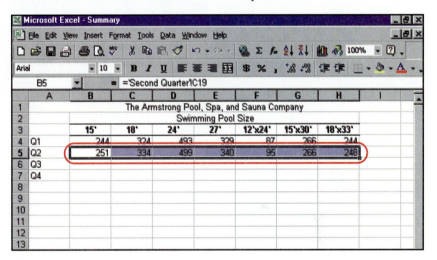

9 Repeat this process in rows **6** and **7** to display the values from the **Third Quarter** and **Fourth Quarter** sheets.

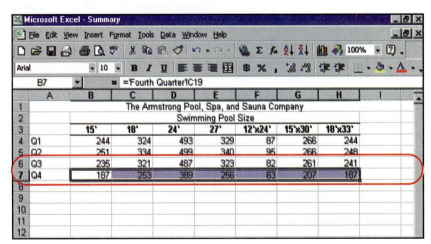

LESSON 8   CREATING CONNECTIONS   255

10 Select cell **A8**. Type **Total Sold** and press Tab.

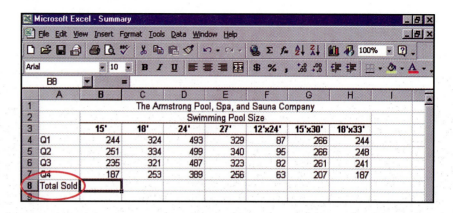

11 Confirm that cell **B8** is selected, and double-click the **AutoSum** button to sum the contents of cells **B4** through **B7**.

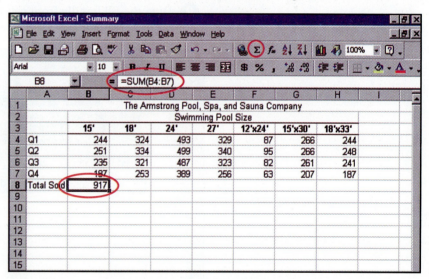

12 Drag the fill handle from cell **B8** to **H8** and release the mouse. Sales for each size of pool are summed. Save your work.

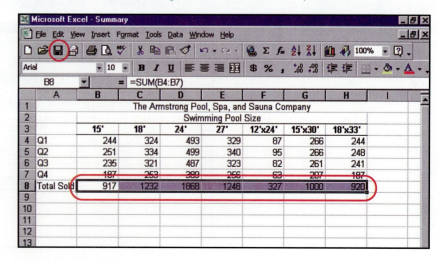

TASK 4

Inserting a Hyperlink to Another Workbook

Why would I do this?

Sometimes it is important to look at data from someone else's workbook, Word document, or Web page. A convenient way to do this is to insert a *hyperlink*. A hyperlink is a connection between a word or label in one location to a file in another location. When you click on a word or label that has been made into a hyperlink, it connects you directly to information in another file. Using hyperlinks to connect to other files can increase your efficiency by locating the information you need quickly. In this example, the warehouse keeps a record of the pool inventory. The number of pools that they shipped should match the number of pools sold.

In this task, you will insert a hyperlink in this summary sheet to compare their records with your records.

1 In the **Year-End Summary** sheet, select cell **A9.** Type **Shipped**, and press ↵Enter.

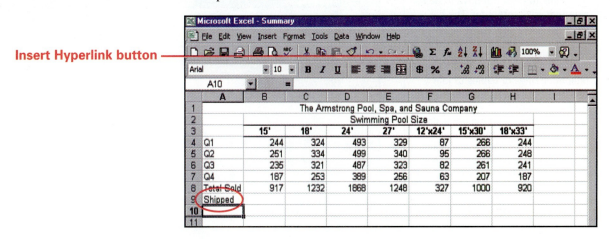

Insert Hyperlink button

2 Select cell **A9** and click the **Insert Hyperlink** button on the Standard toolbar. The Insert Hyperlink dialog box opens.

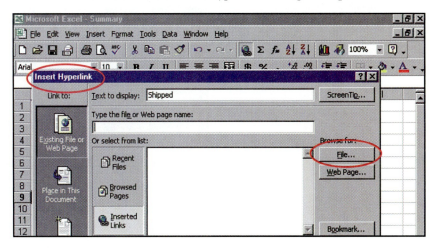

LESSON 8   CREATING CONNECTIONS   257

3 Click the <u>F</u>ile button in the **Browse for** area. The Link to File dialog box opens. (Note: It is likely that your dialog box displays files that are different from those in the figure.) This dialog box works like the Open dialog box and helps you find files in folders.

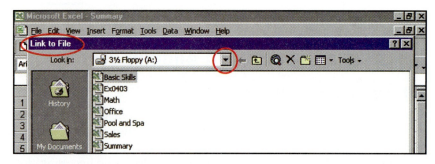

4 Find the file **Less0802** in the **Student\Lesson08** folder on the CD-ROM disc. Select it and click **OK**. The location of the file is displayed in the Type the fil<u>e</u> or Web page name box.

In Depth: When you create a hyperlink, the file that you link to does not have to be located on your computer. The file could be located anywhere on the Internet or on the *local area network* (LAN) to which you have access. A LAN is a system that uses telephone lines or cables to join two or more personal computers, enabling them to communicate with each other. The hyperlink creates a reference to the drive and folder where the file resides or to its *uniform resource locator* (*URL*), which is its address on the Internet. You use the Browse button to find that file location or URL.

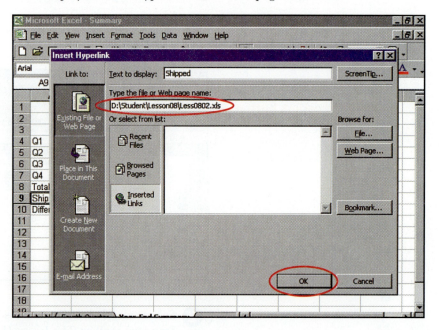

5 Click **OK**. The text in cell A9 changes color and is underlined.

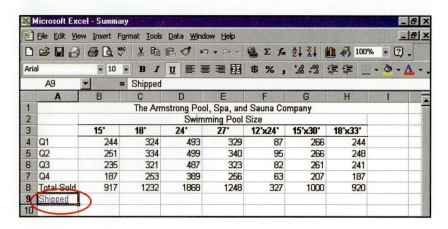

258   LEARN EXCEL 2000

6 Select a different cell to move the selection off of cell **A9**. Move the pointer to cell **A9**. The pointer changes to a small hand and the location of the file is displayed in a *ScreenTip*.

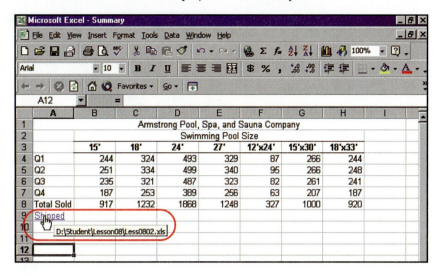

7 Click the hyperlink in cell **A9**. The **Less0802** sheet opens. It contains an inventory of swimming pools.

> **In Depth:** You may notice that the phrase **Read Only** is displayed in the title bar. When you open a file directly from the CD-ROM, you do not have the option of changing it on the CD, since the CD-ROM is created as a read-only medium.

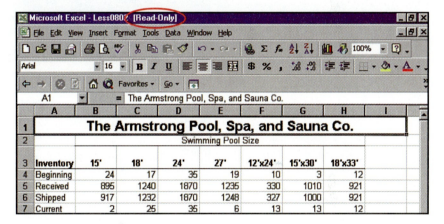

8 Select cells **B6** through **H6.** Click the **Copy** button.

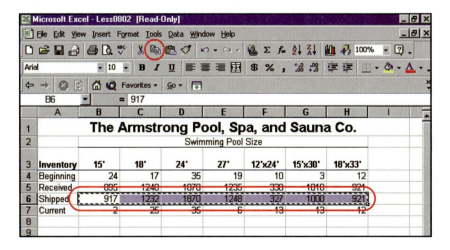

LESSON 8   CREATING CONNECTIONS   **259**

9 Close **Less0802**. Click **No** when you are prompted to save the changes. Select cell **B9** and click the **Paste** button. The number of pools shipped is placed below the total number of pools sold.

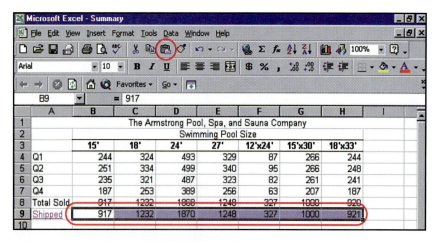

10 Select cell **A10**, type **Difference**, and press Tab.

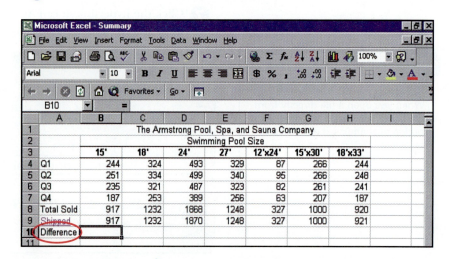

11 Type **=B9-B8** in cell **B10**, and click the **Enter** button on the formula bar.

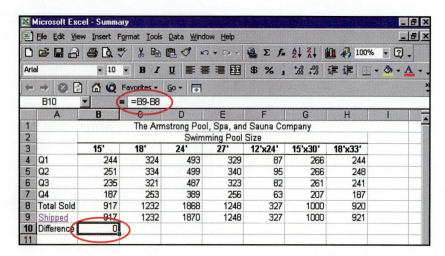

12 Drag the fill handle to the right to cell **H10** and release the mouse. The cells that have a value other than zero indicate a problem. In this case, there are three more pools shipped than were sold.

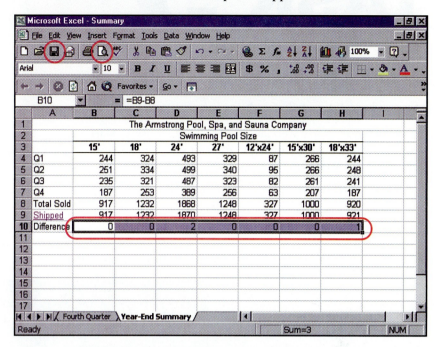

13 Save your work. Add your name to the header as shown in the figure. Preview the sheet and select **Zoom** to enlarge it.

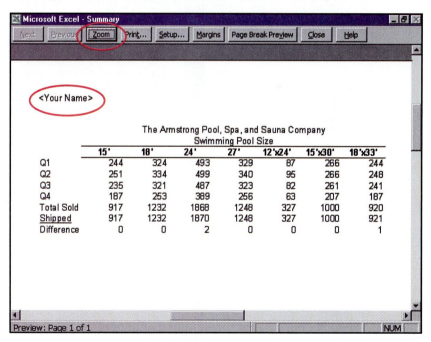

14 Print the sheet. Close the workbook and save your changes.

LESSON 8 CREATING CONNECTIONS

TASK 5

Saving a Worksheet as a Web Page

Why would I do this?

Excel 2000 uses a new Web language called Extensible Markup Language, or *XML*, that allows you to interact with a worksheet using a browser. You can save your worksheet as an interactive Web page that can be used by anyone on the Web who has permission to view your site.

In this task, you save a worksheet as a web page to provide contest information.

1 Open **Less0803** from the **Student\Lesson08** folder on the CD-ROM disc and save the file on your floppy disk as **Contest**. The new title appears in the title bar.

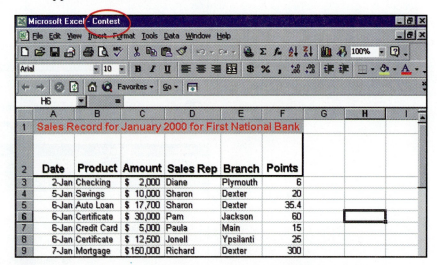

2 Choose **File**, **Save as Web Page**. The Save As dialog box opens.

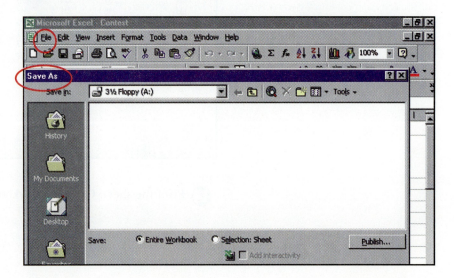

LEARN EXCEL 2000

3 Type the name **WebBank** in the **File name** box.

4 Click the **Selection: Sheet** option and the **Add interactivity** option.

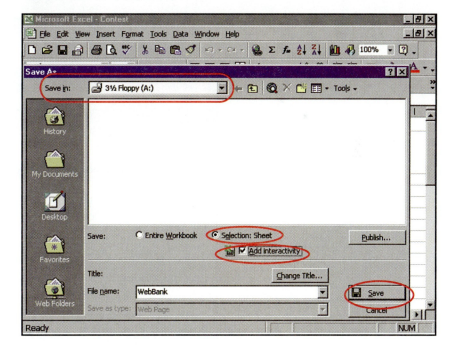

LESSON 8   CREATING CONNECTIONS   263

5 Click the **Change Title** button. Type the title **Bank Sales Contest.**

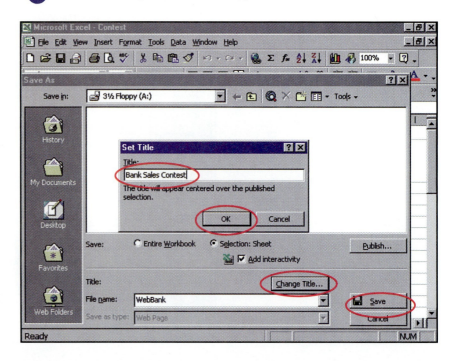

6 Click **OK**. Confirm that the file will be saved to your floppy disk. Click **Save**. The Web page is saved on your disk.

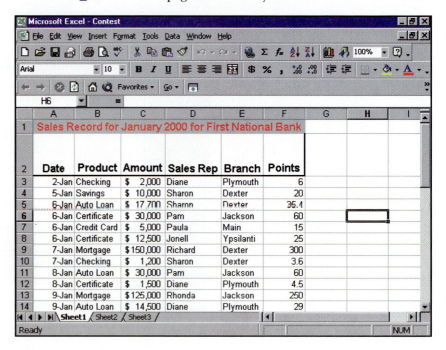

7 Close the workbook and save the changes. Close **Excel**.

TASK 6

Using a Worksheet on the Web

Why would I do this?

Recent versions of Web browsers, such as Microsoft's Internet Explorer 5.0, can read files that have XML features. Older browsers display a static page. Using the XML feature, you can interact with a worksheet on the Web in new ways.

In this task, you launch Internet Explorer 5 and browse the WebBank.htm file on your disk as if it were posted to a Web server.

1 Launch **Microsoft Internet Explorer** 5.0 or another browser that supports XML. The browser opens and displays the home page that it is set to display.

> **Caution:** If you are not connected to the Internet, the browser may display an error message. You do not need to be connected to the Internet to practice using this feature.

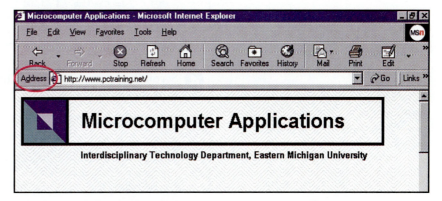

2 Type the location of the WebBank.htm file that you created in the previous task. If you saved it on your floppy disk in drive **A**, type **A:\WebBank.htm** in the A**d**dress box.

LESSON 8 CREATING CONNECTIONS 265

③ Press `Enter`. The worksheet opens in the browser as an interactive Web page.

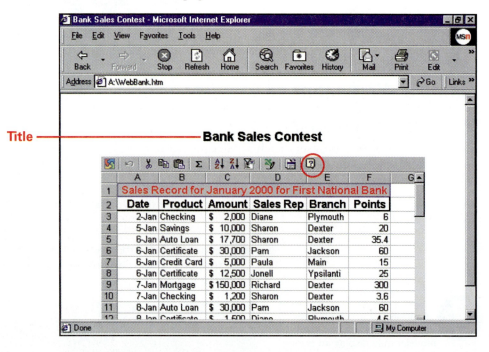

Title — **Bank Sales Contest**

In Depth: Click the **Help** button on the Web worksheet to see a nice example of how a Web worksheet can be used interactively on the Internet.

④ Scroll the browser window, if necessary, to display the entire worksheet window.

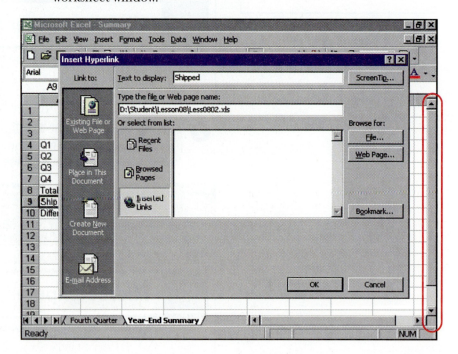

5 Click anywhere in the data below row 2. Click the **Sort Ascending** button and choose **Product** from the list. The rows of data are sorted alpabetically by product name.

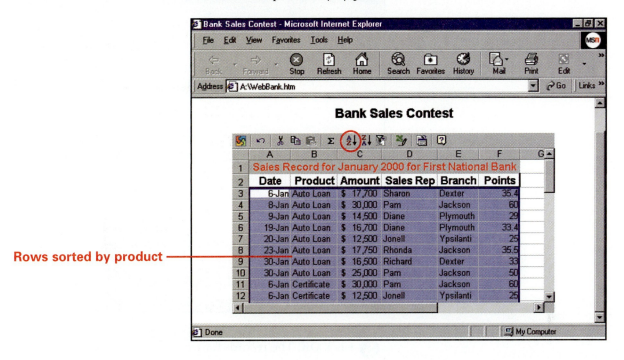

Rows sorted by product

6 Click on any of the column headings in row **2**. Click the **AutoFilter** button. AutoFilter arrows are added to each column.

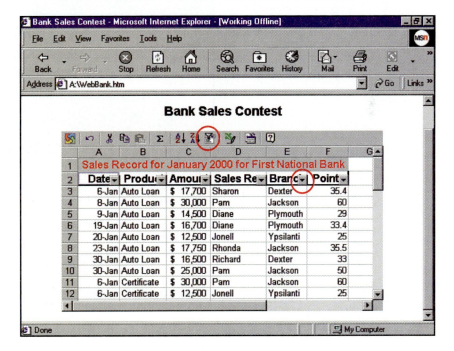

7 Click the **AutoFilter** arrow at the top of the **Branch** column. Deselect all the branches except **Main**.

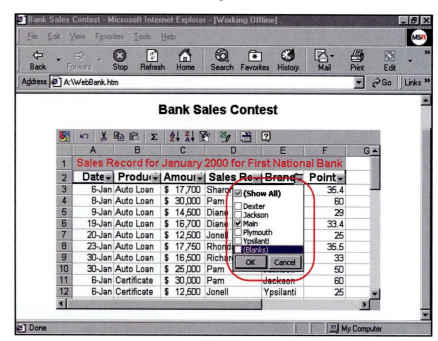

8 Click **OK**. The records for the Main Branch are displayed.

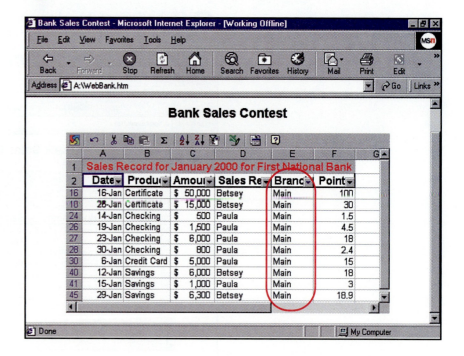

9 Click the **AutoFilter** arrow on the **Branch** column. Select the **Show All** option and click **OK**. All the rows are displayed.

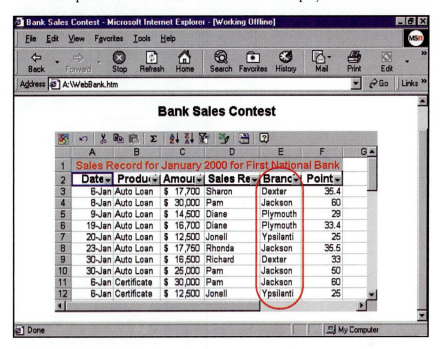

10 Scroll to the bottom of the worksheet and select the empty cell below the **Amount** column.

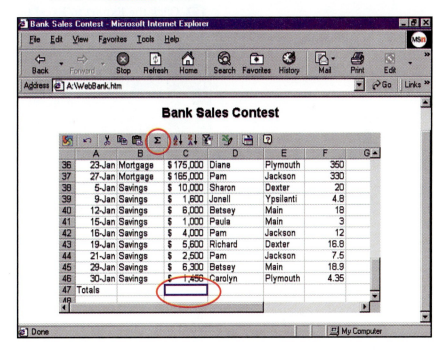

11. Double-click the **AutoSum** button. The cell displays the total of the amounts in the column above it. (If it displays a row of pound signs, double-click the boundary between the headings for columns **C** and **D** to adjust the width.)

AutoSum button

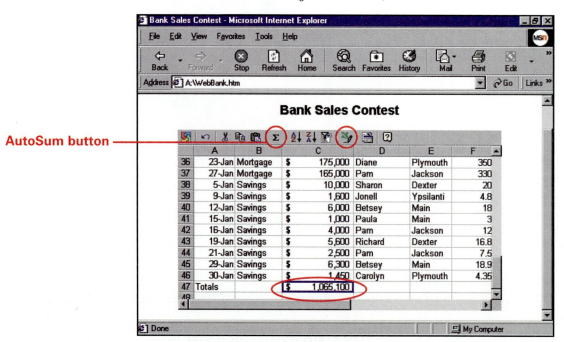

12. Click the **Export to Excel** button. The Excel program launches, and the worksheet opens in **Read Only** mode.

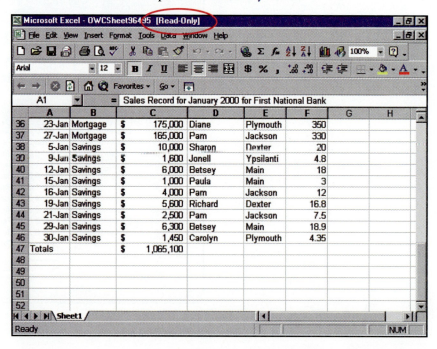

13. Choose **File**, **Save As**. Use the name **WebBank2** and set the **Save as type** box to **Microsoft Excel Workbook**. Save the workbook on your floppy disk. Close the workbook. Close **Excel**. Close the browser.

Comprehension Exercises

Comprehension exercises are designed to check your memory and understanding of the basic concepts in this lesson. You distinguish between true and false statements, identify new screen elements, and match terms with related statements. If you are uncertain of the correct answer, refer to the task number following each item (for example, T4 refers to Task 4) and review that task until you are confident that you can provide a correct response.

True-False

Circle either T or F.

T F 1. To move a worksheet in Excel, you click and drag the sheet tab to a new position. **(T1)**

T F 2. If you want cells in one worksheet to reflect changes that are made in another worksheet, you must start with an equal sign in the destination cell. **(T3)**

T F 3. In a formula, a reference to another worksheet is indicated by an exclamation point at the beginning and the end of the worksheet name. **(T3)**

T F 4. To copy data in a cell from one worksheet to another, choose **Edit**, **Worksheet**. **(T2)**

T F 5. To copy a row of cells from one worksheet to another, the entire row of cells on the source worksheet must be selected. **(T2)**

T F 6. To insert a hyperlink in a worksheet, click the Web button. **(T4)**

T F 7. To save the sheet as an interactive page suitable for publishing on the Internet, choose **File**, **Save as HTML**. **(T5)**

T F 8. You can tell when a worksheet label is a hyperlink because the label appears on the worksheet in a different color. **(T4)**

T F 8. If a worksheet is saved as an interactive Web page, you can sort the data on the sheet when viewing it with a Web browser. **(T6)**

T F 10. The Extensible Markup Language that makes interactive worksheets possible is known by the acronym EML. **(T6)**

Identifying Parts of the Excel Screen

Refer to the figure and identify the numbered parts of the screen. Write the letter of the correct label in the space next to the number.

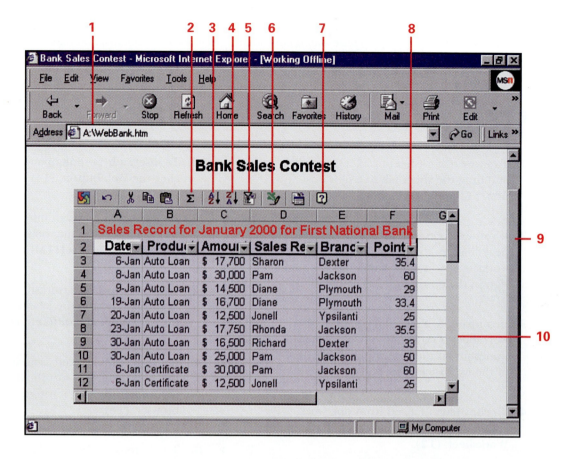

1. _____
2. _____
3. _____
4. _____
5. _____
6. _____
7. _____
8. _____
9. _____
10. _____

A. Help on the Web worksheet (**T6**)
B. Location of the file (in this case, it is on a disk drive, but could also be on an Internet server) (**T6**)
C. Browser's vertical scrollbar (**T6**)
D. AutoSum (**T6**)
E. Worksheet's vertical scrollbar (**T6**)
F. Sort Ascending (alphabetical order) (**T6**)
G. AutoFilter button (**T6**)
H. AutoFilter arrow (**T6**)
I. Sort Descending (**T6**)
J. Export to Excel (**T6**)

Matching

Match the statements below to the word or phrase that is the best match from the list. Write the letter of the matching word or phrase in the space provided next to the number.

1. ___ Used to move a sheet tab into view so it can be selected (**T1**)
2. ___ In a dialog box, this button is used to locate a file (**T4**)
3. ___ A button on an interactive Web page that sends a worksheet to Excel (**T6**)
4. ___ A formula showing a reference to a cell on another worksheet (**T3**)
5. ___ A worldwide network of computer connections that allows people to have access to thousands of online resources (**Introduction**)
6. ___ Used to designate the beginning of a formula (**T3**)
7. ___ A language used to make worksheets interactive on the Internet (**T5**)
8. ___ A file property of files on a CD-Rom disc (**T4**)
9. ___ Used to link a word or a label to a file (**T4**)
10. ___ Uniform resource locator (**T4**)

A. URL
B. Browse button
C. Insert Hyperlink button
D. Read-only
E. Export to Excel
F. ='Sheet1!A2'
G. =
H. eXtensible Markup Language
I. Internet
J. Tab scrolling buttons
K. Browser

Reinforcement Exercises

Reinforcement exercises are designed to reinforce the skills you have learned by applying them to a new situation. Detailed instructions are provided along with a figure, where appropriate, to illustrate the final result. The Reinforcement exercises that follow should be completed sequentially. Leave the workbook open at the end of each exercise for use in the next exercise until you are specifically directed to close it.

The Reinforcement exercises use the same file. Open **Less0804** from the **Student\Lesson08** folder on the CD-ROM disc and save it on your floppy disk as **Ex0801**.

R1—Summarize Income and Expenses by Quarter

Many companies provide quarterly reports to stockholders. The data provided in the first sheet displays the income and expenses by month. You summarize this data on Sheet2 into three-month periods (quarters).

1. Select **Sheet2**. Select cell **B4**, where the sum of the income for the months of January, February, and March should be displayed.
2. Click the **AutoSum** button once to place the sum function in cell **B4**.
3. Click the **2000** sheet tab and drag across cells **B9** though **D9** to identify the total income for the first three months of the year.
4. Press ⏎Enter or click the **Enter** button on the formula bar. The total income for those three months, 66699, displays in cell B4 of Sheet2.
5. Repeat this process to represent the total income for April, May, and June in cell **C4**. The number, 74549, displays in cell C4. (Do not use the fill handle for this exercise.)

LESSON 8   CREATING CONNECTIONS

6. Repeat this process to find the remaining two quarterly summations of income and the four quarterly expenses.

7. Select cell **F4** and use the **AutoSum** function to add the four quarters of income. (The total should be 321668.) Repeat this process for the total expenses in cell **F5**.

8. Rename Sheet2 as **Quarterly Report**. Save the workbook and leave it open for use in the next exercise.

R2—Chart Income and Expense by Quarter

Use the file **Ex0801** created in the previous exercise.

1. Select the **Quarterly Report** sheet, if necessary.

2. Create a column chart to compare the income and expense data in these cells by quarter. Add a chart title, axis labels, and a legend as shown in the figure. Save the chart as a separate sheet named **Quarterly Chart**. Enlarge these to make them more legible.

3. Create a second chart that compares the total income and expenses for the entire year as shown in the figure. (Remember to use Ctrl to select columns that are not next to each other.) Save it on its own sheet named **Annual Chart**. Label it as shown.

4. Save the workbook and leave it open for use in the next exercise.

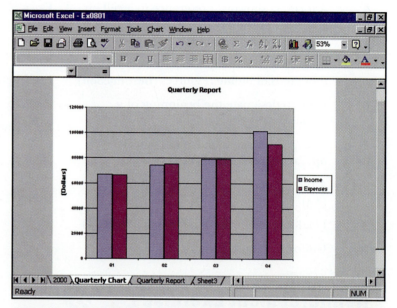

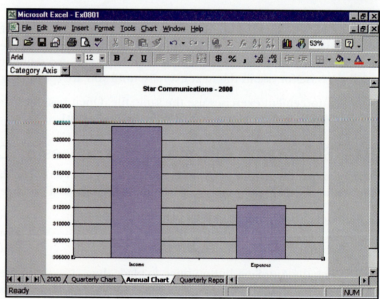

274 LEARN EXCEL 2000

R3—Save a Summary Sheet as an Interactive Web Page

You can share this data with others by saving it as a Web page that can be placed on a Web server or in a folder that is available to others on a local area network.

1. Open the file **Ex0801**. Select the **2000** sheet. Select cells **A1** through **M18**.

2. Save the selected area as a Web page on your floppy disk. Choose the **Add interactivity** option and name it **Ex0801.htm** as shown in the **File name** box.

3. Launch Internet Explorer 5.0 or another browser capapble of reading XML and type the file's location in the browser's **Address** box. It should look like the figure shown.

4. Switch back to Excel. Save the workbook and close it. Close **Excel**.

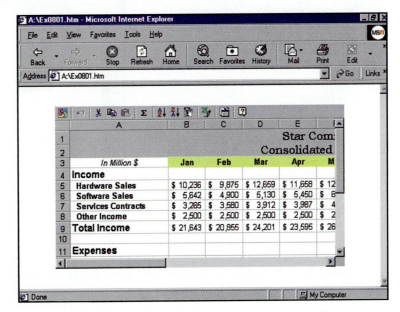

Challenge

Challenge exercises are designed to test your ability to apply your skills to new situations with less detailed instruction. These exercises also challenge you to expand your repertoire of skills by using Excel commands that are similar to those you have already learned. The desired outcome is clearly defined, but you have more freedom to choose the steps needed to achieve the required result.

The following Challenge exercises use the **Summary** file that was created in the lesson. They also use a Word document file, **Less0806.doc**, that is opened in Word.

C1—Pasting a Worksheet into a Document

It is possible to include a worksheet in a Word document in several ways, depending on the application. A worksheet can be copied and pasted in such a way that it is converted into a Word table. It is also possible to paste it as an actual worksheet that you can activate and edit. In this case, you can choose to maintain a link between the document and the parent worksheet so that changes in one are reflected in the other.

Goal: Paste the Armstrong Pool, Spa, and Sauna Co. worksheet into a letter to the employees, then activate the worksheet and look at various sheets within the workbook.

Use the following guidelines:

1. Launch Microsoft Word. Open **Less0805.doc** from the **Student\Lesson08** folder on the CD-ROM disc and save it on your floppy disk as **Ex0802.doc**.

2. Launch Excel and open the **Summary** file on your disk that you created in this lesson.

3. Select the data on the **Year-End Summary** sheet and copy it.

4. Switch to the **Ex0802** document in Word and place the insertion point in one of the blank lines between the paragraphs.

5. Choose **Edit**, **Paste**.

6. Save the document. Leave the document and the workbook open for use in the next exercise.

C2—Using Paste Special to Place a Worksheet Within a Document

In this exercise, you use the Paste Special option to actually place a worksheet in the document.

Goal: Paste the Summary workbook into the Less0806 document without linking them together.

1. Switch to the Word document **Ex0802.doc** if necessary. Save it as **Ex0803.doc** on your floppy disk.

2. Delete the table that was pasted into the document in the previous exercise. (Use **Table**, **Delete**, **Table**.)

3. Switch to the Excel workbook named **Summary** and select the **Year-End Summary** sheet. Select cells that contain data on this sheet and copy them.

4. Switch to the **Ex0803** document in Word and place the insertion point in one of the blank lines between the paragraphs.

5. Choose **Edit**, **Paste Special**. Paste the Microsoft Excel Worksheet object (do not Paste **L**ink it).

6. Delete extra blank lines as needed. Double-click on the table to activate the worksheet.

7. Save the Word document. Close the Word document, but leave the workbook open for use in the next exercise.

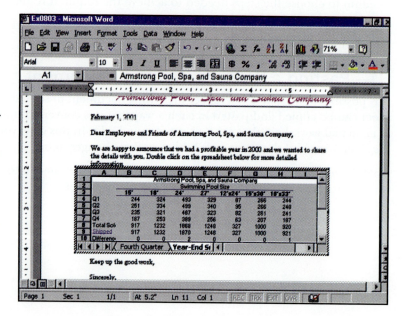

276 LEARN EXCEL 2000

C3—Save a Workbook as a Web Page

If a workbook has several sheets, you can save the entire workbook as a Web page.

Goal: Save the Summary workbook as a series of Web pages that can be selected using navigation buttons.

1. Use the Summary file on yur disk. Use the **File**, **Save as Web page** option to save the entire workbook to your disk. Change the name of the file to **Ex0803.htm** in the **File name** box.

2. Launch your Web browser (Internet Explorer 5.0 or another browser capable of reading XML). Type the location of the file in the browser's address box. (If your file is on the floppy disk, the address is probably **A:\Ex0803.htm**.)

3. Open the Web page. The workbook displays with sheet tabs as shown in the figure.

4. Navigate the different sheets of the workbook using the sheet tabs at the bottom of the page.

5. Close the browser. Close the workbook.

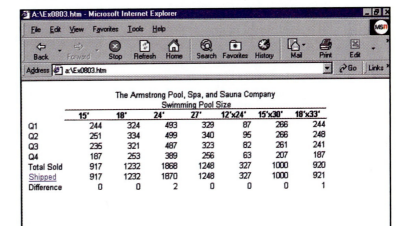

Discovery

Discovery exercises are designed to help you learn how to teach yourself a new skill. In each exercise, you discover something new that is related to the topic taught in this lesson. You may be directed to use built-in wizards or some of the extensive Help features provided in Excel to discover new features and learn new skills with minimum assistance from books or instructors. The required outcome demonstrates your ability to apply the new skill. You determine the choice of topic, worksheet design, and steps of execution.

The following Discovery exercises use the same file. Open the file **Less0806** from the **Student\Lesson08** folder on the CD-ROM disc and save it as **Ex0804** on your floppy disk.

D1—Insert a Hyperlink to a Specific Sheet in Another Worksheet

If you are linking your worksheet to another workbook, you may want to go to a specific sheet or named range within that workbook. Excel allows you to examine a list of sheet names and range names within the target workbook and select the specific place to link to within the workbook.

Goal: Place a hyperlink in a worksheet that links to a specific sheet within another workbook.

1. Open **EX0804** and select a cell in column **A** below the first eleven rows. Type **Go to Pool** and enter it. Select the cell if necessary.

2. Click the **Insert Hyperlink** button. Click the **Browse for File** button and find the **Summary** file on your disk that you created in this lesson. (Check the **File of type** box to make sure the dialog box will display the workbooks.)

3. Once the Summary.xls file is selected, use the **Bookmark** button and select the Fourth Quarter cell reference.

4. Click on the resulting hyperlink to test it. The Summary workbook opens to the Fourth Quarter sheet.

5. Use the **Back** button on the Web toolbar to return to the Ex0804 worksheet.

6. Close the workbook and save your changes.

D2—Change the Properties of a Cell in an Interactive Worksheet

If you are using an interactive Web page that someone else has posted, you can change some of the cell formatting and try different scenarios. In this exercise, you open a Web page on the CD-ROM disc and compare loan balance and resale value of a car. You can change the variables on the left of the screen and then examine the columns on the right to determine if you are ever "upside-down" (loan balance is greater than the resale value) on the loan. In order to make such a comparison easier, you must reformat the columns so that they both display in currency format.

Goal: Learn the limits and abilities of the Web version of the worksheet. Also, format the cells in the Resale Value column to currency to make the comparison easier.

1. Locate the file **Less0807.htm** in the **Student\Lesson08** folder of the CD-ROM disc and copy it to your floppy disk. Rename it **Ex0807** with an XML-enabled browser such as Internet Explorer 5.0 and open the file.

2. Format the cells in column B and column E as shown in the figure. (Right-click on the cell, range of cells, or column heading and use the **Property Toolbox** option.)

3. Scroll down the two columns. Notice that at one point, you owe about $1,000 more on the car than you could get if you sold it (or would get from the insurance company if you totaled it).

4. Write a formula in column G to find the difference between the loan balance and the resale value. See if you can figure out how to copy that formula into the other cells in that column without doing it one cell at a time.

5. Try different amounts of down payment in increments of $500 until you find an amount that is sufficient to ensure that you can always sell the car for more than the balance on the loan.

6. When you have found the down payment that is necessary to prevent a negative or upside-down situation, print the sheet (at least the part that shows in the browser window).

7. Use the Export to Excel feature, then save the worksheet on your disk as **Ex0805.xls**. Close the browser.

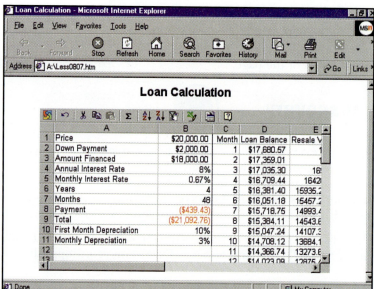

D3—Posting an Interactive Worksheet to a Web Server

To do this exercise, you need to have access to a local area network and a shared folder on that network, or have the permission and software necessary to post a Web page to a Web server. Ask your instructor if either of these is available.

Goal: Place an interactive Web page in a location where others can use it.

1. If you have access to a public folder on your local area server, copy the file **Less0807.htm** to that location. Use your browser to open the file at that location.

2. If you have a user ID and password to post pages to a Web server, transfer the file **Less0807.htm** from the CD-ROM disc to that server. Browse the page on the server.

Glossary

Absolute reference A cell reference that will not change when copied, moved, or filled into other cells.

Argument A variable in a function, to which a value will be assigned when the function is executed.

AutoCorrect A customizable tool that automatically corrects typographical errors or expands user-defined shortcuts.

AutoFilter An option in the Data, Filter menu that adds buttons to field names so data can be restricted based on specified criteria.

Bar chart A chart that compares values across categories. The data bars are horizontal.

Boldface A darker version of characters used to add emphasis.

Browser A program such as Internet Explorer or Netscape Navigator that allows you to connect to the Internet and view Web pages.

Calculations Mathematical operations involving data in the worksheet cells.

Cell The intersection of a row and column.

Chart A graphic representation of a series of numbers; sometimes referred to as a graph.

Chart sub-type A variation on a basic chart type that allows for different emphasis and views of a chart.

Chart Wizard A mini-program that walks you through the steps involved in creating a chart.

Collapsible outline The framework that is created when you add subtotals by using the Data, Sort option. This framework, or outline, at the left side of your spreadsheet can be collapsed or expanded to hide or reveal the details of each change in category.

Column chart A chart that compares values across categories. The data columns are vertical.

Copy A command used to duplicate values or formulas to cells that are not adjacent to the original cell.

Database management A program like Microsoft Access that can manage many pieces of data by sorting, grouping, and filtering the data.

Default A preselected choice.

Display settings The default choices that determine such things as how many rows and columns will be shown on the screen. They can be found by clicking on the **Start** button and choosing **Settings**. It is not proper etiquette to change them if you do not have the permission of the computer's owner.

Field name A column label used in a database to identify a category of information in a database file.

Fill Method used to complete a group of adjacent cells with the same labels, values, formulas, or a series such as dates, numbers, days of the week, or months of the year.

Fill handle A small black square in the lower-right corner of selected cells. When you point to this area, the square turns into a plus sign. You can click on the handle to drag the contents of one cell to other adjacent cells or to create a series, such as a series of dates.

Filter To limit the data shown based on criteria set for a field.

Formatted Data storage areas are already marked electronically on the disk. The disk is ready to receive data.

Formula bar A bar below the Formatting toolbar that displays the address of the currently selected cell and any data in the cell.

Gridlines Lines on a worksheet that separate one cell from another. Gridlines can be turned off both on the worksheet itself and in the printout.

Handle A small black box in the corners and sides of a chart or graphic object.

Headers Letters or numbers used to identify a row or column.

Horizontal scrollbar The scrollbar found at the bottom of the screen.

Hyperlink A link that connects a word or a label in one location to a file in another location. Can be used to go directly to information in another file.

Insertion point A vertical line in the text that marks the current point of text entry.

Internet A worldwide communications network of computer connections that allows people to have access to thousands of online resources.

Launch A synonym for start, begin, or open. Windows 95/98 has a special button named the Start button, so we say that we "launch" a program to avoid using the same word.

Legend A list that identifies a pattern or color used in an Excel worksheet chart.

Line chart A chart that includes a line running through each data point, usually used to show trends.

Linear regression analysis A mathematical procedure that produces a straight line that is the best fit to a group of data points on a an x-y scatter chart where y (value) is dependant on x (category).

Local area network(LAN) A system that uses telephone lines or cables to join two or more personal computers, enabling them to communicate with each other.

Marquee A box of moving, blinking lines that resembles the flashing lights around the marquee of a theater.

Office Assistant An animated feature of Excel that guides the user to additional information.

Paste A command used to insert a label, a value, or formula from another cell or range of cells.

Pie chart Displays the contribution of each value to the total.

Records Rows in a database used to keep all of the relevant data about a single transaction, person, or event.

Registered programs When you install a program, Windows records this fact. Most Windows programs use unique extensions to identify the files they create.

Relative reference A cell reference that will change when the formula is copied, moved, or filled into other cells.

Screen resolution The number of picture elements displayed across and down the screen. The examples in this book represent a resolution of 640 X 480. If your screen is set to a higher resolution, such as 800 X 600, you will see more columns and rows on your screen.

ScreenTip A box that provides additional information when you point at a button or hyperlink.

Select When you click on a cell, it is outlined with a dark border. It is then ready to be edited by entering or changing the data in the cell.

Sheet A synonym for worksheet; identified by tabs at the bottom of the window.

Sheet tab A tab near the bottom of the workbook window that displays the name of the worksheet.

Sort To arrange data in a spreadsheet or a database into ascending or descending order.

Standard toolbar The toolbar at the top of the screen that has the **Save** and **Print** buttons on it.

Toggle A button on a menu bar, toolbar, or in a dialog box that, when clicked, turns a feature or a toolbar on or off.

Uniform resource locator (URL) Address on the Internet.

Vertical scrollbar The scrollbar found at the right side of the screen.

Web Formally known as the World Wide Web or simply WWW, a system of computers and files by which users may view and interact with a variety of information.

Workbook A collection of worksheets saved under one filename.

Worksheet A set of cells that are identified by row and column headers. Also referred to as a sheet.

XML Extensible Markup Language, a Web language that allows the program to attach additional information to data.

Zoom The percent of screen magnification. It may be set using a control found on the right side of the Standard toolbar.

Index

A

absolute formulas
    filling cells, 150-153
    see also formulas
adding
    borders, 61-65
    dates, 119-121
    lines to columns, 61-63
    mathematical calculations, 138-140
    names to headers, 119-121
    shading, 61
adjusting
    cells, 53-55
    columns, 53-55
    fonts, 60-61
    worksheet views, 110-113
    worksheets, 119-121
    zoom, 110-113
aligning text, 56-59
Answer Wizard, 29
Arial fonts, modifying, 60-61
Auditing command (Tools menu), 142
AutoCorrect, 85-86
    dialog box, 85
AutoCorrect command (Tools menu), 85
AutoFilter, 224
AutoSum, 19
axis, formatting, 198

B-C

bar charts, 193, 195
    see also charts
boldface text, 60
    see also text
borders, adding, 61-65

calculating
    formulas, 140-143
        conditioning/counting, 161-167
        filling cells, 144-153
        financial, 156-161
        loan repayments, 154-155
    numbers, 138-140
    see also formulas; functions; mathematical calculations
CD (compact disc), 43
cells
    contents, 81, 113-116
    copying, 113-116
    editing, 15-18, 76-77
    fill handles, 103
    filling, 104
    formulas
        calculating, 140-143
        conditional/counting, 161-167
        filling, 144-153
        financial, 156-161
        loan repayments, 154-155
    groups, 45-48
    magnification, 110-113
    modifying, 53-55
    numbers, 11-15
    numeric series, 104-109
    ranges, 117-119
    references, 138-140
    selecting, 8-9
    text
        aligning, 56-59
        entering, 11-15
Cells command (Format menu), 57, 109
changing
    cells, 53-55
    columns, 53-55

fonts, 60-61
worksheet views, 110-113
worksheets, 119-121
zoom, 110-113
Chart Title command (Format menu), 197
Chart Type dialog box, 201
Chart Wizard dialog box, 187-189
charts, 185
   bar, 193-195
   creating, 185-189
   editing, 196-199
   pie, 190-192
   printing, 204, 206
   trends, 186-189
   types, 200-203
Clear All command (Edit menu), 52
Clear Formats command (Edit menu), 82
closing
   Excel, 31
   workbooks, 24
Collapse dialog box, 125, 158
collapsible outlines, 222
   see also outlines
column charts, 193-195
   see also charts
columns
   comparing, 229-231
   customizing, 61-65
   deleting, 78-79
   freezing, 110-113
   inserting, 78-79
   labels, 124-126
   modifying, 53-55
   selecting, 45, 48
   text, 56-59
Columns command (Insert menu), 79

commands
   Data menu
      Filter, 224
      Sort, 219
      Subtotals, 220
   Edit menu
      Clear All, 52
      Clear Formats, 82
   File menu
      Page Setup, 119, 125, 223
      Print, 118
      Save As, 43
      Save as Web page, 262
   Format menu
      Cells, 57, 109
      Chart Title, 197
   Insert menu
      Columns, 79
      Rows, 79
      Worksheet, 80, 247
   Tools menu
      Auditing, 142
      AutoCorrect, 85
      Options, 12-15
   Windows menu
      Freeze Pane, 112, 228
      Unfreeze Pane, 113
compact disc (CD), 43
comparing
   bar charts, 193-195
   columns, 228-231
conditional formulas, calculating, 161-167
configuring
   charts, 196-199
   summary sheets, 249-251
   worksheets, 119-121
   see also customizing; preferences

contributions, pie charts, 190-192
copying
    cell content, 113-116
    see also moving
correcting
    spelling errors, 86
    see also AutoCorrect
counting formulas
    calculating, 161-167
    see also formulas; functions
currency, formatting, 49-52
customizing
    charts, 196-199
    columns, 61-65
    headers/footers, 121
    text, 60-61
    worksheets, 119-121
    see also configuring; preferences

D

data
    grouping, 220-222
    rows, 224-230
    subtotaling, 220, 222
Data menu commands
    Filter, 224
    Sort, 219
    Subtotal, 220
datasheets
    cells
        aligning text, 56-59
        calculating formulas, 140-143
        conditional/counting formulas, 161-167
        copying, 113-116
        contents, 81, 113-116
        deleting content, 81
        editing, 15-18, 76-77
        entering numbers, 11-15
        entering text, 11-15
        fill handles, 103
        filling, 104
        filling formulas, 144-153

    financial formulas, 156-161
    groups, 45-48
    loan repayment formulas, 154-155
    magnification, 110-113
    modifying, 53-55
    numeric series, 104-109
    ranges, 117-119
    references, 138-140
    selecting, 8-9
column/row labels, 124-126
columns
    comparing, 229-231
    customizing, 61-65
    deleting, 78-79
    freezing, 110-113
    inserting, 78-79
    labels, 124-126
    modifying, 53-55
    selecting, 45, 48
    text, 56, 58-59
data
    comparing columns, 228-231
    filtering, 224-227
    grouping, 220-222
    subtotaling, 220
editing, 15-18
filters, 232, 234
fonts, 60-61
formulas, 168-173
    bar, 17-18
    calculating, 140-143
    editing, 15-18
    entering, 11-15
    filling cells, 144-149
    revising, 78-79
    summing, 19
hyperlinks, 257-261
labels, 102-104
    column/rows, 124-126
    creating, 102-104
    rows, 104-109
    text, 56-59
mathematical calculations, 138-140
navigating, 4-8

numeric series, 104-109
Office Assistant, 25-31
outlines, 232-234
printing, 117-121
rows
   creating labels, 104-109
   data, 224-227
   deleting, 78-79
   freezing, 110-113
   inserting, 78-79
   printing labels, 124-126
   selecting, 45, 48
   sorting, 219-220
selecting, 4-8, 45-48
sheets, 78-79
spelling checker, 90-91
subtotals, 222-224
summary sheets
   configuring, 249-251
   inserting, 246-248
   linking, 252-256
   moving, 246-248
text, 88-89
totals, 232, 234
views, 110-113
Web pages
   saving as, 262-264
   viewing, 265-270
dates
   customizing, 104-109
   formatting, 49-52
   headers, 119-121
   see also numbers
decimal places
   formatting, 49-52
   see also numbers
deleting
   cells, 81
   columns, 78-79
   filters, 232-234
   rows, 78-79
   sheets, 78-79
   totals, 232-234

dialog boxes
   AutoCorrect, 85
   Chart Type, 201
   Chart Wizard, 187-189
   Collapse, 125, 158
   Expand, 126, 158
   Format Cells, 51, 109
   Format Chart Title, 197
   Header, 206
   Insert Hyperlink, 257
   Link to File, 258
   Open, 42
   Page Setup, 149, 206
   Print, 206
   Save As, 43
   Sort, 219
   Spelling, 90
   Subtotals, 220
disks, saving workbooks, 22
dividing (mathematical calculations), 138-140
dragging
   cell content, 114
   see also copying; moving

E

Edit menu commands
   Clear All, 52
   Clear Formats, 82
editing
   AutoCorrect, 85-86
   cells, 15-18, 76-77
   charts, 196-199
   spelling checker, 90-91
entering
   numbers, 11-15
   text, 88-89
errors
   spelling checker, 90-91
   text, 85-86
   undoing, 83-84
   see also troubleshooting

Excel
- closing, 31
- see also cells; worksheets

exercises
- Lesson 1, 33-39
- Lesson 2, 67-73
- Lesson 3, 92, 94-99
- Lesson 4, 128-135
- Lesson 5, 174-182
- Lesson 6, 208-215
- Lesson 7, 236-243
- Lesson 8, 271-278

existing workbooks, opening, 42-43

exiting
- Excel, 31
- workbooks, 24

Expand dialog box, 126, 158

F

fields
- editing, 76-77
- filling, 104
- text, 11-15
- see also cells; columns

File menu commands
- Page Setup, 119-125, 223
- Print, 118
- Save As, 43
- Save as Web Page, 262

files
- cells
  - aligning text, 56-59
  - calculating formulas, 140-143
  - conditional/counting formulas, 161-167
  - contents, 81, 113-116
  - copying, 113-116
  - deleting content, 81
  - editing, 15-18, 76-77
  - entering numbers, 11-15
  - entering text, 11-15
  - fill handles, 103
  - filling, 104
  - filling formulas, 144-153
  - financial formulas, 156-161
  - groups, 45-48
  - loan repayment formulas, 154-155
  - magnification, 110-113
  - modifying, 53-55
  - numeric series, 104-109
  - ranges, 117-119
  - references, 138-140
  - selecting, 8-9
- column/row labels, 124-126
- columns
  - comparing, 229-231
  - customizing, 61-65
  - deleting, 78-79
  - freezing, 110-113
  - inserting, 78-79
  - labels, 124-126
  - modifying, 53-55
  - selecting, 45, 48
  - text, 56-59
- data
  - comparing columns, 228-231
  - filtering, 224-227
  - grouping, 220-222
  - subtotaling, 220
- editing, 15-18
- filters, 232, 234
- fonts, 60-61
- formulas, 168-173
  - bar, 17-18
  - calculating, 140-143
  - editing, 15-18
  - entering, 11-15
  - filling cells, 144-149
  - revising, 78-79
  - summing, 19
- hyperlinks, 257-261
- labels, 102-104
  - column/rows, 124-126
  - creating, 102-104
  - rows, 104-109
  - text, 56-59

mathematical calculations, 138-140
navigating, 4-8
numeric series, 104-109
Office Assistant, 25-31
outlines, 232-234
printing, 117-121
rows
   creating labels, 104-109
   data, 224-227
   deleting, 78-79
   freezing, 110-113
   inserting, 78-79
   printing labels, 124-126
   selecting, 45, 48
   sorting, 219-220
selecting, 4-8, 45-48
sheets, 78-79
spelling checker, 90-91
subtotals, 222-224
summary sheets
   configuring, 249-251
   inserting, 246-248
   linking, 252-256
   moving, 246-248
text, 88-89
totals, 232, 234
views, 110-113
Web pages
   saving as, 262-264
   viewing, 265-270
filling cells, 104, 144-153
fills
   cell content, 113-116
   handles, 103
Filter command (Data menu), 224
filters, deleting, 232, 234
financial formulas, calculating, 156-161
floppy disks, saving workbooks, 22
fonts, modifying, 60-61
footers, customizing, 121
Format Cells dialog box, 51, 109
Format Chart Title dialog box, 197

Format menu commands
   Cells, 57, 109
   Chart Title, 197
formatting
   axis, 198
   columns, 65
   deleting, 81
   numbers, 49-52
   numeric series, 104-109
Formatting toolbar, 65
forms, copying cell content, 113-116
formulas, 168-173
   bar, 17-18
   calculating, 140-143
   editing, 15-18
   entering, 11-15
   filling cells, 144-149
   revising, 78-79
   summing, 19
Freeze Panes command (Windows menu), 228
freezing panes, 110-113
functions, summing, 19

G-H

gridlines, printing, 123
grouping data, 220, 222
groups, selecting, 45, 48

handles, fills, 103
Header dialog box, 206
headers
   customizing, 121
   names, 119
help, 25-31
horizontal scrollbars, 6, 8
hyperlinks, inserting, 257-261

I-J

Insert Hyperlink dialog box, 257
Insert menu commands
   Columns, 79
   Rows, 79
   Worksheet, 80, 247

inserting
    columns, 78-79
    hyperlinks, 257-261
    rows, 78-79
    sheets, 78-79
    summary sheets, 246-248
    text, 11-15
italicized text
    aligning, 56-59
    automatically entering, 88-89
    editing, 15-18, 76-77
    entering, 11-15
    errors, 85-86
    modifying, 60-61
    spelling checker, 90-91
    wrapping, 57

K-L

labels
    column/rows, 124-126
    creating, 102-104
    rows, 104-109
    text, 56-59
length, modifying, 53-55
Lesson 1 exercises, 32-39
Lesson 2 exercises, 67-73
Lesson 3 exercises, 92-99
Lesson 4 exercises, 128-135
Lesson 5 exercises, 174-182
Lesson 6 exercises, 207-215
Lesson 7 exercises, 236-243
Lesson 8 exercises, 271-278
line charts, 186
    trends, 186-189
    see also charts
Link to File dialog box, 258
linking summary sheets, 252-256
links
    inserting, 257-261
    see also hyperlinks
loans, calculating, 154-155

M-N

magnifying worksheets, 110-113
marquees, 19
mathematical calculations, 138-140
    formulas, 140-143, 168-173
modifying
    cells, 53-55
    columns, 53-55
    fonts, 60-61
    worksheet views, 110-113
    worksheets, 119-121
    zoom, 110-113
moving
    cell content, 113-116
    summary sheets, 246-248
    see also copying; dragging
multiplying (mathematical calculations), 138-140

naming, adding, 119-121
navigating workbooks, 4, 6, 8
new features, XML, 262-270
numbers
    editing, 15-18, 76-77
    entering, 11-15
    formatting, 49-52
    mathematical calculations, 138-140
    modifying length, 53-55
    see also data; formulas; functions
numeric series, customizing, 104-109

O-P

Office Assistant, 25-31
Open dialog box, 42
opening workbooks, 42-43
Options command (Tools menu), 12-15
outlines
    collapsible, 222
    deleting, 232, 234

Page Setup command (File menu), 119, 125, 223
Page Setup dialog box, 149, 206
panes, freezing, 110-113

pasting
    cell content, 113-116
    see also copying; moving
pie charts, 190-192
    see also charts
preferences
    charts, 196-199
    summary sheets, 249-251
    worksheets, 119-121
    see also configuring; customizing
previewing
    chart types, 200-203
    worksheets, 117-119
Print command (File menu), 118
Print dialog box, 206
Print Preview toolbar, Page Setup button, 125
printing
    charts, 204-206
    gridlines, 123
    help, 29-31
    transparencies, 206
    workbooks, 24
    worksheets, 117-119
        column/row labels, 124-126
        customizing, 119-121
proofreading, 85-86
    spelling checker, 90-91
    see also revision marks

Q-R

quitting
    Excel, 31
    workbooks, 24

ranges, selecting, 117-119
Read Only Memory (ROM), 43
recording
    workbooks, 21-22
    see also saving
records, 218
    columns, 228-231
    filtering, 224-227
    see also rows

redoing changes, 83-84
relative formulas
    filling cells, 150-153
    see also formulas
removing
    cells, 81
    columns, 78-79
    filters, 232-234
    rows, 78-79
    sheets, 78-79
    totals, 232-234
reversing
    errors, 83-84
    see also deleting
revision marks, 85-86
    spelling checker, 90-91
    formulas, 78-79
    see also proofreading
ROM (Read Only Memory), 43
rounding numbers, 49-52
rows
    data, 224-227
    deleting, 78-79
    freezing, 110-113
    inserting, 78-79
    labels
        creating, 104-109
        printing, 124-126
    selecting, 45, 48
    sorting, 219-220
    see also records
Rows command (Insert menu), 79

S

Save As command (File menu), 43
Save As dialog box, 43
Save as Web page command (File menu), 262
saving
    workbooks, 21-22
    worksheets as Web pages, 262-264
schedules, creating, 105
scrollbars, 6, 8

selecting
- cells, 8-9
  - ranges, 117-119
- groups of cells, 45-48
- worksheets, 4-8

sequential labels
- creating, 102-104
- *see also* labels

shading
- adding, 61-65
- *see also* formatting

sheets
- configuring, 249-251
- deleting, 78-79
- inserting, 78-79
- linking, 252-256
- moving., 246
- *see also* summary sheets; worksheets

Sort command (Data menu), 219
Sort dialog box, 219
sorting
- data, 220-222
- rows, 219-220

spelling
- AutoCorrect, 86
- checker, 90-91
- dialog box, 90

spreadsheets
- cells
  - aligning text, 56-59
  - calculating formulas, 140-143
  - conditional/counting formulas, 161-167
  - copying, 113-116
  - contents, 81, 113-116
  - deleting content, 81
  - editing, 15-18, 76-77
  - entering numbers, 11-15
  - entering text, 11-15
  - fill handles, 103
  - filling, 104
  - filling formulas, 144-153
  - financial formulas, 156-161
  - groups, 45-48
  - loan repayment formulas, 154-155
  - magnification, 110-113
  - modifying, 53-55
  - numeric series, 104-109
  - ranges, 117-119
  - references, 138-140
  - selecting, 8-9
- column/row labels, 124-126
- columns
  - comparing, 229-231
  - customizing, 61-65
  - deleting, 78-79
  - freezing, 110-113
  - inserting, 78-79
  - labels, 124-126
  - modifying, 53-55
  - selecting, 45, 48
  - text, 56, 58-59
- data
  - comparing columns, 228-231
  - filtering, 224-227
  - grouping, 220-222
  - subtotaling, 220
- editing, 15-18
- filters, 232, 234
- fonts, 60-61
- formulas, 168-173
  - bar, 17-18
  - calculating, 140-143
  - editing, 15-18
  - entering, 11-15
  - filling cells, 144-149
  - revising, 78-79
  - summing, 19
- hyperlinks, 257-261
- labels, 102-104
  - column/rows, 124-126
  - creating, 102-104
  - rows, 104-109
  - text, 56-59
- mathematical calculations, 138-140

navigating, 4-8
numeric series, 104-109
Office Assistant, 25-31
outlines, 232-234
printing, 117-121
rows
   creating labels, 104-109
   data, 224-227
   deleting, 78-79
   freezing, 110-113
   inserting, 78-79
   printing labels, 124-126
   selecting, 45, 48
   sorting, 218-220
selecting, 4-8, 45-48
sheets, 78-79
spelling checker, 90-91
subtotals, 222-224
summary sheets
   configuring, 249-251
   inserting, 246-248
   linking, 252-256
   moving, 246-248
text, 88-89
totals, 232, 234
views, 110-113
Web pages
   saving as, 262-264
   viewing, 265-270
Standard toolbar
   AutoSum button, 19
   Copy button, 115-116
   Paste button, 115-116
   Print button, 24
   Undo button, 17
   Zoom box, 110
subtotaling
   data, 220-222
   see also calculating; formulas
subtotals, viewing, 222-224
Subtotals command (Data menu), 220
Subtotal dialog box, 220

subtracting (mathematical calculations), 138-140
summary sheets
   configuring, 249-251
   inserting, 246-248
   linking, 252-256
   see also sheets; worksheets
summing formulas, 19

T

text
   aligning, 56-59
   automatically entering, 88-89
   editing, 15-18, 76-77
   entering, 11-15
   errors, 85-86
   modifying, 60-61
   spelling checker, 90-91
   wrapping, 57
times
   customizing, 104-109
   see also numeric series
Times New Roman font, modifying, 60-61
toolbars
   Formatting, 65
   Print Preview, 125
   Standard
      Copy button, 115-116
      Print button, 24
      Undo, 17
      Zoom box, 110
Tools menu commands
   Auditing, 142
   AutoCorrect, 85
   Options, 12-15
totals, deleting, 232-234
transparencies, printing, 206
trends, creating, 186-189
troubleshooting, 83-84
types (chart) selecting, 200-203

U-V

undoing
    errors, 83-84
    see also deleting
Unfreeze Panes command (Windows menu), 113

values
    cells, 140-143
    see also formulas
vertical scrollbars., 6
    see also scrollbars
viewing
    subtotals, 222-224
    workbooks, 4-8
    worksheets as Web pages, 265-270
views, modifying, 110-113

W-Z

Web pages, 262-270
    saving worksheets as, 262-264
    viewing worksheets, 265-270
width, modifying, 53-55
Window menu commands
    Freeze Pane, 112
    Freeze Panes, 228
    Unfreeze Panes, 113
wizards, Answer, 29
workbooks
    cells
        aligning text, 56-59
        copying, 113-116
        entering numbers, 11-15
        entering text, 11-15
        modifying, 53-55
        selecting, 8-9
    closing, 24
    column/row labels, 124-126
    columns, 61-65
    editing, 15-18
    existing, 42-43
    floppy disks, 22
    fonts, 60-61
    formulas, 19
    labels, 102-104
    navigating, 4-8
    numeric series, 104-109
    Office Assistant, 25-31
    printing, 24, 117-121
    saving, 21-22
    viewing, 4-8
    views, 110-113
    see also worksheets
Worksheet command (Insert menu), 80, 247
worksheets
    cells
        aligning text, 56-59
        calculating formulas, 140-143
        conditional/counting formulas, 161-167
        copying, 113-116
        contents, 81, 113-116
        deleting content, 81
        editing, 15-18, 76-77
        entering numbers, 11-15
        entering text, 11-15
        fill handles, 103
        filling, 104
        filling formulas, 144-153
        financial formulas, 156-161
        groups, 45-48
        loan repayment formulas, 154-155
        magnification, 110-113
        modifying, 53-55
        numeric series, 104-109
        ranges, 117-119
        references, 138-140
        selecting, 8-9
    column/row labels, 124-126
    columns
        comparing, 229-231
        customizing, 61-65
        deleting, 78-79
        freezing, 110-113
        inserting, 78-79
        labels, 124-126
        modifying, 53-55

    selecting, 45, 48
    text, 56-59
data
    comparing columns, 228-231
    filtering, 224-227
    grouping, 220-222
    subtotaling, 220
editing, 15-18
filters, 232, 234
fonts, 60-61
formulas, 168-173
    bar, 17-18
    calculating, 140-143
    editing, 15-18
    entering, 11-15
    filling cells, 144-149
    revising, 78-79
    summing, 19
hyperlinks, 257-261
labels, 102-104
    column/rows, 124-126
    creating, 102-104
    rows, 104-109
    text, 56-59
mathematical calculations, 138-140
navigating, 4-8
numeric series, 104-109
Office Assistant, 25-31
outlines, 232-234
printing, 117-121
rows
    creating labels, 104-109
    data, 224-227
    deleting, 78-79
    freezing, 110-113
    inserting, 78-79
    printing labels, 124-126
    selecting, 45, 48
    sorting, 219-220
selecting, 4-8, 45-48
sheets, 78-79
spelling checker, 90-91
subtotals, 222-224

summary sheets
    configuring, 249-251
    inserting, 246-248
    linking, 252-256
    moving, 246-248
text, 88-89
totals, 232, 234
views, 110-113
Web pages
    saving as, 262-264
    viewing, 265-270
see also workbooks
wrapping text, 57

XML, 262-270

zoom, 110-113